IMAGES IN TIME

FLASHING FORWARD, BACKWARD, IN FRONT AND BEHIND PHOTOGRAPHY IN FASHION, ADVERTISING AND THE PRESS

EDITORS: ÆSA SIGURJÓNSDÓTTIR · MICHAEL A. LANGKJÆR · JO TURNEY

WUNDERKAMMER

Published by:
Wunderkammer Press
Bath School of Art and Design
Bath Spa University
Sion Hill
Bath BA1 5SF

Printed in the United Kingdom

ISBN 978 0 9566462 2 4 [paperback]

Images in Time: Flashing forward, backward, in front and
behind photography in fashion, advertising and the press

Editors: Æsa Sigurjónsdóttir, Michael A. Langkjær, Jo Turney
Includes bibliographical references
40 illustrations
Designed by Paul Minott

Images in Time

CONTENTS

Introduction
Images in Time

ÆSA SIGURJÓNSDÓTTIR AND MICHAEL A. LANGKJÆR

Prefatory remarks

Photography and fashion have much in common; both are expressive visual mediums, constructors of meanings and significations, slippery research objects, the theoretical approaches to which have been subject to much change and some irresolution. Moreover, recent tendencies towards cross-fertilisation in the academic field with newer fashion studies, and studies of visual and material culture, have opened up the possibility of a variety of empirical, technical and methodological, as well as thematic and theoretical approaches and visual references. The present volume consists of eleven papers related to *Images in Time: Flashing forward, backward, in front and behind photography in fashion, advertising and press*, a conference held on 27–28 November 2009 at the University of Iceland in Reykjavik as part of the activities within the Wardrobe network initiated by Associate Professor Lise Skov at The Copenhagen Business School [CBS].[1] The CBS-led Wardrobe network aims to develop new methodologies and perspectives of studying material culture under the rubric of wardrobe.

Images in Time was premised on the need for a sharing of practical experiences and methodologies amongst researchers who deal with photographs as a source of contextual meanings in the field of fashion. The papers published in this volume all contribute to the expanding field of inter-disciplinary studies on the uses of visual material in research.[2] Such uses are indeed problematic, as the truth-value of images depends on hyper-textual approaches to and contextualisation of the visual field. The authors, therefore, all treat current topics within the visual imagery and fashion fields by employing empirical and anthropological methods of using photographs 'as relational objects in the making and telling of histories'[3] – whether it be histories of fashion, photography or media. Contributors have considered photographs as a resource and an object of study, questioning the image as a constructive element, asking what kind of significance an image communicates, confronting specific problems of dating, locating, attributing and identifying, as well as looking at fashion and photography as elements in media systems or in fashion narratives.

The papers have been sorted under the headings 'Beyond the Album', 'Fashioning Identity' and 'Framing Modernity'. They go 'Beyond the Album' to situate photography in other contexts, for instance the photographic archive, or with respect to social, gendered, commercial or political circumstances that prevailed at the time when the photo was taken. In looking at how photography contributes towards 'Fashioning Identity', some papers consider it as a mediator of coveted identities as well as a neutraliser or domesticator of whatever personal characteristics are regarded as unaccustomed or dangerous. 'Framing Modernity' covers different aspects of the photo as reflecting the specifically modern qualities of change and ephemerality, of 'all that is solid melting into air', and of consciously emancipated [as opposed to unconsciously tradition-bound] individuals. The heading also covers the post-modern re-use of modern media. Fashion was chosen as a unifying theme, in so far as it is part of the circumstances, identity or modernity expressed in the photographs.

Of the two conference organisers, Æsa Sigurjónsdóttir is an art and photo historian, while Michael A. Langkjær is a general historian specialising in popular culture, costume and fashion. Following a précis of the principal subject matter of each paper, we jointly comment on what our contributors have written about methodology, theory, and the empirics of images and fashion. In doing so, we call attention to similarities and differences in their observations on image sourcing, on images in time and space, and on performativity of the image, and we conclude by considering some inherent negations and opposites, or tensions. It is our hope that the material presented here has a broad appeal to students and established scholars in the fields of fashion, historical, cultural and visual studies, as well as all who are interested in the epistemologies of interdisciplinary research and the creative industries.

Summary of the *Images in Time* papers

The papers represent a wide spectrum of interrogative and theoretical approaches and discipline-related methodologies. For instance, Charlotte Bik Bandlien has in 'On the Style Site' chosen to focus on the street-style blog *Face Hunter*, in order to examine fashion photo mechanisms and their connections with the information and attention economies. Bandlien utilises anthropological consumption theory, while Henning Bender has in 'The Heinrich Tønnies Collection' drawn on his laborious experiences of establishing and presenting a nineteenth-century photography archive for a present-day public. Bender considers the historical significance of Tønnies' work as a photographer along with issues raised by the problematic analogue, as opposed to digitalised, representation of images conserved almost entirely as a material glass-plate archive. In 'Surpassing the Reified Film Star' Ingeborg Thaanum Carlsen treats film icons of modern culture, which have been caught like snapshots through the medium of ekphrastic poetic language, thereby bringing us 'voyeuristically closer to the life of the real person within or behind the icon'. Anna Dahlgren uses a biographical outline, from which she in 'Tact and Tactics' has inferred an explanatory context comprising factors and limitations connected with norms of gendered behaviour, developments in the photographic profession and changing aesthetics.

As seen by Lidia Marte, when text and image are treated as a unit, it subtly tells us how to interpret the images of domesticated Blackness in relation to current American racial politics; in 'Domesticating Blackness', Marte speaks of 'piercing the dream-imaged narratives'. Per Nielsen's primary focus in 'Dressing for Europe' deals with the representing of skin colour and other physical features, heritage, folklore and fashion, questioning the colonial interest of displaying and creating a *positive* stereotype image of Danish West Indians through photography and dress. For Tone Rasch, the texts accompanying photos in a selection of Norwegian fashion journals examined in 'Making Clothes Desirable' emphasise the descriptive aspects – the written fashion – closely connected with our understanding of the fashionable, in addition to which fashion reports show the rhetoric between the international stylish fashion world and the economic need of creating national fashion mythologies in the Nordic countries during the 1960s and 1970s. Stephanie Sadre-Orafai bases 'Fashion's Other Images' on ethnographic fieldwork at a leading fashion casting agency in New York City: 'I interrogate the discourses of objectivity and "realness" ... as [casting professionals] produce, rank, and assess forms of evidence in their practice.' From casting encounter to casting archive, Sadre-Orafai places the images within a broader visual economy in order to shed light on the motivations and constraints that structure the process.

Merja Salo deals with the topic of image-embedded values and assumptions of Finnish fashion photos in 'On Location'; it is the rhetoric of location which has held her particular attention in using a semiotic approach to reveal complex sign systems, dense with values and assumptions, as being an important element in a national discourse of Finnishness. In 'Playing for the Camera' Eugenie Shinkle goes beyond semiotics to investigate the introduction of the playful body in twentieth-century fashion photography. Shinkle points to 'affect' as a way of thinking about images in terms of their effect – not just what they signify or communicate in linguistic terms. While using John Huizinga to heuristically reflect on the appearance of the newly mobile female body in early twentieth-century fashion images, Shinkle argues the limitations of his concept of play in *Homo Ludens*.

When seen as *aides-mémoire*, photographs do not by themselves provide us with the entire picture, thus Joanne Turney has in her contribution 'In the Picture' taken into account some of the feelings and attitudes that have also gone into our past choices of what to wear; when revisiting the clothes that we have worn, whether it be through photographic evidence or through the garment itself, the ironical distance between the 'here and now' and 'there and then' is apparent. In her study, meaning is articulated in the space between these two different mediums of visual memory, the snapshot and the garment.

Archives: Challenges and prospects in sourcing images

There are some basic sets of rules in dating, locating, attributing and identifying images as empirical documents, as well as in interpreting fashion and understanding their information in a broader political and socio-economic frame. The researcher has to deal with the where and when, how and why of images. Historical awareness, the archival desire, is not always in concert with the silence of the archive or the visible circulation of images – or the noise made by an image. The apparent perfection of a particular archive, as in the case of the Tønnies Collection, does not necessarily make it more accessible visibly to the user than the incomplete Sohlberg Foto archive. Yet it should be remembered that as an historian, Bender, in dealing with the Tønnies archive – what it tells us about old technologies, techniques and attitudes connected with the act of taking photos – is dealing with history for history's own sake: it is our interest in how different things were then, and our ability to appreciate the *differentness* of it all that is the *raison d'être* behind the preservation and exhibition of Tønnies' archive and atelier. Bender asks: how are we to comprehend nineteenth-century mass-production, an 'industrial madness',[4] on the basis of a perfectly preserved archive of glass plates through randomly surviving examples of positive prints?

Much closer in time, in connection with the Sohlberg Foto archive at the Norwegian Museum of Science and Technology, Rasch is struggling with lack of information, as no records accompany the fashion prints, apart from an occasional entry noting the journal and the volume in which a particular photo appeared. For Dahlgren, the state of preservation has been much worse: what remains of the images from the Lenkert archive are a few vintage prints; most of the rest had been consigned to the dustbin, causing Dahlgren to comment that 'a short career could prove fatal for a female photographer's work, in particular its preservation'. On the other hand, Dahlgren does note that the work of another female photography atelier, the Studio Deux Sœurs, is well preserved. This may have been due to continuation of that atelier's business into the 1970s when 'historical awareness took over', a serendipitous incidence of archival desire remarkably similar to that experienced by the huge Tønnies archive, as has been remarked on by Bender.

In this volume, construction of knowledge is articulated between case-studies of local histories confronted with studies of international genres. Rasch calls our attention to the generally low status of fashion photography, explaining the meagre interest fashion photography has had for Norwegian photo-history. This is in accordance with what Sadre-Orafai has remarked about the few that have focused on the documentary practices which precede fashion's fantastic and frequently controversial iconography. Finnish fashion photographers remain unmentioned in the international histories of fashion photography; Salo would even go so far as to call fashion photography in Finland 'a quite cruel practice' seeing as it 'ephemeralises photographers at the same hectic pace as it consumes fashion'. The state of being disregarded is something which Dahlgren has noted about Swedish female photographers: their work was undervalued and simply discarded. By contrast, no Polaroid images shot or layouts were ever discarded by the casting agencies treated by Sadre-Orafai, but the fragility of a Polaroid archive and its suspension in time make it difficult as an object of research. Notably, Rasch finds that much of our knowledge about the fashion of the 1960s is based on fashion photography and publications, and that it is the *clothes* that have often disappeared.

Fashion and photography operate in this space of appearance/disappearance – remembering and reconstructing the past – factual or fictional. Then again, if we deal with mental images, rather than with [lack of] physical evidence, the problem is entirely different as we are not dealing with material objects but with literary readings: the ekphrastic poems about Audrey Hepburn and Marilyn Monroe take for granted that readers of the poems would in their mind's eye see the image of the poetically described film icons, as Carlsen has shown. Marte takes it even further: 'what makes this image so powerful is what is *not* there'.

For Nielsen the basic problem in 'Dressing for Europe' was that of identifying the individuals in the picture. Identification is, in this case, the key to meaning as well as for Bender, where loss of knowable identity leads to the loss of intrinsic interest in portraits of the past. For both, a frequent problem in dealing with images in local archives is that these have no information about who the portrayed individuals were, or when the picture was taken. And, to reiterate our point made above about abstract symbolic evidence, positive image identification is not necessarily always a priority: Bandlien speaks of the symbolic power of style; of aesthetically influential fashion blogs when anonymous individuals are turned into fashion icons.

Turning towards the study of the history of photography and genres, Shinkle has remarked on how the originally radical outdoor snapshot style of Hungarian photojournalist Martin Munkásci back in the 1930s evolved into the animated, playful images of femininity that were to become a staple within the genre of fashion photography as they expressed fashionable symbolic qualities at the time intrinsic with modernity. Theatricality became the language of fashion photography, mirroring the spontaneity and often-awkward postures of amateur snapshot photography.

The family snapshot has become a subject of increased scholarship and is seen by Turney as offering an insight into 'a temporal genre', that is, one associated with popular styles of dress and the technologies available at the time of taking the photo, as well as the distinctive character of the snapshot genre itself being [as pointed out by Batchen] 'cloyingly sentimental in content and repetitively uncreative as pictures, having little value in the marketplace of either ideas or commodities'.[5] Turney makes use of the relational quality of fashion, its sentimentality, by matching it with personal narratives of the family album. Her approach emphasises the orality of the vernacular genre, the importance of constructing a personal fashion narrative, a visual image through the spoken word.

Rasch has stressed that the genre of fashion-promotional pictures cannot be looked at as isolated images, but that they must be considered in their commercial contexts, just as Sadre-Orafai argues the necessity of having a sense of the larger visual economy in which the images of the present-day casting agencies operate. The marketplace as matrix for the internal development of a genre is also put forward in the analysis of Finnish fashion photography by Salo. Shinkle's view is that play can also be bound up with commercial interests, the playful experimentation of the Spiel-Raum, and that, among other things, it is here that Huizinga fails to account for the broader context within which fashion images such as those of playful female bodies circulate. Placement of the image according to genre and genre-context forms an intermediate link to framing the image in time and space, to which we shall now turn.

Shifts: Framing the image in time and place

All our contributors operate within a modern and post-modern time frame which, irrespective of topic, is, in some cases, fairly wide, in others quite narrow. Although focusing on a single Danish photographic atelier, Bender covers Aalborg from the 1860s to the present; within the span of 150 years he notes several shifts in aesthetics, fashions and technologies related to photographic images. Salo covers Finland from 1917–1991, focusing on the important national identity construction related to the specific economic demands of the Cold War period. Shinkle situates her analysis in the context of early twentieth-century North America and Western Europe, with especial focus on fashion photography of the 1930s. Wide time frames can tell us something about overall trends, of course, or they can shed light on a shift, as with Bender, or Shinkle: 'The fashion photography of the 1930s can be understood ... as marking the beginning of a general shift away from images that were designed to be read, and towards images that were also intended to be felt.'

Narrowing the time frame provides a detailed picture of the uses and receptions of certain types of images. Nielsen considers how photography in 1888 and 1905 had been used to represent an exotic, yet suitably 'Danish', image of the black Danish West Indians. Rasch has focused on the mixed reception of the Norwegian 'Fjord Look' together with five fashion reports published in 1968 and 1969. We have taken note of some hybrid approaches to the time element as well: Carlsen shifts ekphrastically backwards/forwards between a contemporary Danish poet and her post-World War II film-icon material. Bandlien, Marte and Sadre-Orafai have all set themselves firmly within a post-millennial time frame while remarking on tendencies and trends in their particular areas of study.

Time inevitably turns out to be a destructive factor. More often than not it is by sheer luck that images have survived the vicissitudes of time. Their perceived value depends on a particular, but changeable, state of mind, attitude or taste; time ephemeralises style in photography, just as it renders fashion *per se* outmoded. Shinkle indicates that even if the legacy of the formal studio pose persisted in early fashion photographs, it would to some extent be superseded by the taste for open-air action photograph spontaneity embodied in Munkásci's 'snapshot' style photos. Bender mentions that *carte-de-visite* images went out of fashion, because changes in technology led to changes in what customers required. This has also had consequences for the attitudes of present-day museums and their patrons towards the exhibition 'value' of these materials.

Lost and found: Visual economies

The tension between fashion and photography can be compared to that between lost and found, intersecting in suggestive ways. On the ephemeral nature of street-style image blogs, Bandlien remarks that they are continuously updated, that there is no permanence on the style site. Yet they are at the same time in a classic photographic sense a frozen moment in time. This brings to mind another time-suspending factor: icons and iconicity transcend and so to speak neutralise time. Although the film stars Marilyn Monroe and Audrey Hepburn are no longer with us, Carlsen recalls Barthes in noting that we speak of them in a manner as if they were still alive: when we stand before the photo or watch the film, the dead persons featured in them are very much alive to us; they acquire the simultaneity of icons. This is in contradistinction to Sadre-Orafai's casting images which have no 'present', only a past and a future.

Turning now from time towards space, we see how the latter, too, imposes limits when it is not widening the bounds of the possible. Bender observes that 'the technology that these [nineteenth-century] photographers worked with was quite limited, and as a consequence the original prints appear small'. By way of comparison, according to Sadre-Orafai it is the very limitations of Polaroids – a single 'take', no negative, aesthetic starkness – that has provided casting agencies with their opportunities to present clients with a greater range and number of models than they can see directly. As already noted, the ephemerality in time and extreme instability of street fashion is, in Bandlien's view, offset by the firm context of shared urban space as well as transnational symbolic value of the blogging images. So we see how new technologies contribute towards opening up and widening the field of image-production as famously stated by Benjamin.[6]

A particularly intriguing aspect is the dialectical relationship that unfolds within a given space. This is interestingly remarked on by Marte, in what she has termed a 'counterpoint narration' which [in the focus of her research, the fashion, lifestyle and beauty magazine for African-American women, *Essence*] emerges from the space of the page and within the subtle relation among the pages where advertisements and photo-images speak uneasily to each other, and where the text/image dialogue raises some pertinent questions as to the real purpose of the message. About the political economy of *Essence*'s images, we would suggest that the editors were not necessarily 'domesticating Blackness' [as was the case with the photographs studied by Nielsen], but were in fact well aware that by their juxtaposing images they would be challenging their readers to 'rethink' their own social position. Marte also emphasises that the image-accompanying text limits the interpretive meanings the reader can make. 'Space' for Marte becomes a matter of boundaries and tensions proposed by the representation.

Images can also be situated on an interface or nexus of time and space. Bandlien has observed that 'these blogs distribute worldwide with a click', thus aiding the establishment of a sense of a transnational community. Carlsen speaks of the ekphrastic impulse, viz. the aspiration of language and its inherent temporality towards the immediate sensibility and spatiality of the visual arts. Another way of looking at the temporal/spatial nexus is when Sadre-Orafai notes the striking repletion and volume of Polaroid images of tens of thousands of fleeting encounters that have and continue to occur in the space of a given casting agency. Marte points out how the re-production of certain representations of Blackness 'domesticates'; if repeated often enough it becomes 'true' in the sense of 'familiar' and hence 'safe'. Still, according to Marte, even though two images of African-Americans are operating within the same space/time frame of the magazine representationally, they can seem to inhabit different worlds, as marking out two separate paths to the American Dream, which brings us to the concept of the performative image.

'Fixing' the effectively performative image

Images are inherently performative, and those of fashion photographs are particularly so. Shinkle states that as a cultural actor, the fashion image needs to be understood in terms of what it – affectively – does, and what its audience – affectively – does with it: 'what makes a particular show package promoting models so interesting is the way it prioritises affect over visual information in defining an edgy, playful image by embodying a feeling'. However, she asks, is it an emblem of freedom or an agent of control? The images of Obama juxtaposed with those of Black youth are, according to Marte, relating to readers through a process of self-identification, while at the same time advertisements in apparent contradiction 'echo beyond the frame' to illustrate the growing gap in wealth among African-Americans. As a constructive element or constituting force, these images can be seen as possibly too effective. However, images can for some reason or other also fall short of their intended effect. Nielsen concludes that, for reasons extrinsic to the photos and themes, the use of clothing and photography were not successful in creating a sustainable image of the dignified and equal West Indian citizens; photographic images did not prove to be sufficient to unite the black and white Danes. Rasch explains the lack of effectiveness of the images of the Norwegian-made 'Fjord Look' with the far too naturalistic character of these photos.

Apart from what has already been established in connection with the casting images of Sadre-Orafai and the style blogs of Bandlien, we find that Salo, Rasch and Shinkle are in basic agreement about the importance for success in fashion photography of having a certain, often indefinable, 'look'. Salo notes that the 'ideal' fashion image of a tall, blonde, young woman with flowing hair and long legs may not have resembled the majority of Finns, but that she nonetheless could promote Finnish design successfully. In addition to having long legs, Rasch's Norwegian models look playful which, in accordance with Shinkle's view, would signify freedom, maturity and individuality, projecting the political aspirations of a young nation.

Some of our contributors look more closely into what constitutes the effective underlying 'something else' in a motif. Marte connects Obama's visual attractiveness with the trope of respectability. Bender notes that garments that followed reigning fashion often were rented for the occasion of taking a portrait photo, thereby lending respectability to the person pictured. At least as important to Rasch as the garments and model for the visual expression of fashion photography are the locations chosen, as is demonstrated by the Norwegian exploration vessel *Fram* symbolically providing the ready-made clothes with an extra or added value by means of embedding them in a historical national discourse. Like Rasch, Salo has seen nature as a symbolic location, but one which had been combined with Finnish nationalism to form a synthesis that became part of Finnish export rhetoric. Here, the striving for respectability – witnessed by the choice of apparel by the individuals or the national image-branding of those fashion designs photographed – has apparently retained its value, to which one then can engraft the somewhat less familiar added [symbolic] value of location.

Yet, on the other hand, there are always ways of creating a conflict between garment and location, such as showing high fashion in rustic surroundings. By 'putting fashion in a wrong place', one is supposedly imparting a sense of irony, a cool and detached attitude towards both fashion and the world. However, could this not just as well be an example of what Barthes has designated as constituting 'rhetorical contrast'? And: is it not precisely the clash and rhetorical blurring of limits that sparks the fun and the desire?[7]

Moving on to the effective afterlife of images, one of the oldest, most fundamental ones is related to what Bender has characterised as 'retouching to make a suitably improved likeness'. Turney agrees that snapshots and clothing are the articulation of aspects of personal and fantasy narratives, coded, controlled and communicated to a particular audience at a particular time, and that both media are performative, in so far as they are staging, showing off how we would like to be remembered; it all of course depends on who does the remembering. In contrast to Bender's portrait photographs, what fulfilled a specific aesthetic goal in Sadre-Orafai's casting images was an apparent lack of 'artistry', so that models might be evenly evaluated and judged. Yet, whether it is portrait photography or casting agency Polaroids, the agreement between photographer and subject as to what one wants or needs remains direct.

In considering intent or purpose, Rasch notes that the magazine, the ready-to-wear industry and the photographer each had a role that it is necessary to discuss further in order to understand the meaning of the pictures in a given journal. It is evident to Marte that whoever controls the means of media production will shape, or at least influence, the kinds of representations privileged in them. Apart from commercially motivated intent, there are national and global issues leading to the need to manufacture safely de-historicised and de-politicised images as well as positive representations that open up to the imagination. Marte also suggests that images are meant as a legacy and an attempt to join mainstream historical archives, and that history must be the judge of the success of this endeavour. One is reminded of Nielsen's emphasis that some individuals and organisations in Danish society possibly had a special interest in representing the Danish West Indians, including their dress, as a natural part of the Kingdom of Denmark, while at the same time focusing on cultural differences – the cosmopolitan character – of that same kingdom. Unlike Marte, it is the advantage of historical hindsight which has enabled Nielsen to determine the success of this Danish venture.

Conclusion: The *Images in Time* experience

Photographic images can never be studied alone, especially when the subject is fashion. They are always embedded in other systems of knowledge. Barthes called them concurrent messages, and their important relation to narration, to orality and to written text, has been scrutinised in the papers of this volume. What the *Images in Time* experience has demonstrated is that using images as research material is not unproblematic, and that there also are some useful methodologies. Eleven papers cannot furnish us with the whole picture, but they have led us to some interesting and valuable new insights. Has this made the topic any less slippery? Has the irresolution reduced? To some degree, we feel that we can answer both questions affirmatively.

We have identified and established the nature of some problems in the investigation of images. Many are connected with random survivals and gendered disparity, imbalance or the meagre interest shown by posterity to aspects of the history and sociology of photographic images and their subject matter, as here: fashion. This has consequences for the representativeness of one's data, as is seen in some of the papers. At first sight, it does appear that sourcing and documentation of images have become easier, through the mass of digitalised photographic data – however dubious or misleading some of it may be owing to conscious manipulation [*pace* Bender].[8] Nevertheless, a standing discussion, and concern, among professional archivists is that the sheer mass of imaged data, as well as the changes in the technologies of the storage of such data every ten years or so, has created yet another twentieth-century 'monster', with which we must learn to deal in the twenty-first century!

Art historian Geoffrey Batchen wrote in 1998 in a much-cited article that 'in the near future, electronic reproduction is the only kind that is going to matter'.[9] Paul Frosh reached a somewhat similar conclusion in his thoroughly studied tome *The Image Factory* [2003]. Citing the film historian Anton Kaes about how 'The past is in danger of becoming a rapidly expanding collection of images … available in an eternal present', Frosh, in calling this 'really a state of luxury which we have not yet achieved', insisted on the reduction of the visual through the digitalisation of photographic archives by stock agencies, commercial image providers and the like.[10] Frosh explains how a global, visual-content industry increasingly controls images supplied to advertisers, marketers and designers, yet so far the process has, paradoxically, evaded the public eye. He has argued that:

> the distinction commercial/non-commercial has become thoroughly internalized – it has become a distinction between *content* and *non-content*. It has entered the historical archive, leading irrevocably to the conclusion that our image of history – the collective visual memory of the past that depends upon access to its images and their public dissemination – will be increasingly determined and constrained by the rhetorical needs of consumer advertising and marketing.[11]

This distinction, pointed out by Frosh, between the problematic construction of content and non-content is particularly striking when dealing with photographic source material which has lost its voice, as in the case of the studies by Bender, Rasch, Dahlgren and Salo. Digitalisation seems, however [as in the case-study by Bandlien of the fashion blogs], to be making it possible to reconfigure the relationship between photography and history, opening new fields of research. By juxtaposing the study by Bandlien with that by Bender, we observe how the photographic image has abandoned the age of mechanical reproduction and turned towards digital cultural uses, and in this process has overturned certain presumptions and conceptions of the uses of photography in the study of fashion.

Among newer [or less familiar] approaches, the affective turn and ekphrastic analysis stand out as promising ways of interpreting images and fashion. New [or less familiar] concepts such as that of 'temporal genre' and 'counterpoint narration' show potential. Time and space and the close connections they have been seen to have with the limits and opportunities presented by photographic technology are, together with 'ephemerality', demonstrably relevant for interpreting photographic material. Iconicity, a subject for research in itself, would appear to be the very opposite of ephemerality, although this, too, raises questions as to representativeness.

Contextualising remains a must, and this has been brought to our attention once more with respect to the commercial side of fashion photography; the latter is already proving to be a fruitful field for inquiry. The power of images as agents of freedom or control, along with the matter of what constitutes effective and ineffective images, are important issues.

Our work with the contributions to the present volume has, along with uncovering image-embedded values and assumptions, made us aware of inherent negations and opposites. Turney points out how photography and dress, both being of the moment lost, simultaneously embrace both life and death. Bandlien notes that, while particular styles of fashion might be presented as unique by street-style blogs, the converse is true of their representation: street-style blogs have absorbed the visual language of straight photography, in addition to which subculture similarities across cultures are emphasised by the city acting as a unifying and uniform backdrop. Another tension is apparent when Dahlgren sees the invisibility of women photographers in [Swedish] history of photography as 'real', despite the fact that women demonstrably played a large role as professionals, and were in fact appreciated as such by their male colleagues. Yet a third contradiction turns up when Rasch notes that the Norwegian fashion pictures seem fresher and more imaginative than the clothes of the Norwegian fashion trade they were meant to sell.

Regarded as historical, aesthetic or social symptoms, photographic images present a multifaceted material for studying the rhetoric of fashion. Having read through the *Images in Time* papers, it can be concluded that archival deaths, fashion reminiscences and surviving icons are important agents which have to be incorporated when using visual material as a point of departure in contemporary cultural studies.

ENDNOTES

1 The Wardrobe network is funded by NordForsk; see the afterword by Jo Turney.

2 Æsa Sigurjónsdóttir presented 'Gesture and expressions of desire in popular photography in the 1930s'. Michael A. Langkjær's presentation at the Reykjavik conference is to be published under the title 'Déjà Vu Desperados: Embattled survivor imagery of Crosby, Stills, Nash & Young in the setting of youth rebellion America 1968-1972', in Joanne Turney [ed.], *Fashion Crimes: Fashion and Crime* [London: I. B. Taurus Publishers, anticipated 2012].

3 As discussed in Elisabeth Edwards, 'Photographs and the sound of history',

Visual Anthropology Review, 21:1/2 [2005], pp. 27–46.

4 Elizabeth Anne McCauley, *Industrial Madness: Commercial Photography in Paris, 1848–1871* [New Haven: Yale University Press, 1994] p. 1, p. 8, quotes Charles Baudelaire ['The Salon of 1859'] who had complained that the medium of [commercial] photography was 'part of the "industrial madness" that the Bonapartism [of Napoleon III] had fostered' and she remarks how he thus had 'lashed out at the products of the industrial revolution without understanding that he was attacking a worldwide movement'.

5 As discussed in Geoffrey Batchen, 'Snapshots', *Photographies*, 1:2 [2008], [pp. 121–42], p. 123.

6 Walter Benjamin, 'The work of art in the age of mechanical reproduction', in Howard Eiland and Michael W. Jennings [eds.], *Selected Writings, vol. 4, 1938–1940* [Cambridge, Massachusetts and London: Belknap Press of Harvard University Press, 2003], p. 253.

7 At the conference we discussed the element of understated sexual message in the images Salo was showing; it might be interesting to look for the sexual connotation in the image 'girl in a wrong place'; or 'interposing the urban into the rural'; or 'Cold War irony against "Finlandization"'.

8 Associate Professor Arild Fetveit [Department of Media, Cognition and Communication, University of Copenhagen] dealt with some of these questions in his presentation at the *Images in Time* conference of 'The digital revolution in photography'.

9 Geoffrey Batchen, 'Photogenics/fotogenik', *Camera Austria*, 62/63 [1998], [pp. 5–16], p. 8.

10 Paul Frosh, *The Image Factory. Consumer culture, photography and the visual content industry* [Oxford and New York: Berg, 2003], p. 204, where Frosh cites A. Kaes, 'History and film: Public memory in the age of electronic dissemination', *History and Memory*, 2:1, p. 120.

11 Frosh, *The Image Factory*, p. 204.

Beyond the Album

The papers under the heading 'Beyond the album' deal with the relationship between the professionally produced image and the market, showing how these relationships are dictated by economic interests of the marketplace, pushing the borders of personal uses and interests limited to the intimacy of the album. Being 'beyond the album' should be more properly understood in the sense of looking at the historical contexts and economic realities behind the photographic images that constituted albums and archives, viz. social, gendered, commercial or political circumstances that prevailed at the time of taking the photo. It must be kept in mind that, the aim of the production of these images was in all cases to sell, whether it be a modern identity in the case of Tønnies, or a national identity, or simply fashion. The studio photograph and the fashion image can thus shift between the commercial and the political without much effort on the behalf of the viewer/consumer. A national identity mediated in fashion photography can be considered as part of a national photo album, comprising shots of the models as part of an extended national family in scenic surroundings of the wild Finnish outdoors and Norwegian fjords.

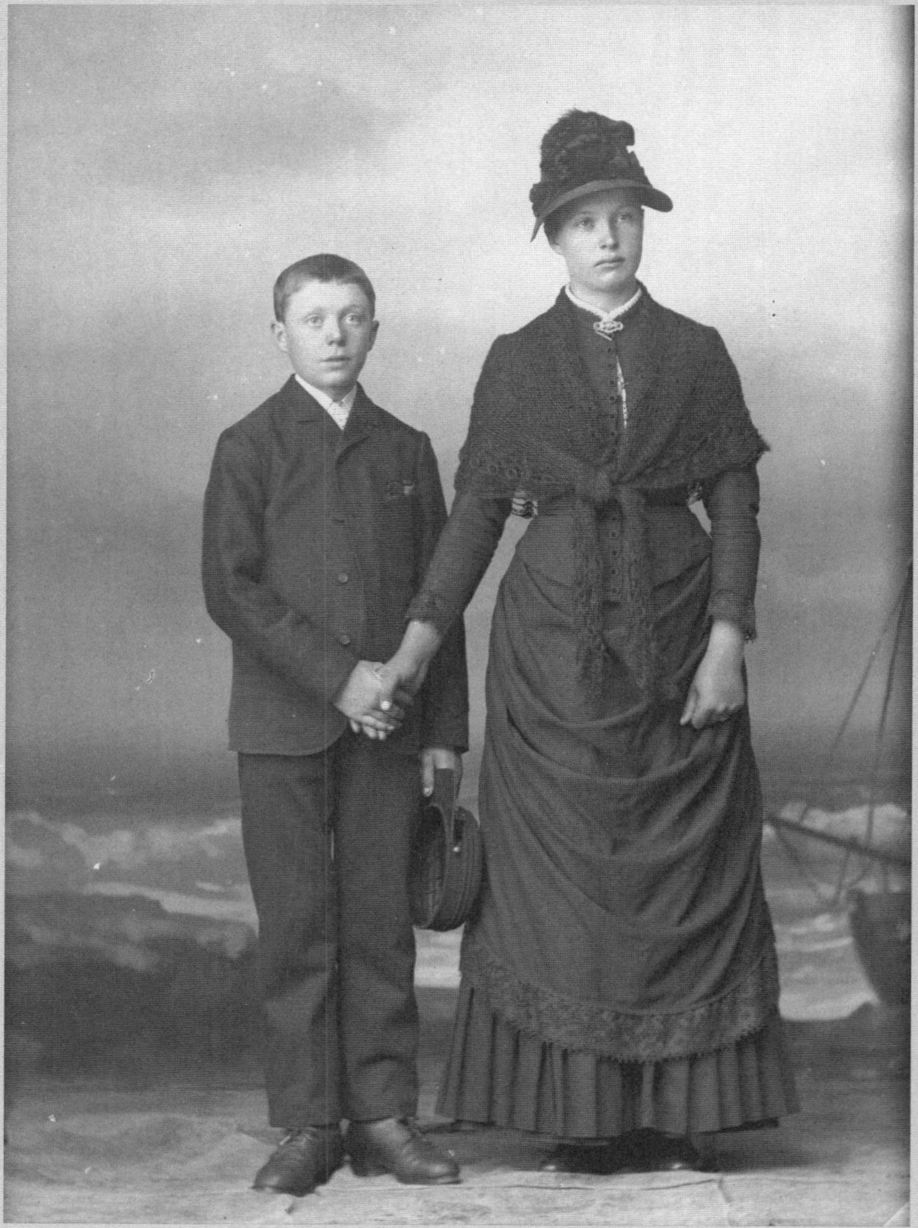

Fig.1:
Brother and sister on the eve of emigrating to Utah. Thousands of people had their photo taken before they travelled across the Atlantic.
From original negative plate, taken 17 July 1888.

The Heinrich Tønnies Collection
Photography as the market wants it

HENNING BENDER

Introduction: *Carte-de-visite* portraits and the Tønnies archive
Developments in photography around the mid-nineteenth century created an explosion in the demand for portraits. The new photographic method using a negative imprint meant that a motive now could be turned into an infinite number of positive prints. It also led to a revolutionary democratisation of the portrait, through mass production at a price that roughly corresponded to a day's wages of an average worker. The price of painted portraits and daguerreotypes had previously limited the availability of personal portraits to the well-to-do, but now just about anybody could afford to be depicted at least once during his or her lifetime and collect pictures of other people or places. It was in particular with the *carte-de-visite* format [5.5 x 9 cm] that pictures became a common property, and together with pictures in the larger *cabinet* format [10.3 x 14 cm] they constituted the majority of all photographs produced in the years 1856–1918.[1]

Within just a few decades, photographic ateliers were opened in every town all over the world. In Aalborg alone [a town which between 1856 and 1914 would grow from ten thousand to fifty thousand inhabitants to make it the second largest town in Denmark and the most industrialised after Copenhagen], more than five hundred portrait photographers established themselves during this timeframe for a shorter or longer period. The market consisted not only of the strongly growing population in the town, but to an even larger degree of peasants from the surrounding countryside during the years when the export of dairy products and bacon to England was beginning to make Denmark a rich nation.[2]

Most of the photographers did not consider themselves as artists, but rather as tradesmen, artisans whose task it was to deliver to the customer what he/she wanted: a portrait that was a good, suitably 'improved' likeness, but which above all had to be offered at a suitably low price. Style and composition were taken over from portrait paintings, but the products could hardly be varied much, seeing as the photographer, in order to keep the price down, would have had to turn out literally dozens of individual portraits – per day. But that was less important, as the portraits were not expected to, and indeed, by preference *should* not, deviate from the established norm. They were made for the purpose of inspiring respect and were collected in photo albums or would be hung up on the walls in private homes where they were displayed with pride. In this way the pictures bespoke the solidity and respectability of the subject, his family and his circle, as well as the solidity of the society to which he belonged; thus the portrait photograph became one of the most important material symbols of the age.

At the same time, the technology that these photographers worked with was quite limited, and as a consequence the original prints appear small, finicky and faded until enlarged via modern methods from the original negatives. The dress, settings and props used in the portraits are often mismatched and marked by a compromise between what the customer desired and what the photographer would have happened to have at hand. The portrait subjects often look serious, not because they were afraid to be depicted, but simply due to the long period of exposure, where any movement would blur the picture, meaning that neither the hands nor the facial muscles were to be moved during the taking. The subject's head was, until the mid 1880s, tied to a support and the arms kept absolutely still by being supported by props in the atelier, but movements of the eyelids could not be prevented and so the pupils had to be painted in. The garments were often rented for the occasion, so the clothes followed reigning fashion and thus lent respectability to the person pictured. Such was also the case when work clothes and implements were used to signify the capable and well-established tradesman. So it is no matter for surprise that the photos filled every available space on tables, shelves, and the walls of rooms and halls, as well as being exchanged among relatives whom the large population movements during the this time-period had scattered to different parts of the world. As a consequence, you can today find photographs by a single photographer, such as Heinrich Tønnies, wherever Danes have settled in the United States,[3] and vice versa: portraits exist in Danish homes which had been sent home by Danes who had emigrated to North America, Australia and New Zealand [Fig. 1].

Considering their great prevalence it may seem strange that researchers have not until fairly recently shown much interest in the *carte-de-visite* portraits. The explanation is that in the period between the two world wars these photographs had been made outdated by the new methods used by professional photographers, by the privately owned box-camera, as well as by the new media contexts of illustrated journals, cinema and so forth. Being thus outmoded, the old portraits were now seen as standardised and anonymous – also by the descendents of the subjects portrayed, who had no relationship to their ancestors. The *carte-de-visite* portraits were discarded along with most of the old glass negatives and reorder books. Why keep archives when nobody was reordering prints any longer from the old negatives that were taking up so much storage space? The fact of having so relatively few, anonymous original prints that by chance have survived the vicissitudes of time has meant that historians would experience great difficulty in understanding and describing the mass-production of portraits in its very beginnings.

The problem consists in having to comprehend a revolutionary mass-production on the basis of randomly surviving, often anonymous and faded examples of positive prints. As luck would have it, by a singular combination of events, we have come to possess twenty-nine completely intact photographic archives at Aalborg's City Archives. The oldest and the largest archive covers the years 1856–1974. Its preservation is partly due to its having been owned during the entire period by the same Tønnies family; Heinrich Tønnies [from 1856–1903], his son Emil Tønnies [from 1903–1923] and the grandchildren Lili and Verner Tønnies [from 1923–1974]: and partly due to its having been kept in the years 1881–1961 in the largest photographic atelier ever built in Scandinavia. There had been space enough and neither the need nor the will to scrap anything, even after atelier-photography had gone out of fashion.

Heinrich Tønnies: From immigrant to established and renowned photographer

Heinrich Tønnies [1825–1903][4] was born at the glassworks of Grünenplan, south of Hannover in Germany, but when the region was hit by the great potato rot and famine in northern Europe in the mid 1840s, a large part of the population emigrated. Some of them moved to Voigtländer's newly started optical works in Braunschweig [also known as Brunswick in English]; others became glassworkers in Bay City, Michigan, USA.[5] Tønnies himself went in 1847 to the Conradsminde glassworks in North Jutland in Denmark in order to work there as a glass-cutter and painter. When this glassworks changed over to producing only green glass bottles in 1853, Tønnies was dismissed. On 4 August 1853 he was married at the American Consulate in Hamburg to Emma Müller [1830–1911] from Grünenplan *en route* to joining relatives in Michigan. But, just prior to their departure, Tønnies received an offer of five thousand rixdollars from a new glassworks in Aalborg if he would turn back and work there as the chief glass-cutter.[6] So, Tønnies and his new wife went to Aalborg instead of Bay City, but when in 1855/56 the Aalborg works scaled down its production to making only green glass bottles, there was no longer need for a glass-cutter and Tønnies, once again, had to leave. He became an apprentice to the first photographer with an established atelier in Aalborg, Carl Fritsche of Berlin. Fritsche, who wanted to establish himself in Hamburg instead, sold his atelier and equipment to Tønnies on 9 December 1856. The purchase price was half of the five thousand rixdollars Tønnies had been given for coming to Aalborg. Apart from whatever training as a photographer Tønnies had received from Fritsche, his knowledge of glass-cutting enabled him to judge the quality of a camera lens, while his work as a miniature painter on glass meant that he knew precisely how to arrange a picture 'drawn' with light on the small, glass plate he placed in his camera.[7]

Tønnies soon made a great breakthrough in Aalborg, when, in December of 1857, he ran a big advertising campaign in the newspapers of the town, inviting the readers to 'let the Christmas gift of the year be a photographic portrait'. The Tønnies Company could deliver portraits that were more beautiful and at a lower price than anybody else. Some of these *carte-de-visite* portraits from December 1857 are actually preserved, making them the oldest dated photographs of this type in Denmark.[8] It should be noted, however, that they were not produced according to the method patented back in 1854 in Paris by André Disdéri, with up to twelve portraits per negative plate. Instead they were produced by a method that allowed only two portraits per negative, a method Heinrich Tønnies had learnt in Berlin, where he had stayed during November of 1857.[9]

All in all, it was in Berlin that Tønnies acquired the knowledge and inspiration as photographer during his yearly travels on business to that city, the capital of Prussia. In particular, he sought out the Royal, later Imperial Court, photographer Carl Suck, Unter den Linden 24, from whom he learned a great deal. And it was here that Heinrich's son and successor, Emil Tønnies [1860–1923], was educated and in 1887 married the *retoucheuse*[10] of the atelier, Bertha Andrée [1863–1948]. The Tønnies family represents the development of photography in the German capital, and is thus representative of a central European photographic tradition as well. This is a tradition we do not know so much about, as the source material to that tradition consisting of negative plates and order books disappeared during the Allied bombing on 3 February 1945, which obliterated the photographers' district in central Berlin. That of course increases the value of the Tønnies collection from the perspective of international research, where the British, French and American materials otherwise predominate.

Along with what Tønnies learned in Berlin – which can be traced through the prints, equipment and books he brought home to Aalborg – he expanded his photographic activities in the 1860s with topographic pictures from Aalborg. They were sold all over Denmark, making the old and picturesque buildings of the town well known. With the arrival of industrialisation in the following decade and the disappearance of the old houses, Tønnies changed over to documenting thoroughly the new factories along with their machinery and workers. This cannot be ascribed to any especial interest in photographically documenting the development of the town *per se*; instead it must be understood as having been a lucrative business to work as an advertisement photographer making *carte-de-visite* pictures of the industrial products, steam engines, castings, textiles, etc. that were collected in albums for use by the travelling salesmen of the factories.[11]

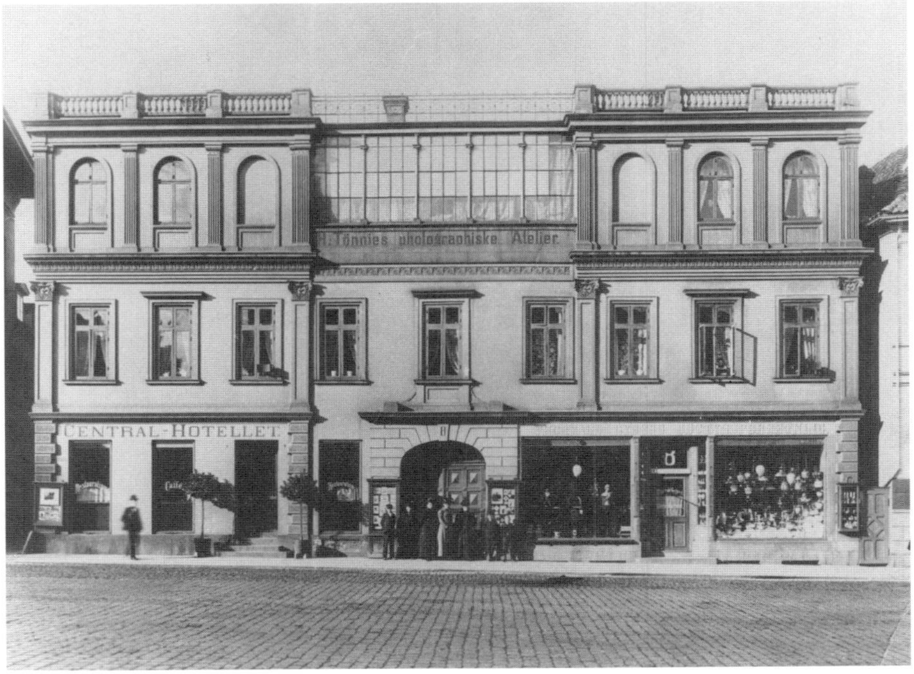

Fig.2:
Tønnies' atelier located in Nytorv, Aalborg, c.1907.
From original negative plate.

Fig.3:
Emil and Frank Tønnies working on positive *retouche* in the studio, c.1900
From original negative plate.

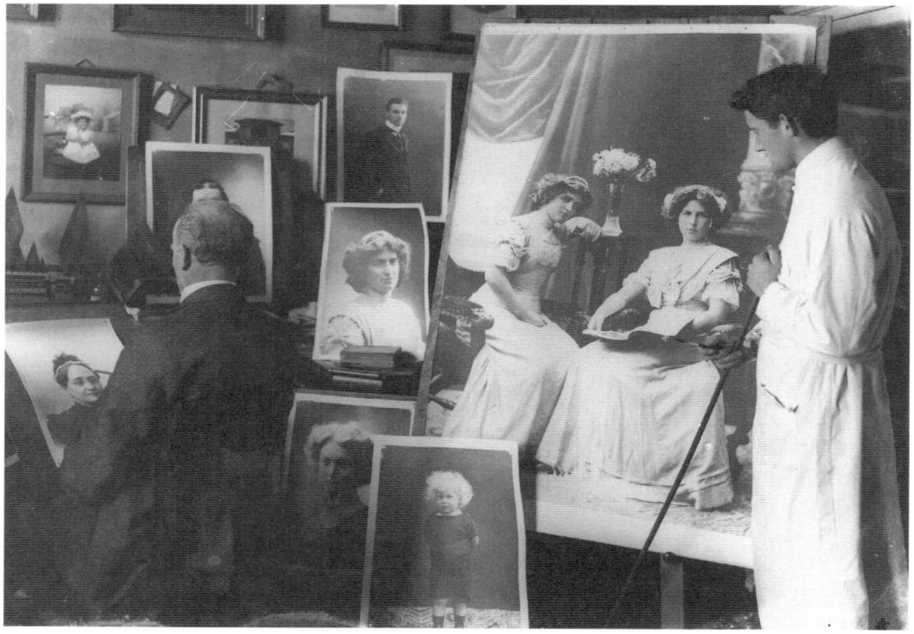

These activities, when added together with the flourishing business of making portraits, made Tønnies one of the richest men in Aalborg with a yearly income of about five thousand rixdollars. This was why, in 1881, he could afford to erect a new, three-storey atelier building in the very centre and main marketplace of Aalborg, with huge wings for storage, a factory for negative-plates and darkrooms, along with *retouche* and framing workshops [Fig. 2]. Here, from Tønnies' negative factory, most of the photographers from Jutland were from 1883 provided with the new and more light-sensitive 'dry' gelatine plates, always ready for use, instead of the 'wet' collodium plates which had to be specially prepared immediately prior to each picture taking. As possibly the largest photographic enterprise in Scandinavia, the buildings had rooms for storing the whole and Heinrich Tønnies' descendents did just that with great piety.[12] All these buildings were demolished in 1961 to be replaced by a shopping centre, but the plates, books and equipment were for the greater part preserved, as the Tønnies Company stayed in business until 1974. It was therefore possible for us to receive the entire collection when the City Archives of Aalborg was established that same year. Cameras, darkroom implements, atelier properties, and curtains all the way back to the start of the company, plus 250,000 negatives on glass. All the negatives after 1864 were numbered, dated and identified in the reorder books, and together with the main book-keeping records that also start in 1864, this means that you can on a day to day basis for a period of 110 years follow the number of exposures, the profits and the names and addresses of the customers. On average fifteen photographs per day were taken – all year round. But on the occasion of special events, such as fairs, Tønnies became part of the entertainment; when people travelled to Aalborg from the big surrounding countryside in order to attend the markets or cattle shows, 'Tønnies at the Market' could manage up to two hundred exposures per day, with the help of up to fifteen employees.[13]

At the time of receiving the Tønnies collection at the newly established Aalborg City Archives, not everybody could see the value of preserving such a vast collection in its entirety. This scepticism was also present with the local public authorities and so, as director of the institution, I was forced to figure out how to convince the public that this collection was something truly unique. The original interior of the atelier could be pretty well reconstructed and exhibited, and as such was received with much interest, as were the topographical pictures. But the main part of the collection, the portraits, proved more difficult to make popular other than to genealogical researchers. Neither the many glass negatives nor the rather few original prints were in their original state very suitable for exhibition. The original negative plates would therefore have to be enlarged and printed on modern photographic paper and be retouched for contrast and light. But it could not be denied that this procedure had a major drawback, namely that you change the original picture completely by methods that are totally different from the intentions and technical possibilities of the original photographer [Fig. 3].

What the market demands – today!

What the customers wanted at the time when Tønnies created his portraits was, as mentioned above, not 'the reality' but 'a reality', that is to say as beautified, respectable and inexpensive a picture of themselves as possible. But what about today's 'customers', who are the patrons of institutions of cultural history? What they wish for is an arranged and easily understandable tale from the past, which can speak to new audiences of exhibitions, their own imagination, and not just a simple summoning-up of some previous era's reality in the shape of original artefacts presented in the form in which they have been preserved.

This dilemma has made its mark on the long row of Tønnies exhibitions, which since the mid 1970s have been shown in both Europe and the USA. Titles like *The best preserved photo-collection in the World* have, of course, attracted attendance but not necessarily satisfied the public. What they preferred were exhibitions where they themselves were photographed in the reconstructed 'Tønnies atelier'. At the exhibition *Heinrich Tønnies – the photo album of Aalborg*, visitors could acquire a digital photo of themselves after trying to retouch it by means of a photo-editing program. Added to this was the possibility to search directly in Tønnies' order books on the web. These activities ensured sufficient grants to enable careful registration, packing and storage of the enormous material.[14]

Such initiatives were, however, only technically possible from the mid 1990s. Previously, the big eye-opener had been a broadcast in 1974 of the Tønnies collection on the sole TV channel at the time in Denmark. Here it was possible to give the pictures a life of their own through the use of sound, music, and different enlargements and zoomings in a medium that the whole population knew. And when this TV broadcast was shown in the USA in 1975, it caught the attention of an American photographer.

Alexander Alland Sr [1902–1989] was the photographer who in the 1940s found the negative-plates of the Danish-born journalist Jacob A. Riis [1868–1914], author of the book *How the Other Half Lives. Studies Among the Tenements of New York* [1890]. Riis did not consider himself as a photographer; he was a crime reporter at the *New York Tribune*. The pictures that he took with a flash camera [invented in 1887] were to be used here and now as a strong exhortation to solve the slum problems of the city. His appeal was followed by a strong reaction among his socially conscious contemporaries and inspired not least the progressive president Theodore Roosevelt, but after that both Riis and his pictures were forgotten.[15]

The oblivion was rectified by Alexander Alland who made heavily edited new prints from the old negatives. This was done through enlargement, cropping, new framing from the negatives and substantial changes in light and contrast effects made in the darkroom. It was done to such a degree that The Museum of the City of New York, where the negatives were kept, refused to buy Alland's new prints, as they, according to the management of the museum, differed so much as to be unrecognisable from the original negatives. Nevertheless it was Alland's positive prints that made the collection famous and lifted Riis from relative obscurity to being considered the very founder of the photo-documentary tradition since followed by Lewis Hine [1874–1940] and others. It was a role that

Riis himself had never contemplated; on the contrary, he thought that: 'I am no good at all as a photographer... I am clumsy and impatient of details.'[16] But the fame was underlined in Alexander Alland's *Jacob A. Riis. Photographer and Citizen* [1974], where Riis' pictures quite rightly stand strong, beautiful and well composed with a social appeal that was interpreted – mistakenly! – as being something especially Danish.

Alexander Alland sought the roots of this social appeal in an earlier Danish photographer – the German-born Heinrich Tønnies – and, after a long stay at the City Archives of Aalborg, he published *Heinrich Tønnies. Cartes-de-visite Photographer Extraordinaire* [1978]. Alland chose a number of negative plates from the Tønnies collection, but the work had to stop, at least partly, when he started to remove the original *retouche* from the original negatives to reveal what Tønnies had seen behind his camera. As was the case with Jacob Riis' negatives, Alland's prints were reinterpreted and re-edited as his own pictures rather than those of Tønnies. Or as the then director of the Royal Library's photo-collection, Bjørn Ochsner, expressed it in the foreword of the book: 'Alexander Alland has been able to reveal the images as truly as the two photographers actually saw them.'[17]

That is a very problematic view when it concerns reproduction of original material, but the book meant that Heinrich Tønnies, as edited by Alexander Alland, became known in the US.

When the Nordic Council in 1980 asked the director of Walker Art Center in Minneapolis, Martin Friedman, to be in charge of the great travelling exhibition *Scandinavia – the Frozen Image* touring in the USA and the Nordic countries, it was not surprising that Heinrich Tønnies was chosen to represent the Scandinavian photographic portrait of the nineteenth century. When Martin Friedman, during his preparations for the exhibition, reached Aalborg he – somewhat taken aback – noted the difference between those original negatives and those of Alland's prints which he had seen, but he decided to reproduce from the original negatives using only original paper and methods, but as enlargements. It did not diminish the pictures in any way, as the negatives were in fact of a high quality. It is of course still a problem that you have to use electrical light to enlarge the prints as Heinrich Tønnies himself had no electricity installed before 1899 and as time goes by you will have still more problems to find original paper and use original methods as analogue photography is now being replaced by the digital. In short: it becomes ever more difficult to avoid manipulating in the process from original negative to contemporary print.

Concluding remarks

Thus the *carte-de-visite* photographer was accused of manipulating reality in order to offer the customer the picture he wanted and was willing to pay for. The question is whether we behave very differently when we mediate old pictures. They are being constantly adapted in order to make the greatest impression on our modern audiences so as to encourage funding and grants for our institutions. But we can, of course, try to deconstruct photographic history of its overlay of later myths. Heinrich Tønnies did not produce his pictures driven by his social conscience, but because he could make money from it. Models and inspirations were taken over from the German photographic tradition that also provided the background of the later, so-well-known German photographer August Sander [1876–1964]. When both Tønnies and Sander are regarded today as being unique, this may be due to the fact that so much source material for the wider history of German photography is lost or missing.

The internet has given us radically new possibilities for providing access to this important source material to the public, which the cultural institutions must serve. This is done partly by opening Tønnies' order books to everybody on www.aalborgkommune.dk/tonnies – and partly, as the scanning of the pictures themselves progresses, on www.danpa.dk.

ENDNOTES

1 Henning Bender, 'Heinrich Tønnies negativarkiv. Omfang og overlevering' in Nina Hobolth [ed.], *Heinrich Tønnies. Et fotografisk atelier* [Aalborg: Nordjyllands Kunstmuseum, 2004], pp. 115–19.

2 Henning Bender, *Aalborgs industrielle udvikling 1735–1940* [Aalborg: Aalborg Kommune, 1987], p. 264.

3 I have particularly found Tønnies' photos in Utah, Sanpete County, where the Danish Mormons especially settled. Aalborg was one of the key points of the Mormon mission in Denmark and Tønnies had a contract to photograph all converted saints before departure for the US.

4 The Tønnies family and company records 1813–1975 are kept at the City Archives of Aalborg. See www.danpa.dk and search 'Tønnies, Heinrich' or 'fotograffirma' to see the registry [# 326].

5 Cornelia Pohlmann, *Die Auswanderung aus dem Herzogthum Braunschweig* [Stuttgart: Franz Steiner Verlag, 2002], pp. 152–8. [Die Kolonie des Grünenplaners im US-Bundesstaat Michigan], http://books.google.dk/.

6 Five thousand rixdollars was a very large sum of money. The annual wage for a skilled worker at the time was about four hundred rixdollars. A white-glass factory however, could not operate without a skilled glass-cutter and glass-painter.

7 Henning Bender, 'Fotografen Heinrich Tønnies' in Hobolth [ed.], *Heinrich Tønnies. Et fotografisk atelier*, pp. 86–91.

8 Henning Bender, 'Danmarks ældste fotoalbum', *Objektiv. Dansk Fotohistorisk Selskab*, 60 [1993], pp. 4–8.

9 The many trips to Germany can be followed in the passport records of Aalborg's chief constable.

10 A *retoucheuse* would paint directly on the glass plate to correct flaws and marks of age on the face of the sitter before the photograph was printed.

11 Henning Bender, *From Birth to Global Expansion. Metallic Industries for 175 years* [Suzhou: Suzhou Huafang Printing, 2009], pp. 54–7.

12 When in 1980 I interviewed Lili Tønnies [1888–1984], she told about daily life and how it was to be a photo assistant in the famous studio of her grandfather [Heinrich Tønnies 1825–1903] and father [Emil Tønnies 1860–1923].

13 Bender, 'Heinrich Tønnies negativarkiv. Omfang og overlevering', pp. 115–19.

14 Henning Bender, 'Heinrich Tönnies negativsamling reddet', *Objektiv. Dansk Fotohistorisk Selskab*, 54 [1991], pp. 10–20.

15 Lauren Jensen, 'The photographs of Jacob Riis: History in relation to truth', *Constructing the Past*, 5:1 [2004], http://digitalcommons.iwu.edu/constructing/vol5/iss16.

16 Bonnie Yochelson,'The Masked Image Recapturing the Work of Reformer Jacob Riis', *Humanities*, 19:3 [1998], pp. 16–21, www.neh.gov/news/humanities/1998-05/riis.html.

17 Alland, Alexander, *Heinrich Tönnies. Cartes-de-Visites Photographer Extraordinaire*, Camera, Graphic Press, New York, 1978, 'Foreword', unpaginated p. [3].

BIBLIOGRAPHY

Alland, Alexander, *Jacob A. Riis. Photographer and Citizen* [New York: Aperture, 1974].

Alland, Alexander, *Heinrich Tönnies. Cartes-de-Visites Photographer Extraordinaire* [New York: Camera/Graphic Press, 1978].

Bender, Henning, 'Portraits by Heinrich Tønnies', in Martin Friedman [ed.], *The Frozen Image – Scandinavian Photography* [New York: Abbeville Press Publishers, 1982].

Bender, Henning, 'Heinrich Tønnies negativsamling reddet', *Objektiv*, 54 [1991].

Bender, Henning, 'Landets ældste visitkortalbum', *Objektiv*, 60 [1993].

Bender, Henning, *Aalborgs industrielle udvikling 1735–1940* [Aalborg: Aalborg Kommune, 1987].

Bender, Henning, 'Fotografen Heinrich Tønnies', in Nina Hobolth [ed.], *Heinrich Tønnies – Et fotografisk Atelier* [Aalborg: Nordjyllands Kunstmuseum, 2004].

Bender, Henning, 'Heinrich Tønnies' negativarkiv – Omfang og overlevering' in Nina Hobolth [ed.], *Heinrich Tønnies – Et fotografisk Atelier* [Aalborg: Nordjyllands Kunstmuseum, 2004].

Bender, Henning, *From Birth to Global Expansion. Metallic Industries for 175 years* [Suzhou: Suzhou Huafang Printing, 2009].

Frizot, Michel, *A new History of Photography* [Köln: Körnemann Verlag, 1998].

Jensen, Lauren, 'The photographs of Jacob Riis: History in relation to truth', *Constructing the Past*, 5:1 [2004], http://digitalcommons.iwu.edu/constructing/vol5/iss16.

Mortensen, Mette, 'Folkets fotograf', in Nina Hobolth [ed.], *Heinrich Tønnies – Et fotografisk Atelier* [Aalborg: Nordjyllands Kunstmuseum, [2004].

Pohlmann, Cornelia, *Die Auswanderung aus dem Herzogthum Braunschweig* [Stuttgart: Franz Steiner Verlag, 2002].

Wolthers, Louise, 'Original og kopi – Gamle fotografier i nye fortællinger', in Nina Hobolth [ed.], *Heinrich Tønnies – Et fotografisk Atelier* [Aalborg: Nordjyllands Kunstmuseum, 2004].

Yochelson, Bonnie, 'The Masked Image Recapturing the Work of Reformer Jacob

Riis', *Humanities*, 19:3 [1998], http://www.neh.gov/news/humanities/1998-05/riis.html.

www.aalborgkommune.dk/tonnies – search database on Tønnies' order books, City Archives of Aalborg.

www.berliner-fotografenateliers.de – search database on photographers in Berlin By Prof Dr Sibylle Einholz, Fachhochschule für Teknik und Wirtschaft, Museumskunde.

www.danpa.dk – search database on Danish private records. For the records of The Tønnies Company, search 'fotograffirma', City Archives of Aalborg.

Fig.1:
Fashion photograph from
the studio Deux Sœurs, 1965.
[Image courtesy of
Göteborgs landsarkiv]

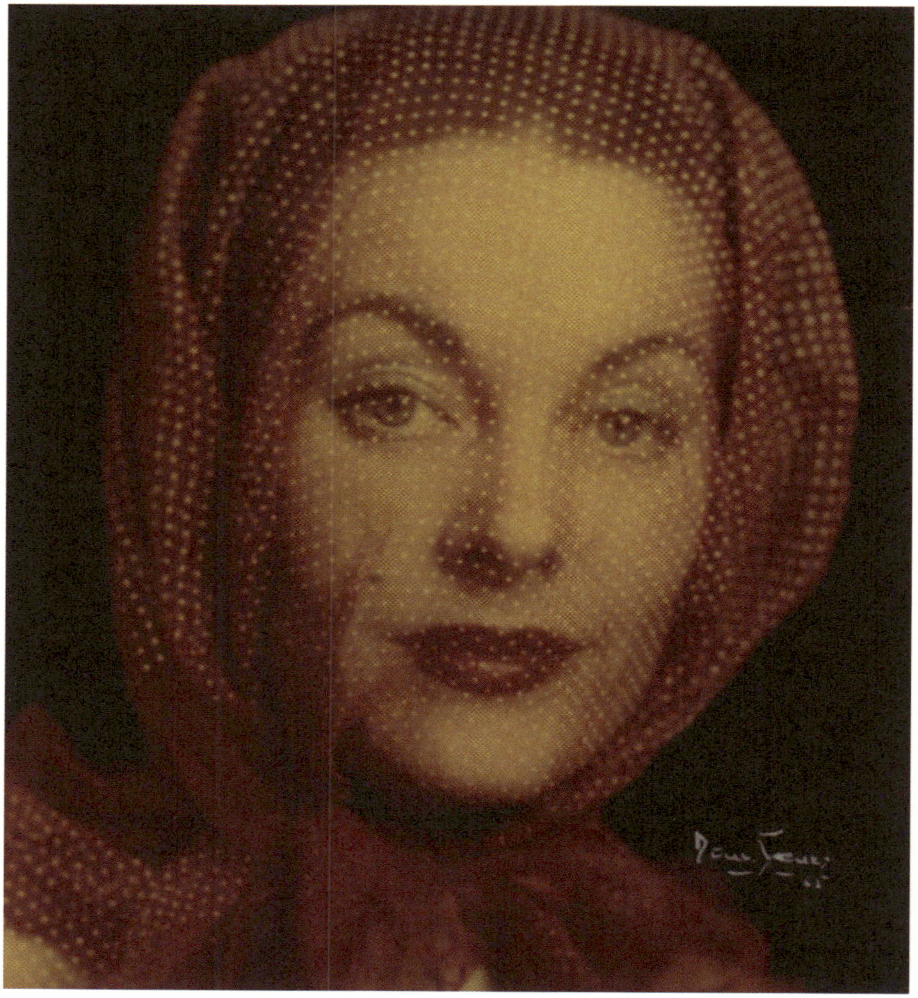

Tact and Tactics
The gendered life stories of four Swedish female photographers

ANNA DAHLGREN

Tact and tactics

In the collection at Moderna museet in Sweden there are some album pages that belonged to the Swedish photographer Edvard Welinder.[1] The album was presumably a gift of honour to Welinder in his role as chairman of the Association of Swedish Professional Photographers [Svenska Fotografers Förbund] in 1955. Each page contains a photograph and a message from his fellow photographers. On one of these pages is a photograph and a handwritten greeting from one of Sweden's most active fashion and advertising photographers in the 1950s that reads:

I have tried to find an image worthy of your fine album for half a year, and have now rested for this, which I offer with a warm hand. [2]
Olle

The greeting is signed 'Olle', a very common Swedish male surname at the time. In this particular case, it is, however, a short name for the family name Olofsdotter, and behind this male signature stands in fact the female photographer Karin Olofsdotter. Among fellow colleagues she was always called Olle.

Olle is one of the main characters in this essay that deals with the circumstances and strategies of four Swedish female fashion photographers during the first half of the twentieth century, who are to date more or less unknown.[3] As pointed out in a recent study of Swedish women photographers, women entered the profession of photography early and constituted a considerable portion of its practitioners in the country from the 1890s to the 1930s, especially in the countryside. Still they were in the minority and many of them were employed, i.e. not running a studio in their own name. Later on, especially after 1945, the associations, and trade in general, were increasingly dominated by men.[4] Despite the fact that there were quite a few women working in the photography business, they were consequently underrepresented in the professional journals, organisations and competitions and even more so in later histories of the field. The reason for the omission of women in Swedish photo history writing is complex and due to a combination of factors, and the aim of this essay is thus to trace some of them.

This essay falls into two parts. The first part contains short biographies, i.e. presentations of four individual women's careers and circumstances as professional photographers in the middle of the twentieth century in Sweden. The second part, traces features and recurrent patterns in these micro stories as gendered structures.

The intention here is to present the tact and tactics of four women photographers in Sweden in the 1930s and onwards, and furthermore to discuss the recurrent patterns in their professional careers and their implications and effects. The four women, Karin Olofsdotter, Inga Runnquist, and Ebba-Lisa and Ulla Roberg, are chosen for several reasons. Most importantly they are among the few visible women in professional associations, journals, education, exhibitions and competitions from the 1930s onwards.[5] Yet they have been given little, if any, attention by the writers of Swedish photographic history.[6] By their contemporaries, however, they seem to have been quite well known. One of them for example, Inga Runnquist, is responsible for one of the few writings on the techniques and aesthetics of fashion photography published in the Swedish professional press in the 1930s.[7] Essentially, this is an account of four more or less unknown women photographers who entered the professional photographic scene in Sweden around 1930. Furthermore they exemplify quite different fates as professional photographers. Therefore, the intention is to describe and analyse their individual strategies for coping with and maintaining their profession within a patriarchal framework, which privileged the traditional women's role of wife and mother. Initially, the investigation presents a biographical framework of each study from which subsequent discourse arising from norms of gendered behaviour, developments within the photographic profession and changing aesthetic and/or forms of representation can be contextualised. Thus a further aim of this essay is to analyse the relations between the micro stories of individual photographers and the macro stories of photo history writing.

Micro stories

Karin Olofsdotter [1915–1998], born in the southern part of Sweden in Åhus in 1915, started her career as a photographer in 1935 as an apprentice at Atelier Lenkert.[8] The Lenkert Studio had been run by the female

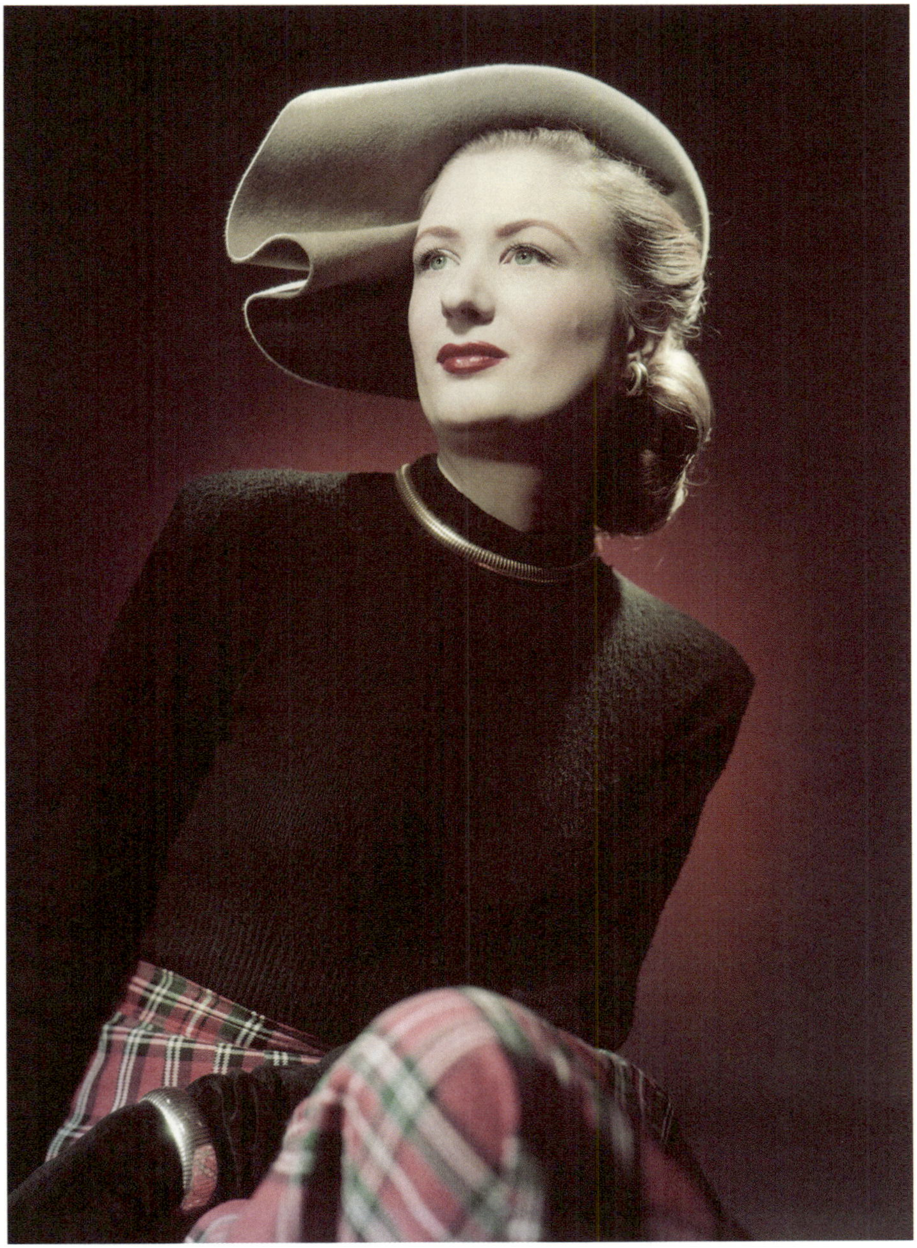

Fig.2:
Undated fashion photograph,
Karin Olofsdotter.
[Image courtesy of Malmö museer.]

photographer Sigrid Lenkert [1885–1958] since 1927 at the fashionable address Stureplan 4 in Stockholm. Sigrid Lenkert was married to Gunnar Lenkert, who owned a clothing shop, which might have influenced her ability to run a photo studio specialising in fashion and portraits.[9] Olofsdotter got her job as assistent to Mrs Lenkert after she had tried to get a position as apprentice to a male photographer. At Lenkert's studio she felt welcome. In a later interview she reported: 'I did not feel lost since she only had female personnel.'[10]

After working at Lenkert, Karin Olofsdotter moved to The Uggla Studio in 1938, which specialised in advertising.[11] In 1941 she moved on to be chief photographer at the newly opened studio at Nordisk Rotogravyr also specialising in advertising photography.[12] Subsequently, in 1945, she moved on to Åhlen & Åkerlunds photo studio owned by the publishing house Bonniers, where she was primarily working with fashion.[13] By now Karin was a name in the business and promoted as 'the well-known advertising photographer'.[14] In 1960 she was head-hunted by the flourishing studio Färgfoto in Lund where she stayed until she retired in 1970. Although she did not continue to work professionally as a photographer after 1970, she was registered as such at her home address for the rest of her life.[15] After her death a fellow photographer saw that her negatives, prints and other documents were donated to the regional museum close to her hometown. This means that some of her *oeuvre* has been saved for posterity, yet little information is saved on individual photographs. The image reproduced here is typical in this sense. Neither year of production, client or publication is noted. The only thing that is known is that it is taken by Karin Olofsdotter, probably in the 1940s on the basis of the depicted dress [Fig. 2].

The Lenkert studio was also the locus for another Swedish female fashion photographer, Inga Runnquist [1913–].[16] Runnquist came to Stockholm in the early 1930s to take a paid position as assistant to the highly esteemed male photographer Herman Sylwander at Atelier Jaeger. Following this she had a paid apprenticeship at the Elliot & Fry studio in London, and some years later went to Kodak's 'School of Commercial Photography'. In 1932 she started to work at Atelier Lenkert and four years later, in 1936, at the age of twenty-three she took over the business from Sigrid Lenkert. At the time she had two employees and one apprentice, one of who was Karin Olofsdotter. Atelier Lenkert received commissions from different Swedish fashion magazines, i.e. *Veckojournalen*, *Månadsjournalen* and *Bonniers Månadstidning.* They also worked with catalogue images and for tailors such as Augusta Lundin and Femina in Stockholm. Moreover, clothing companies, like Erling Richard, ordered photographs of their new collections for travelling salesmen to take on their sales journeys. Her studio was then taken over by two male photographers. One took over the studio while the other took over the image archives. Inga subsequently

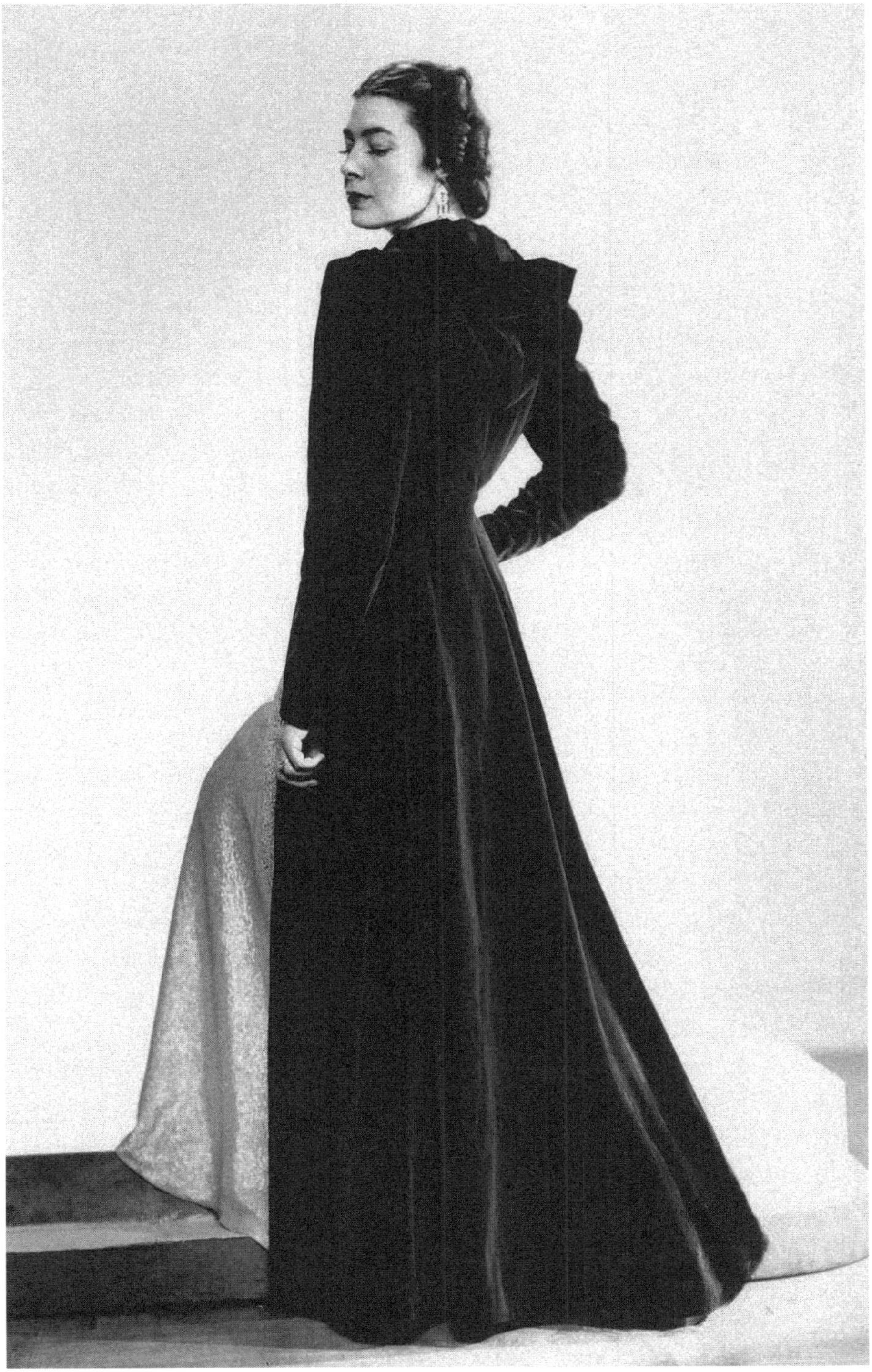

Fig.3:
One of the few surviving examples of fashion photography from the Studio Lenkert published in *Nordisk Tidskrift för Fotografi* in 1938.
Inga Runnquist.
[Image courtesy of Inga Ohlsén.]

had more children and continued to work on a small scale in her home. Yet she was continually active in the field with teaching and engagements in the photographers' association. Unfortunately the photographer who took over her studio eventually consigned the whole Lenkert archive to the dustbin. What remain of the images from Atelier Lenkert today are the original paper-prints that were published or exhibited at the photographers' association in Sweden. The photograph reproduced here [Fig. 3] initially illustrated Inga's article on fashion photography in *Nordisk Tidskrift*, 1938, and is one of very few fashion photographs by her that remains today.[17]

The last individuals to be presented in this essay are sisters Ebba-Lisa and Ulla Roberg, to date the most acknowledged of the four in Swedish photo history writing. The younger, Ulla, was interviewed in 2000 as a part of the Swedish research project 'Women Photographers. European Experiences' that aimed to give prominence to the role and work of some European women photographers.[18]

Ebba Lisa [1903–1993] and Ulla Roberg [1907–2003] grew up in a wealthy family in Gothenburg. On the initiative and at the financial expense of their father they got an exclusive education and opened up a photographic studio together in their home town. They were first trained at the local male photographer Erik Hendriksson's studio. After some months there Ebba-Lisa and later also Ulla were sent to practice at the studio Mesdames Morter in London, run by the two sisters Dorothy and Rita Morter. From London they went to Paris to work for Mademoiselle Ergy Landeau and their apprentice time was closed by a period in Berlin at the male photographer Nicola Perscheid.

By the end of 1926 the two sisters returned to Sweden to start up their own studio, financially supported by their father. He ordered exclusive photographic equipment from Germany and provided studio space in his own building in the centre of Gothenburg. In October 1928 their elegant Studio Deux Sœurs opened, specialising in portraits and becoming famous for their images of actors, members of high society in Gothenburg and children.[19] In addition they took on advertising and fashion work. Among their customers were the Wezäta, Nordiska trikåbolaget, Gillblads and Lidbecks companies. While the writings and archival material emphasise their portraits, Ulla notes that approximately a third of their business was advertising photography.[20] Indeed, they consistently presented their business from the 1930s to the 1970s as *Deux Sœurs. Portrait and advertising photography* [Deux Sœurs. Porträtt- och reklamfotografering].[21]

The two sisters ran the studio together until 1950. That Ulla, who had been married since 1938 and had four children, kept her professional career was much due to her financial ability to employ a nanny at home, but when the fifth child was on its way she finally had to leave her profession. The combination of family and professional life did not work. Nevertheless Ebba-Lisa managed to continue the business on her own for another twenty-three years, until 1973, when the studio was closed.[22] In contrast to the first two photographers described in this essay, what remains from their business is well preserved in the regional archives. It holds around twenty thousand negatives, hundreds of prints and rich documentation on the daily business in the studio. Nevertheless, the remaining part of their business is dominated by their portrait commissions. The reason for this is hinted at in a contract from an advertising producer in 1936, kept in their archive. The contract declares that all adverting commissions were strictly confidential. For example, Deux Sœurs were prohibited to expose their advertising work for others or use them in any marketing actions for the studio.[23]

Take it like a man

Despite the fact that a considerable portion of the professional photographers and photography workers were women in the early twentieth century, the profession was male dominated. The norm was in various ways a male photographer, whilst a woman photographer was considered a deviation from that norm.[24] There were a number of possible strategies for women to make their way in the business. In the case of photographer Karin Olofsdotter the use of a male nickname, 'Olle', with friends and colleagues was, perhaps, an attempt to stifle prejudice. The business name, always printed on the photographs she produced, was her family name Olofsdotter. But this was a clear statement. Karin was born Andersson, the daughter of the barber Olof Andersson, and took the name Olofsdotter later in life.[25] Her reasons for changing her name are not known, but one might be that the family name Andersson is a very common name in Sweden. It is anonymous and connotes ordinariness. The name Olofsdotter literally means 'the daughter of Olof'. By using this family name, Karin emphasised that she was a woman, a daughter. In her professional career Karin Olofsdotter consistently used her family name alone with the effect that she was simultaneously, though not overtly, emphasising and concealing the fact that she was a woman. This point was made to such an extent that when the Swedish fashion photographers from the twentieth century were presented in the book *Bilden av modet* [*The Image of Fashion*] in 2009 her surname was not known – and consequently neither was her sex. The authors write:

Atelier Uggla started in 1939 ... the studio photographers were Olofsdotter, Stig Holmes and Rolf Winqvst. Among the famous assistants were Rune Hassner, Hans Gedda, Bo Appeltoft and Carl Johan Rönn.[26]

Everybody except Olofsdotter was presented with their male surnames. Karin was obviously the only women photographer at the studio at the time and the only one that was not presented by her full name. I do not know if this was a strategy on her own part or simply neglect on the part of historians, but the fact remains: the woman who was termed 'the only female advertising photographer of Sweden' in 1943 is today very anonymous.

But her tactics were not limited to the use of name. She dressed in trousers, a recurrent topic in the press during the 1940s. In one interview, the trouser girl ['Byxtös'], as she was called, declared that: 'trousers are a part of the necessary professional equipment for a photographer. Initially I worked in skirts and I managed to destroy a pair of nylons every day.'[27] In another interview she gives one more rationale. The skirt would draw attention when working in the field. Karin remarks: 'Of course you may draw some attention when you come out to a factory, but I have started to use trousers, so nowadays the workers don't have to stand and look when I climb ladders.'[28]

The same article is illustrated with a photograph of Karin standing legs spread with a pair of trousers and a jacket holding a large format camera [Fig. 4]. Thus the image bears a peculiar paradox, for while Karin is dressed and poses like a man, one cannot neglect the fact that her pose also connects her to what is, for the period, a very feminine act. She is holding her camera on her hip in exactly the same way as a small child is carried. Thus she is simultaneously acting like a professional photographer and a mother in the same pose. In a sense this image is a condensed visualisation of the female photographer's tension between private and professional life. This photographic image of Karin can also be seen literally as a proof; it proves the contemporary male fashion photographer Horst P. Horst wrong. Talking on fashion photography in the 1930s he argued that 'the 8 x 10 in

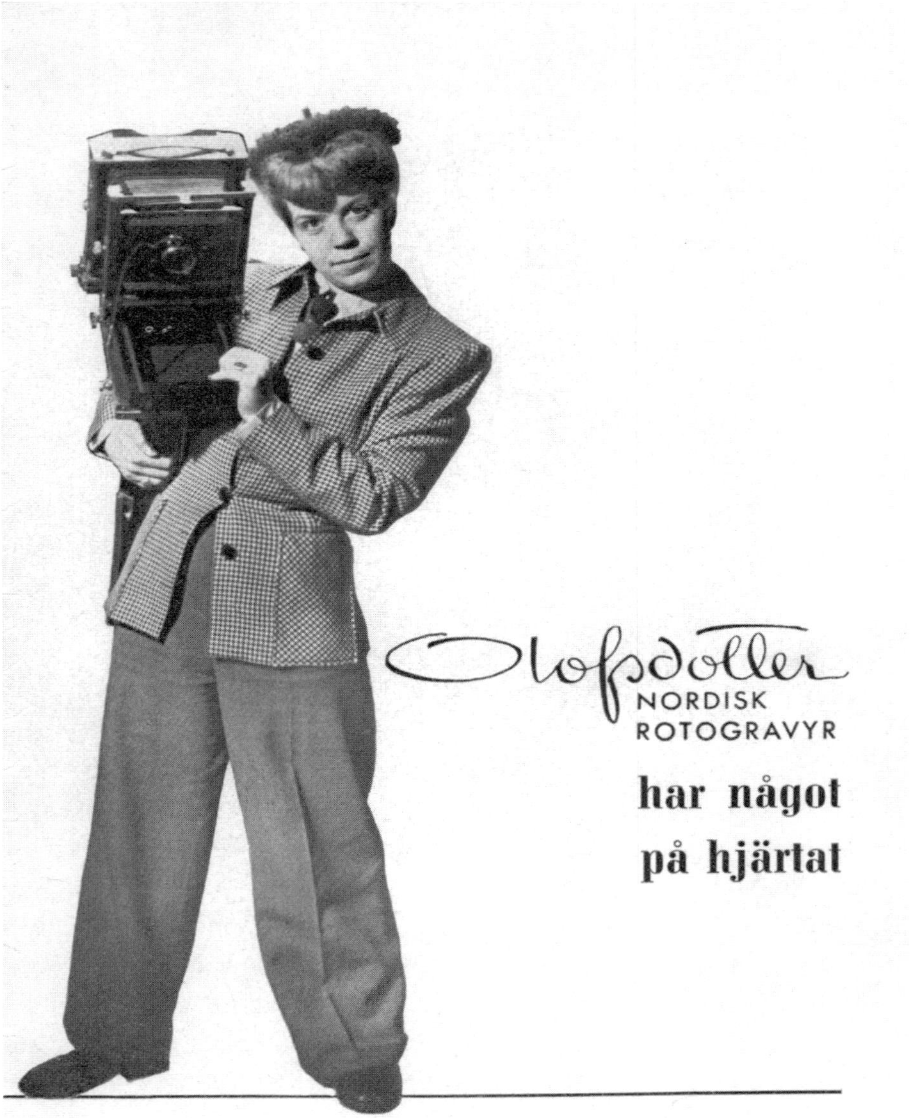

Fig.4:
Advertising brochure for Studio Nordisk Rotogravyr, 1941–1945.
Photographer unknown.
[Image courtesy of Malmö museer]

camera was so heavy and unwieldy that it was assumed that no woman could ever be a *Vogue* photographer'.[29] To be a *Vogue* photographer was a mark of distinction, it implied photographs of the highest technical and aesthetic standard and in the period this kind of fashion photography was synonymous with the large-format camera and advanced lighting technique. What is telling with Horst's remark is that he connects the photographer's skill and success with technical resources and physical strength and presumes that this excludes women in general. Of course there were several women photographers who handled heavy studio cameras at the time, among others were Toni Frissell, Louise Dahl-Wolfe, Deborah Turbeville, Mme d'Ora, Toni von Horn, Lillian Bassman, Lee Miller and Frances McLaughlin-Gill.[30] From this perspective the image of Karin Olofsdotter can be read as a quality assurance. Karin proves to be strong enough, both literally and figuratively speaking. She has what it takes to be a highly skilled and successful photographer.

Professional life or family life

From the case studies of these four women it is evident that it was quite hard to combine family life and a professional career as a photographer in Sweden at this time. To have children and continue to work was almost impossible.[31] According to Inga Ohlsén this was the reason why Sigrid Lenkert had to leave her studio.[32] Similarly, for Inga Ohlsén and Ulla Roberg marriage and children more or less put an end to their professional careers. Worth noting though is that they chose to start a family quite late in life.[33] Ulla Roberg acknowledges this in an interview many years later: 'Five children in six years and two months! That is quite close, but I was over thirty when I married.'[34] Ebba-Lisa, who successfully kept her studio, remained unmarried.

In an interview in 1943, Olofsdotter stated that she loved her work and would not stop in the event of her getting married. The male journalist and fellow photograper, Karl Sandels, closed the article with the laconic remark: 'So now every man knows that.'[35] Many years later her daughter described her experience of life with a professional photographer for a mother: 'I came to the world a sunny morning. But life had to go on. Work was waiting. Kajsa met all kinds of nice people while I went to school and was taken care of.'[36] Even though Karin Olofsdotter Nylund [her full name after marriage] left her employment as a photographer at the age of fifty-five and divorced in 1953 she kept the same appellation in the phone directory until her death in 1998: 'Karin Olofsdotter, photographer, wife.'[37] This, short, simple text clearly displays the tension between being a professional and a private woman.

What is evident is that when these women photographers appeared in the professional press and daily papers they were exceptions from the norm. The fact that they were women was always mentioned, they were constantly presented as 'female photographers' rather than just 'photographers'. Furthermore, the reports on their professional work and careers were always interwoven with descriptions of their private lives. Concerns about their appearance, marriage, children and skills as housewives were recurrent themes in interviews, as if they constantly had to reassure the readers that they were still 'normal' women, despite being successful and talented professionals.[38] An exemplar of which is the account of Ebba-Lisa Roberg's talents in cooking and table decoration in the regional daily paper *Göteborgsposten*. The article opens by declaring that:

[she] is not only a talented photographer with a famous studio in Gothenburg. She ... will still save time for her large circle of friends. She is in her element when she plans parties, tries new recipes and plans lavish table settings.[39]

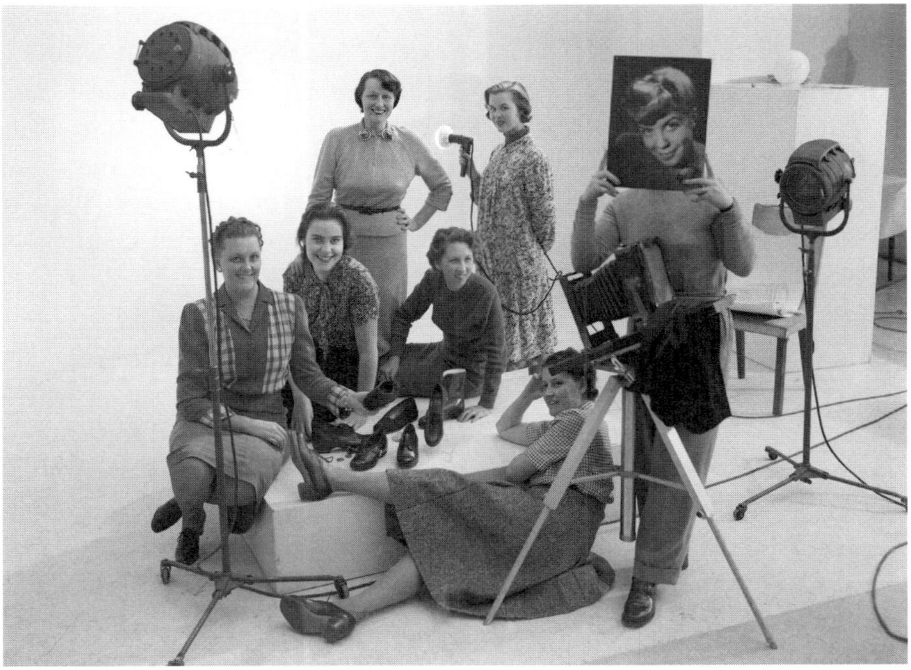

Fig.5:
Karin Olofsdotter with assistants and models in the studio. Not dated.
Karin Olofsdotter.
[Image courtesy of Malmö museer]

A woman's world

The undated photograph from Karin Olofsdotter's studio, probably from the 1950s, is telling: the studio is, without exception, filled with women, [Fig. 5]. They are posing around a white podium typically used for shooting accessories like the shoes that are on display in this image. The technical equipment is there; two studio lamps are visible as is the studio camera on a stand. It is not clear from the photo what function the women had, some may be models, others assistants or fellow photographers. Nevertheless it is obvious that this is a group of professionals in the photography business. Karin herself poses by the camera. She is obviously the photographer, but she keeps her hands in the air so she is not pulling the trigger. Her left hand waves to the beholder, while the right holds a photographic portrait of herself that completely covers her face. The choice of this particular portrait is important. It is the official image of Karin Olofsdotter that appeared over and over again in the press when she made her breakthrough in the early 1940s. This is the Karin Olofsdotter 'brand' so to speak. In a sense her use of the official, and by the time this particular image was taken probably old, photograph serves the same purpose as her consequent use of her family name in professional contexts. By using the image of Karin Olofsdotter, and hiding her 'real' face she actually keeps her privacy. Her play with the portrait, masking herself, also emphasises her position as a beholder rather than object for the gaze. This image provides evidence to support the earlier biographical outlines that it seemed to have been a strategy among women photographers to work together, utilising their professional networks. Furthermore the image is symbolic in the sense that it simultaneously displays and conceals Karin Olofsdotter. Thus it illustrates the paradox of being invisible while constantly making others visible that typically characterises the photographer.

The amassing of women in particular photo studios may or may not not have been an avowed strategy, but nevertheless it is telling. In this respect Sweden followed patterns seen in other Western countries where the concept of female photographers who employed female apprentices was recurrent.[40] Olofsdotter, Runnquist and the Robergs all underwent apprenticeships at studios run by women, in London, Paris and Stockholm. Consequently it is no coincidence that Sigrid Lenkert, born of an older generation, welcomed both Inga Runnquist and Karin Olofsdotter to her studio in the 1930s.[41] Getting an apprenticeship was of vital importance if you could not afford to pay for an education at a studio. In this respect the circumstances appear to have been somewhat different for the four women presented here. The Roberg sisters and Inga Runnquist were from wealthy backgrounds and their parents paid for their apprenticeships at highly esteemed photo studios in Sweden and abroad, while Karin Olofsdotter had no previous training when she arrived at Atelier Lenkert. For her the opportunity offered by a fellow woman was crucial. In short, financial support, i.e. class background, was a decisive factor for being able to be a woman photographer and run a studio in the period. Karin Olofsdotter later returned the favour when she became the head of the new advertising photography studio at Nordisk Rotogravyr in 1941. Within two years she had employed three other women.[42] Later on she had several female assistants, among others Kerstin Björkström and Lisa Kallós. The latter became one of Sweden's most famous female fashion photographers in the next generation. The Roberg sisters in turn also had female assistants, even though Ulla Salén did not recall this as a conscious choice when interviewed much later.[43] One obvious rationale could be that it was considered more respectable that young women worked with women.[44]

According to studies of the photographic field in Britain, women were especially active in the field between 1920 and 1940, and the flow of women into studio portrait and commercial practice was 'enormous' in this period.[45] The situation in Sweden seems to have been somewhat different. Despite the fact that women made up a considerable portion of the photographic trade they were, in fact, scarcely visible in the contemporary professional journals and organisations. Women photographers were the exception. Karin Olofsdotter was, for example, described as the *only* female advertising photographer in Sweden in the 1940s.[46] In the subsequent writing of fashion photography histories this is even more pronounced.[47] In the *Swedish History of Photography [Den svenska fotografins historia]*, published in 1983, women photographers are very few and the field of fashion photography is completely omitted. In consequence none of the photographers presented here are in it.[48] In the more recent publication particularly dedicated to Swedish fashion photography 1940–2000, *Bilden av modet* [2009], one female photographer is mentioned, Kerstin Bernhard.[49]

The interesting question is why have all of these women fashion photographers not been included in later photo-historical narratives, when they were appreciated by their male colleagues and had an active, productive contemporary role? As these case-studies imply, the reasons are neither simple nor conclusive. As with many examples of women's work, examples are undervalued and consequently discarded. In the case of Inga Runnquist, a short career as a studio owner proved fatal for her work. As it was custom to keep the negatives at the studio, to enable customers to order new prints, leaving the studio also meant leaving all your work. Her male successor subsequently discarded both her and her predecessor Sigrid Lenkert's accumulated work. Male photographers, on the other hand, probably more often kept their businesses throughout their life. Longevity and control ensured their work was preserved and it was more than likely that their collected works would either be passed on to a fellow colleague or donated to an archive or museum.

Another influential factor could result from male domination within the photographic organisations, including professional associations and journals. This was crucial as the events, exhibitions and writing from these agencies has formed the basis of later history writing. Like their male colleagues, women photographers took a wide range of assignments, among them portraits, fashion and reportage. When interviewed, the female photographers often emphasised that photography was a suitable trade for a woman. 'It's a fashionable work and it suits women perfectly', as the Roberg sisters said in an interview in 1943.[50]

This might be understood as a constant defence for their own professional activity as the photographic trade's 'other'. Yet there was a hierarchy between the genres. Women photographers were more often assigned to 'women's issues', subjects connected to domestic life like children, food and interior decoration.[51]

Artworks and portraits were held in higher esteem than advertising and fashion.[52] This is evidenced in a description of the work of the Nordisk Rotogravyr studio in 1943: 'in the advertising studio Ms Olofsdotter arranges goods and mannequins in a seductive way, but also as a change from this hard work she portraits actors and other real people skillfully, like a modern photo artist'[53] [Fig. 6]. Working in a studio with portraits and objects was considered more suitable for women than working in the field as a press photographer or travelling photographer, even though there existed woman photographers in these genres too.[54] Fashion photography, being about clothes and accessories, was eventually one field of photography that could be labelled feminine. According to Karin Olofsdotter, women were especially suited for fashion photography as 'A woman likes to potter about with clothes and has a completely different feeling for them. She is by nature accurate and maybe even finicky, but all in all these qualities are useful in advertising photography'.[55] The repeated emphasis by women photographers on being *suitable* may be interpreted as a reassurance of them being worthy of the task.

Moreover, women were needed in the studio, where so-called female qualities were vital in the communication with the customers. This is hinted at in the letters of recommendation written for Karin Olofsdotter in

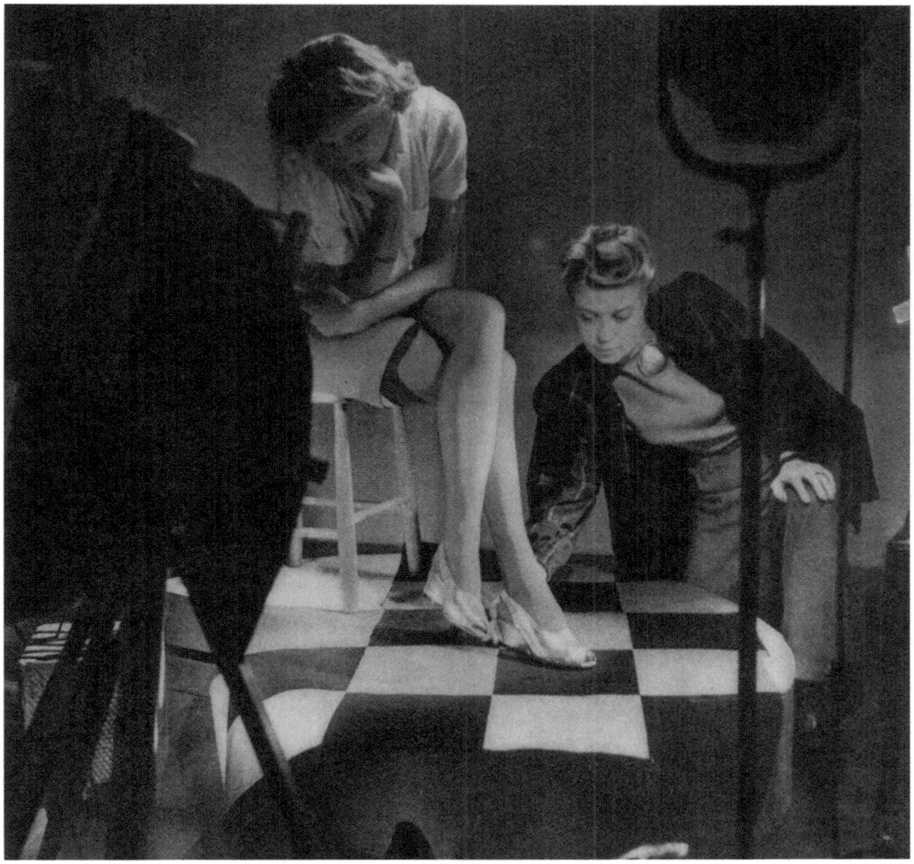

Fig.6:
'In the advertising studio Ms Olofsdotter arranges goods and mannequins in a seductive way' photograph of the studio at Nordisk Rotogravyr, 1943.
Photographer unknown.
[Image courtesy of The Royal Library of Sweden]

the 1930s and 1940s. She is praised for her technical skills but invariably also for her 'agreeable manner, which is of utmost importance in the daily contact with the customers'.[56]

Working as a photographer in the 1930s to the 1950s, it seems, was not easily combined with traditional female duties of taking care of children and a home. The two women presented in this essay who actually had longer careers as photographers put almost all their energy into their work. Indeed, long working hours and stress is a recurrent theme in interviews with Karin Olofsdotter. She acknowledged in an interview in 1961: 'Work consumes almost all my time.'[57] The other successful photographer, Ebba-Lisa Roberg, who was neither married nor had children, described the successful photographer as a '*flâneur*', a classical male figure:

You have to move out in the crowds. See clothes and people in milieus. Neither as a portrait nor as an advertising photographer can one achieve good results just by working in the studio. One has to meet a lot of people and see as much as possible.[58]

Ebba-Lisa Roberg lived by her ideals. But for most women, the gendered responsibilities that tied them to the home likewise hindered the development of a photographic career with any longevity. You had to choose either/or. Opportunities for *flânerie* were severely restricted for women who could not commit wholly to their career, particularly as photography moved from the studio to on-location assignments. Later, from the 1950s, women [fashion] photographers became even more anachronistic in the photographic field as a new image of photographers grew strong. With photographers like Irving Penn and Richard Avedon, fashion photography was typically described as the result of the meeting between a male artist and his female muse. The female photographers obviously did not fit into this heterosexually saturated matrix, with a male observer and a woman to be observed.[59] The result is paradoxical and yet evident. Simultaneously as photography as a medium was re-evaluated and written into art history, women photographers were written out of this history.

Conclusion

The micro stories presented in this essay on the professional careers of four female photographers in Sweden in the 1930s and onwards show a diversity of strategies and tactics for entering, maintaining and eventually leaving a position in the photographic field. Nevertheless there are some recurrent patterns in these life stories. One of them is the difficulty in combining a professional career and an expected life as a wife and mother. In many cases women had to choose either/or. In some cases this was professional suicide as it shortened their time in the business and, as a consequence, their control over their work. Another recurrent theme is that the women photographers constantly had to relate to a male norm in the profession. The one extreme is Karin Olofsdotter who used a male nickname and consistently dressed in trousers. But I would argue that even less spectacular features fulfilled the same purpose. Every time these women had to argue why they were acting as professional photographers or were asked about their private lives in professional contexts, they were in fact being questioned on the basis of their gender.

In general women were in the minority within the photographic profession in Sweden in the period, but there were certainly some very successful and highly accomplished women in the field. The overall question asked in this essay is how and why women photographers were so invisible in contemporary media and even more so in the later photo history writing? As this essay shows, this neglect cannot solely be explained by the fact that the majority of the photographers, as well as the writers of photo history, were male. As these four micro stories show, almost all aspects of the female photographers' professional careers were flavoured by gendered structures – from getting an education, maintaining a studio, working in the different genres and keeping control of one's *œuvre* – structures that in turn proved to be crucial for the inclusion of exclusion in the history writing on the professional photographer.

ENDNOTES

1 Moderna museet, collection of Edvard Welinder.

2 The Swedish text reads: 'Efter ett halvårs fruktlösa försök att åstadkomma en bild värdig Ditt fina album har jag på grund av tidsbegränsning måst stanna inför denna, som jag överlämnar med varm hand.' Edvard Welinder collection at Moderna museet, Sweden.

3 None of them are mentioned in R. Söderberg and P. Rittsel, *Den svenska fotografins historia* [Stockholm: Bonnier Fakta, 1983], the only comprehensive Swedish photo history to date.

4 G. Knape, 'Some notes', in L. Johannesson, G. Knape and E. Dahlman [eds.], *Women Photographers: European Experience* [Gothenburg: Acta Universitatis Gothoburgensis, 2004], pp. 9–10.

5 This is a result of my own survey on the writings on commercial photography in the three Swedish photo journals, *Fotografisk Tidskrift, Nordisk Tidskrift för Fotografi* and *Foto*, during the period 1888–1990.

6 All four are briefly mentioned in *Women Photographers – European Experience*. The education and working conditions of the Roberg sisters are described in this publication. Furthermore Karin Olofsdotter's name is mentioned and there is a reference to a short interview with her from 1975. Finally Inga Runnquist's name is mentioned once. See: L. Johannesson, 'Photo exile. On the European experience and women photographers in Germany and Sweden', in Johannesson, Knape and Dahlman [eds.], *Women photographers: European Experience*, p. 34 and p. 60; and J. Tedroff, 'Women photographers in the Swedish professional and public press 1930–2000. An

analytical inventory', *ibid.*, pp. 223–4. In this respect they differ from other contemporary Swedish women photographers, like Anna Riwkin and Kerstin Bernard, whose work to date is covered by numerous catalogues and books.

7 I. Rundquist, 'Några synpunkter på mannekängfotografering', *Nordisk Tidskrift för Fotografi*, 3 [1938], pp. 52–3.

8 R. Berner, 'Lund fångade landets första modefoto-kvinna', *Arbetet*, 8 [1961], p. 9; Shot, 'Mitt yrke. Fotograf och byxtös' [My profession: Photographer and trouser girl], *Stockholms Tidningen* [18 August 1944].

9 Initially she and her husband shared offices, at Birger Jarlsgatan 16 in Stockholm, where he had his clothing business and she her photo studio. *Rikstelefonkatalogen* Stockholmsdelen, 1930; Interview with Hans Lenkert, 18 November 2008.

10 Letter of recommendation from Ateljé Lenkert, in Karin Olofsdotter archives, Malmö museer.

11 Letter of recommendation from Ateljé Uggla, in Karin Olofsdotter archives, Malmö museer

12 K. Sandels, 'Karin Olofsdotter', *Svensk Fotografisk Tidskrift*, 395 [1943], pp. 272–3.

13 'Nya män – nya uppgifter', *Reklam-nyheterna*, 2 [1945], p. 4.

14 Advert for Åhlen & Åkerlund Studio in the journal *Reklamnyheterna*, 2 [1945].

15 R. Berner, 'Lund fångade landets första modefoto-kvinna'; C. Friberg, 'Fem kvinnliga fotografer ser på sitt jobb', *FOTO*, 1 [1975], pp. 20–1; and *Telefonkatalogen* Lund, 1961–1997.

16 All data in the following paragraph come from my interview with Inga Ohlsén [born Runnquist]. Interview conducted by the author in Norrtälje, 15 November 2008.

17 I. Runnquist, 'Några synpunkter på mannekäng fotografering', *Nordisk Tidskrift för Fotografi*, 3 [1938], pp. 52–3. Thanks to the journal editor Helmer Bäckström, who donated his private collection to the Moderna museet in 1966, including many of the published photographs from the journal, two fashion photographs by Runnquist are kept in the collection at Moderna

Museet in Stockholm.

18 Interview with Ulla Salén, née Roberg, conducted by Ann-Charlotte Glasberg on 25 May 2000 as a part of the research project 'Woman Photographers – European Experience'. Some information from the interview was used in the anthology of the same name: Johannesson, Knape and Dahlman [eds.], *Women Photographers: European Experience*.

19 K. Sandels, 'Deux Sœurs', *Svensk Fotografisk Tidskrift*, 389 [1943], pp. 116–17; The Studio Deux Sœurs' archives, Göteborgs landsarkiv.

20 Interview with Ulla Salén, née Roberg, conducted by Ann-Charlotte Glasberg on 25 May 2000.

21 This is evident from advertising, bills, letters and other printed material from the business that remains in Studio Deux Sœurs archives, Göteborgs landsarkiv.

22 L. Fahlén, 'Två systrar – en epok', *FOTO*, 1 [1975], pp. 44–5.

23 Contract between The Studio Deux Sœurs and the advertising department at Göteborgs litografiska AB, dated 13 March 1936. Deux Sœurs archives, Göteborgs landsarkiv.

24 E. Dahlman, 'Kvinnliga pionjärer osynliga i fotohistorien', *Kvinnovetenskaplig Tidskrift*, 3:4 [1995], pp. 45–54; A. Tellgren, 'Förnyelse av formen i femtiotalets fotografi', *Kvinnovetenskaplig Tidskrift*, 3:4 [1995], pp. 55–66.

25 Data on when Karin took her new family name are contradictory. In her school leaving marks from 1928, when she was fourteen years old, she still had the family name Andersson. When she and her sisters, Anna-Britta and Gunnel, appear in the telephone directory of Stockholm in 1942 they all have the family name Olofsdotter.

26 L. Lewenhaupt and T. Lewenhaupt, *Bilden av modet* [Malmö: Arena, 2009], p. 9.

27 Shot, 'Mitt yrke. Fotograf och byxtös', *Stockholms Tidningen* [18 August 1944].

28 K. Sandels, 'Karin Olofsdotter', *Svensk Fotografisk Tidskrift*, 395 [1943], pp. 272–3.

29 N. Hall-Duncan, *The History of Fashion Photography* [New York: Alpine Book Company, 1979], p. 77. For the Horst quote Hall-Duncan quotes Horst P. Horst,

N. Hall-Duncan, *Salute to the Thirties*, [New York: The Viking Press, 1971], p. 13.

30 Hall-Duncan, *The History of Fashion Photography*, p. 77.

31 Their fellow colleague, Kerstin Berhard, a contemporary successful woman photographer, admitted that she could never have combined family life with her profession. See: Tellgren, 'Förnyelse av formen i femtiotalets fotografi', p. 65.

32 Interview with Inga Ohlsén [born Runnquist], Norrtälje, by the author, 15 November 2008.

33 Inga Ohlsén was twenty-eight when she had her first child, Karin Olofsdotter thirty-one, and Ulla Roberg married at thirty-one.

34 Interview with Ulla Salén, née Roberg, conducted by Ann-Charlotte Glasberg on 25 May 2000.

35 Sandels, 'Karin Olofsdotter', p. 273.

36 'Berättelsen om Kajsa Kavaj', dated 1965, The Karin Olofsdotter archive at Malmö museer.

37 *Telefonkatalogen*, Lund, 1961–1997.

38 When their male colleagues where presented they were neither designated 'male photographers', nor were their private lives, eventual spouses or children mentioned. See, for example, the presentation of their contemporary colleague Erik Holmén. K. Sandels, 'Erik Holmén', *Svensk Fotografisk Tidskrift*, 385 [1943], pp. 12–13.

39 Signature Eivor, 'Kall vinterdag pigags upp med kul bordsdukning, het löksoppa och sallad från medelhavet', *Göteborgstidningen*, 1 [1962]. The text reads in Swedish: 'Ebba-Lisa Roberg är inte bara en skicklig fotograf med känd studio i Göteborg. Hon är också en mycket aktiv föreningskvinna – Zonta och Yrkeskvinnors klubb – men ger sig ändå god tid att sköta sin stora vänkrets. Hon är i sitt esse när hon rustar till fest, prövar nya recept och tänker ut piffiga borddukningar.'

40 N. Rosenblum, *A History of Women Photographers* [New York: Abbeville Press, 1994], p. 115; V. Williams, *The Other Observers. Woman Photographers in Britain 1900 to the Present* [London: Virago Press, 1986]. pp. 93–9.

41 Olofsdotter tells in an interview in 1943 that she initially went to an artistic male photographer but he declined her while Sigrid Lenkert took her on. Sandels, 'Karin Olofsdotter', pp. 272–3.

42 They were Ester Bondesson, E. Hedrén Andersson and Lillian York. See *Nordisk Rotogravyr 1918–1943*, [Stockholm, 1943] p. 2.

43 They were Mabel Colliander and Gerd Wennersten. Interview with Ulla Salén, née Roberg, conducted by Ann-Charlotte Glasberg on 25 May 2000.

44 Women have been working professionally with photography since the invention of the medium, yet more often as assistants or employees than as studio owners due to the fact that women seldom had the resources to set up a studio for themselves. See, for example, Mary Warner Marian, *Photography. A Cultural History* [London: Laurence King Publishing, 2002], pp. 161–2; Johannesson, Knape and Dahlman [eds.], *Women Photographers: European Experience*; Rosenblum, *A History of Women Photographers*.

45 Williams, *The Other Observers. Woman Photographers in Britain 1900 to the Present*, pp. 89–90. This is based on her studies on the development in Britain, but is arguably applicable to other European countries. The Swedish case-studies presented in this essay strengthen this conclusion.

46 Sandels, 'Karin Olofsdotter', pp. 273.

47 This is true for Nancy Hall-Duncan's classic, *The History of Fashion Photography* [1979], as well as the more recent survey of the history of fashion photography in Michel Frizot's *A New History of Photography* [1998]. See: Francoise Ducros, 'The dream of beauty. Fashion and fantasy' in Michel Frizot [ed.], *A New History of Photography* [Köln: Könemann, 1998], pp. 535–53; and Hall-Duncan, *The History of Fashion Photography*.

48 Söderberg and Rittsel, *Den svenska fotografins historia*.

49 Lewenhaupt and Lewenhaupt, *Bilden av modet*.

50 Sandels, 'Deux Sœurs', pp. 116-17.

51 Rosenblum, *A History of women Photographers*, p. 144.

52 The contemporary female photographer, Anna Riwkin, has, for example, been remembered for her reportage photographs and expressive images of dance while she was actually quite active as an advertising photographer. She was,

for example, working with advertising at the studio Rotogravyr and was one of the few photographers who was a member of the Swedish advertising association in the 1930s. See: *Svenska reklamförbundets medlemsmatrikel*, 1937.

53 *Nordisk Rotogravyr 1918–1943*, p. 15.

54 See, for example, K. Becker, 'Det skarpa perspektivet och könsproblematiken inom dokumentärfotografin', *Kvinnovetenskaplig Tidskrift*, 3:4 [1995], pp. 17-35.

55 The text reads in Swedish: 'En kvinna tycker om att pyssla med kläder, och har en helt annan känsla för dem än männen. Hon är dessutom av naturen noggrann och kanske litet petig, men just dessa egenskaper kommer väl till pass vid all slags reklamfotografering.' Sandels, 'Karin Olofsdotter', p. 273.

56 Letter of recommendation from Atelier Uggla, dated 30 January 1940. See also letter of recommendation from Atelier Lenkert, dated 1 September 1938. Both in the Karin Olofsdotter archive at Malmö museer.

57 A. Heinberg, 'Mesterfotografen er en dame', *Flitige Hender*, 27 [1961], p. 45.

58 L. Gräslund, 'Kvinnoyrket på modet. Bra yrke för rätt kvinna', *Damernas Värld*, 26/7–2/8 [1956], pp. 22–3, p. 36, p. 38.

59 This is, for example, evident in the descriptions of the work by Irving Penn and Richard Avedon, but also Helmut Newton, David Bailey and others. See: Francoise Ducros, 'The dream of beauty. Fashion and fantasy' in Michel Frizot [ed.], *A New History of Photography*.

BIBLIOGRAPHY

Becker, K., 'Det skarpa perspektivet och könsproblematiken inom dokumentärfotografin', *Kvinnovetenskaplig Tidskrift*, 3:4 [1995].

Berner, R., 'Lund fångade landets första modefoto-kvinna', *Arbetet*, 8 [1961].

Dahlman, E., 'Kvinnliga pionjärer osynliga i fotohistorien', *Kvinnovetenskaplig Tidskrift*, 3:4 [1995].

Ducros, F., 'The dream of beauty. Fashion and fantasy', in M. Frizot [ed.], *A New History of Photography* [Cologne: Könemann, 1998].

Eivor, 'Kall vinterdag piggar upp med kul bordsdukning, het löksoppa och sallad från medelhavet', *Göteborgstidningen*, 1 [1962].

Fahlén, L., 'Två systrar – en epok', *FOTO*, 1 [1975].

Friberg, C., 'Fem kvinnliga fotografer ser på sitt jobb', *FOTO*, 1 [1975].

Gräslund, L., 'Kvinnoyrket på modet. Bra yrke för rätt kvinna', *Damernas Värld*, 26/7–2/8 [1956].

Hall-Duncan, N., *The History of Fashion Photography* [New York: Alpine Book Company, 1979].

Heinberg, A., 'Mesterfotografen er en dame', *Flitige Hender*, 27 [1961].

Johannesson, L., 'Photo exile. On the European experience and women photographers in Germany and Sweden', in L. Johannesson, G. Knape and E. Dahlman [eds.], *Women Photographers: European Experience* [Gothenburg: Acta Universitatis Gothoburgensis, 2004].

Knape, G., 'Some notes', in L. Johannesson, G. Knape and E. Dahlman [eds.], *Women Photographers: European Experience* [Gothenburg: Acta Universitatis Gothoburgensis, 2004].

Lewenhaupt, L. and T. Lewenhaupt, *Bilden av modet* [Malmö: Arena, 2009].

Nordisk Rotogravyr 1918–1943, Stockholm, 1943.

'Nya män – nya uppgifter', *Reklam-nyheterna*, 2 [1945].

Rikstelefonkatalogen Stockholmsdelen, 1930 and 1942.

Runnquist, I., 'Några synpunkter på mannekäng fotografering', *Nordisk Tidskrift för Fotografi*, 3 [1938].

Rosenblum, N., *A History of Women Photographers* [New York: Abbeville Press, 1994].

Sandels, K., 'Erik Holmén', *Svensk Fotografisk Tidskrift*, 385 [1943].

Sandels, K., 'Karin Olofsdotter', *Svensk Fotografisk Tidskrift*, 395 [1943].

Sandels, K., 'Deux Sœurs', *Svensk Fotografisk Tidskrift*, 389 [1943].

Shot, 'Mitt yrke. Fotograf och byxtös', *Stockholms Tidningen*, [18 August 1944].

Svenska reklamförbundets medlemsmatrikel, 1937.

Söderberg, P. and P. Rittsel, *Den svenska fotografins historia* [Stockholm: Bonnier Fakta, 1983].

Telefonkatalogen Lund, 1961–1997.

Tedroff, J., 'Woman photographers in Swedish professional and public press 1930–2000', in L. Johannesson, G. Knape and E. Dahlman [eds.], *Women Photographers: European Experience* [Gothenburg: Acta Universitatis Gothoburgensis, 2004].

Tellgren, A., 'Förnyelse av formen i femtiotalets fotografi', *Kvinnovetenskaplig Tidskrift*, 3:4 [1995].

Warner Marien, M., *Photography. A Cultural History* [London: Laurence King Publishing, 2002].

Williams, V., *The Other Observers. Woman Photographers in Britain 1900 to the Present* [London: Virago Press, 1986].

ARCHIVES

Göteborgs landsarkiv, Gothenburg, Studio Deux Sœurs' archives.

Hasselblads stiftelsen, Gothenburg. Interview with Ulla Salén, née Roberg, conducted by Ann-Charlotte Glasberg, 25 May 2000, as a part of the research project 'Woman Photographers – European Experience'.

Malmö museer, Malmö, Karin Olofsdotter archives.

Moderna museet, Stockholm, collection of the photographers Edvard Welinder, Karin Olofdotter, Inga Runnquist and Studio Deux Sœurs.

Telephone interview with Hans Lenkert, Stockholm, 18 November 2008.

Interview with Inga Ohlsén [born Runnquist], Norrtälje, 15 November 2008.

On Location
Proper and not so proper places of fashion in Finnish fashion photography

MERJA SALO

Finnish fashion and photography

Finland may not be one of the big fashion nations, but the fashion industry was of great importance to the industrial development of the country in the twentieth century. From its modest beginnings after the republic was born in 1917, the national fashion industry grew to a remarkable size. The climax came in the 1970s when there were over five hundred Finnish fashion companies and the exports exceeded imports. Having relied on mass orders from the former Soviet Union [in exchange for oil] the industry collapsed in 1991 as exports to this eastern neighbouring country dwindled concurrently with the fall of the Socialist State. There has been no real recovery since, and the role of the fashion industry has remained marginal.[1] However, Finnish design still has an outstanding image as a brand and as a strong style.

Where there is a fashion industry, there are also fashion photography and fashion magazines. I have studied the history of Finnish fashion photography from its beginnings in the 1920s to the present.[2] Being located on the fringes of Europe, Finland mainly followed international trends in fashion photography. The industry and fashion magazines did keep an eye on what was happening elsewhere and the best photographers studied or worked abroad either before or during their career, but none of them made a truly international career and they remained unmentioned in the international histories of fashion photography. There have been several professional Finnish fashion photographers with careers of ten to twenty years, but most worked in the fashion business for a shorter period. It seems that fashion photography in Finland is quite a cruel practice, it ephemeralises photographers at the same hectic pace as it consumes fashions.

In considering the image-embedded values and assumptions of Finnish fashion photographs, this investigation discusses the rhetoric[3] of location. As research material shows, the choice of location has been an important way to embed values, such as functionality, modernity and even ideas of nationality, which will be discussed in detail, in both images and fashion. Although based on Finnish material, it is hoped that this article will stimulate more detailed analyses of uses of location in international fashion photography.

'On location' is a term widely used in fashion photography. It means that the pictures are not taken in a professional photographer's studio, but that the garments are depicted in various real-life surroundings. 'On location' strongly references cinema/staging/playing in front of the camera, but these aspects of staging and playing take place in all fashion photography, whether done in the studio or outdoors. One might suggest, therefore, that fashion photography is inherently performed and performative, establishing a clear distance between fashion, model and scenario and the audience, whilst simultaneously maintaining interest through the guises of familiarity, desire and wish fulfilment. Location can be seen as a framing device; an aspect of *mise en scène* that proposes a fantasy anchored in 'the real'.

Locations are not specially emphasised in existing histories of fashion photography. Naomi Rosenblum lists, in *A World History of Photography*, four basic elements of a fashion photograph: garment, model, pose and décor. She calls them 'pictorial configurations' but does not discuss what kind of meanings, values and attitudes they bear. [4]

Martin Harrison stresses, in *Appearances: Fashion Photography since 1945*, the significance of gesture, suggesting that fashion photography is emphatically aware of the importance of gestures. He writes about three 'principal elements' of fashion photography and defines them to be an actor [model], dress and gesture.[5] Further developing Rosenblum's four configurations, one can say that garments show what is fashionable at the moment. Models represent the contemporary ideals of femininity and beauty. Pose presents the garment, and it provides a fascinating register of gestures as well, ranging from flirting and seduction to cool distance.

When compared to the ideals of femininity and beauty and the different gestures of seduction, the issues conveyed by décor seem less charged. Décor means props and accessories that accompany fashion, but also larger settings that are built around garments and models, either in the studio or outside, in existing real-life environments. These choices give fashion its place and tell us where it belongs – and where it definitely does not belong. Starting modestly with gloves, scarves and studio props, the domain of décor expands at its other end into large-scale stagings and arguments of entire ways of life. Therefore, one could assume: Décor connects fashion to the world.

Here it can be suggested that there are three different ways of using locations in fashion photography that create a framework for discussing the connotations that locations transmit to the clothing depicted and to fashion in general. These three types of locations can be termed: *functional* locations, *symbolic* locations and *controversial* locations.

Fashion's proper places

A location can be called *functional* when it is used in order to show the clothes in places where they are actually worn: bathing suits on the beach, winter clothing in the midst of snowy landscapes, etc. The idea of functional locations was developed in the 1930s when fashion photographers left their studios and started photographing clothes outside, using the new, small roll-film cameras like the famous Leica. The trend was universal and, according to Rosenblum, flourished especially in the US, where fashion editors wanted to show American-made products in an informal and democratic way. They wanted to differ from European fashion photography aesthetics, but actually needed a European, the photographer Martin Munkacsi, to create the new, 'candid' style of outdoors fashion photography. He snapped a bathing-suit model running on a beach in 1933 and the picture was published in *Harper's Bazaar* the next year.[6]

My research has shown that in Finland tricot factories like Silo and Suomen Trikoo were the first in the 1930s to take their products outdoors to be photographed on location. Tricot garments were cheap, mass-produced clothing, providing everybody with an easy access to fashionability. They were easy to wear and take care of, practical and functionally designed. All these qualities were emphasised by depicting the clothes in actual use. The fresh, realistic approach challenged existing studio fashion photography, making it appear stiff and posed.[7]

The advantages and disadvantages of this change were particularly clear in photographs of swimsuits. In a studio, lighting and the technical qualities of the image could be easily controlled. Hints to the functional use of the garment were made by using props, like simple paper-cut silhouettes of waves and birds, or by spreading sand onto the studio floor to connote 'beach'. Taking the garment and the model outside to be depicted by the lakeside would have made it much more difficult to control the lighting, and deep shadows fell on different areas of the body, the face and the scenery. But the real-life surroundings did provide the kind of authenticity that was impossible to produce in the studio. There even appeared unexpected elements [like children staring at the photo session] which gave a special feeling of reality and authenticity to the image.[8]

Thus functional locations can be used in fashion photography to create strong illusions of authenticity. They accomplish this by emphasising the practical uses of clothing and by situating fashion as an everyday commodity and as a part of everyday life – which in fact it had become in the 1930s, when the new garment industries manufactured fashionable clothes to the new, growing middle class. The idea behind functional locations assumes that there is a proper garment and dress code available for every situation and that fashion meets all our dressing needs. Functional locations have become a self-evident part of contemporary fashion photography, whenever there is a need to emphasise fashion as a reasonable, practical and commonplace phenomenon.

But the choice of location can be used to communicate more complicated ideas as well; ideas that are sometimes only loosely connected to the actual use of the clothes depicted. I call these locations *symbolic*, because they inevitably add a new level of cultural and rhetorical meaning to the images.

To give an example: In the post-war Finland of the 1950s, airports and ports were symbolical locations depicting the new era with its optimistic, internationally open spirit, which culminated in the Helsinki Olympics in 1952. New buildings and architecture were common settings as well, with all their connotations of rebuilding and modernity.[9] The settings for fashion shots in the 1960s certainly had far-reaching symbolism in the utilisation of space technology and prop themes of conquering the universe. After the space flights, space became a common international theme in both fashion and photography.[10]

Many of these symbolic locations connote progress and modernity and transmit these qualities to the depicted garments as well. Fashion has always presented itself as new, or rather, novel, even when it is recycling details or styles of past periods. Modernity is a natural companion to fashion and modern locations help maintain this illusion of being up to date. Like functional locations, the locations connoting modernity have become a stable continuum in fashion photography. Whenever a new landmark of technology [such as an express train] or a remarkable piece of architecture [such as skyscrapers or museums] is created, there is always a wave of fashion imagery using it as a symbolic location.

The visual signs of modernity in fashion photography would indeed be worth a separate study, but here I shall restrict myself to discussing yet another theme that seems peculiar to Finnish fashion photography: the use of nature as a symbolic location.

Natural, national nature

In Finland, nature has had great symbolic power and potential. Many internationally known Finnish artists, composers like Jean Sibelius and architects like Alvar Aalto, have stated that nature is their main source of inspiration. By the 1950s nature had become a strong theme in Finnish fashion design and fashion photography as well. This coincides with the basic economic change of the country from an agricultural nation to an industrial one.[11]

Following the grim war years of the previous decade, Finnish design was exhibited in major international design exhibitions like the Milan fairs, receiving international acclaim. Part of Finnish design's export rhetoric was its connection to nature. Not any nature, but that of Finland with its forests, snow and ice, and lakeshores. These elements came to carry the meaning of both Finnishness and naturality, combining nationalism with nature.

Two new design-label companies, Vuokko and Marimekko, were established in the 1950s.[12] They started using wild natural settings as backgrounds for their garments. The picture by Max Petrelius[13] from 1975 [Fig.1] offers several of the new symbolic details: a down-to-earth, wholesome-looking woman wandering in an outdoor, natural environment on the beach or among the coastal rocks and reeds. The naturality of this scene is emphasised by small, recurring details: the woman is barefoot, her hair is worn loose, and she is wearing little make-up. She does not look directly at or engage with the photographer/viewer, confronting the camera in a way that art historian Michael Fried calls absorption; an immersion in a world of her own, not posing for or aware of the camera. The opposition of absorption is theatricality or 'facingness', a straight and open pose towards the camera.[14] In *Why Photography Matters as Art as Never Before* Fried discusses contemporary art photography in terms of absorption and theatricality. Although these two concepts are grounded in Fried's ideas of modernist art, they could be applied to other genres of photography and visual culture as well.

Fig.1:
Vuokko 1975
Max Petrelius
[Image courtesy of Otava]

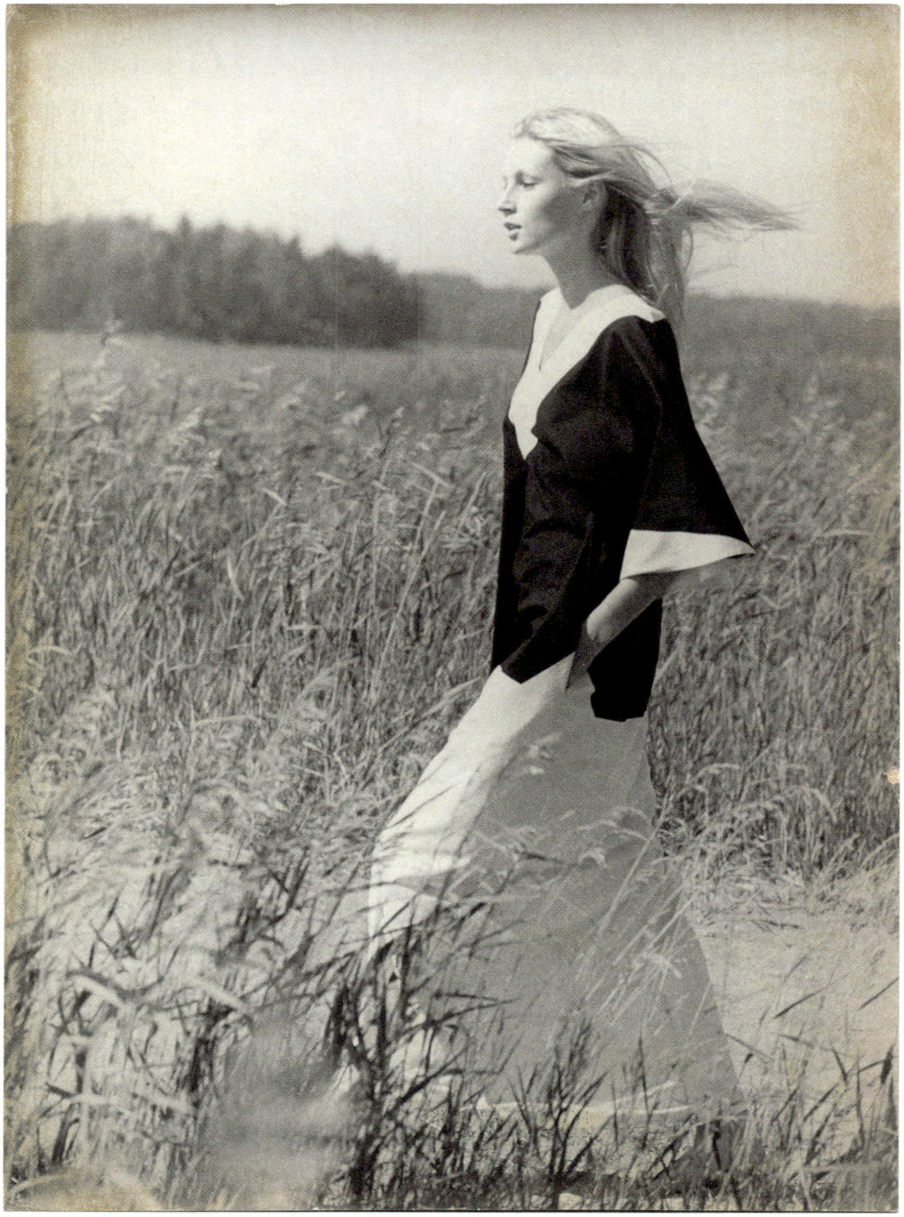

The motif of a natural-looking woman wandering in the middle of reeds, wearing a Vuokko or a Marimekko dress, has an archetypal reference image in Finnish culture: a woman standing amidst a rye field dressed in a national costume.[15] This was a popular motif in the 1930s and had strong nationalist and patriotic values embedded in it. National dress is timeless in itself, opposed to the rapid changes of fashion; the rye field connotes good harvest and abundance of nature. These values were not repeated, but transformed in the later images of the 1950s. The rye, which has been a staple diet for Finns since ancient times, was replaced by the graphic, but useless, reed. The 'plenty of reeds' does not have the same meaning as the 'abundance of rye'. But the value that remained was nationality, now depicted in a lighter and less agricultural way. Is this a statement about the wealth of the nation and the uselessness of the consumption of fashionable goods?

Vuokko and Marimekko produced garments made of printed cotton fabrics that were strong and durable. The printed patterns were often big and the colours bright. Both brands identified themselves with more general ideas of Finnish design that made an international breakthrough in the 1950s. Both proclaimed themselves as design [that is, lasting] not fashion [that is, ephemeral]. By doing, so both labels promoted the idea of being something 'national' – maybe not the new national dresses of Finland, but clothes with a strong national connotation. Fashion photography served this purpose by depicting the fabric and garments within a specific, recognisable location: the Finnish landscape. And while there may not necessarily be anything especially Finnish in these patterns and designs, the pictures created, or at least attempted to create, the connotation of 'Finnishness'.

When the rye field was replaced by wild reeds, also the connotations changed. The idea of cultivated wealth gave way to a more general idea of naturality. Vuokko Nurmesniemi, the founder of Vuokko label and the former designer of Marimekko, confirms this in an interview:

> I did not want any artificial studio photography, but something that is both natural and has a Finnish spirit. It was quite obvious that the pictures should be taken outside, in the wild. I'm living close to nature and carry nature with me all the time.[16]

Once the combination of naturality and nationality was established, it was repeated for several decades. The photographers changed, but the theme remained the same – and even the same female model was used in Vuokko's pictures for more than ten years.[17] This exportable figure may not have looked like the majority of Finns did or do, but was an ideal type: a tall, blonde, young woman with flowing hair and long legs.

The bond between nature and Finnish design has a mythology that has proved inspirational in Finnish industrial arts, as articulated in many exhibition catalogues, press articles and design-fair statements. Famous designers, such as Tapio Wirkkala, famous for his glassware, have traced their inspiration to nature and see the origins of their forms in ice, wood and water. By choosing and using wild, natural scenery in their fashion photographs, Vuokko and Marimekko aligned themselves with the more general mythical design rhetoric of their time. This rhetoric claims that creative design originates from nature, which guarantees its national, Finnish character.[18] And is indeed the ethos of Scandinavian Modernism.

The mythical idea of Finnish 'natural' design is persistent and has been used in international contexts as well. When *Vogue* presented Finnish fashion in 1965, the photographs [by Gordon Parks, the American photographer known for his photo essays in *Life* magazine and as a freelance photographer for *Vogue*] were taken in the wild. And when the Finnish fur and leather manufacturer Friitala invited Veruschka, the German supermodel, to Finland in the 1970s, she, too, was photographed among the reeds.[19] The 1960s and the 1970s were the golden decades for both Finnish fashion and fashion photography, which explains the new, international scale of activities. After two decades of international interest and acclaim, the business declined in the 1980s. But the rhetoric of nature is still alive and can be found in many Marimekko fashion catalogues from the 2000s and in the fashion stories published in the magazines as well.

My conclusion is that using wild nature as a location in fashion photography can have different, deeply symbolic meanings. It can even link nature on a symbolic level to national ideas as these Finnish examples prove. Although obvious, national identity is based on commonality such as language and landscape, yet nature may connote naturality and by doing so it presents fashion as a 'natural' phenomenon, not as a product of culture and history. According to semiotician Roland Barthes this kind of naturalisation of culture is a myth, and he calls for a critical attitude towards every attempt to present cultural and historical phenomena as natural.[20] This opens up a broader question of the naturalising rhetoric of Finnish design, not just that of Finnish fashion photography. Fashion and design are nothing natural, but complex, historical human sign systems which are dense with values and assumptions.

Fashion in a wrong place

Location may also create controversial and risky connotations in fashion photographs. In this investigation the relationship between fashion and the countryside has also appeared problematic. How does fashion, basically urban, fit into rural locations? The inevitable clash seems often comic or as a form of irony, based on the paradox between traditional countryside and the modern, fashionable clothes [Fig. 2]. But – are we laughing at the countryside or at the fashion?

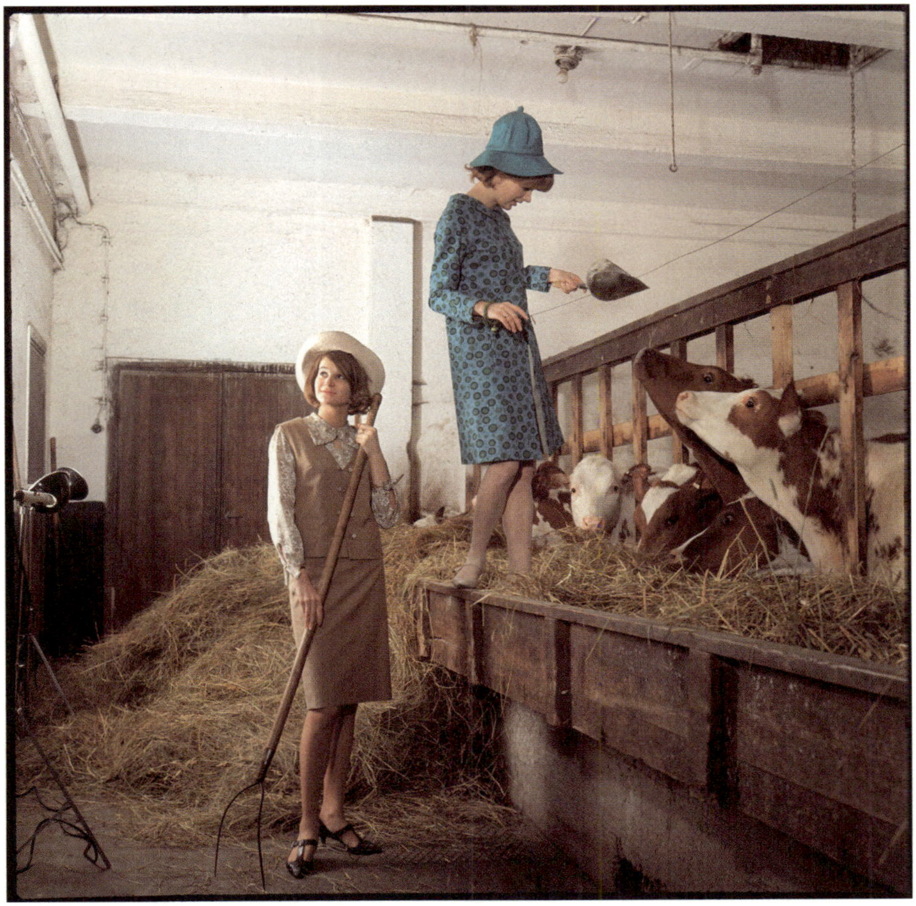

Fig.2:
Seura Magazine 1966
Tuovi Nousiainen
[Image courtesy of
Suomen Kuvapalvelu]

One might conclude that it is fashion that is ridiculed here, not the countryside. The 'follies' of fashion do not seem to fit into rustic, real-life farm environments. There is no functional relationship between the depicted clothes and the location, but the dresses are entirely in a wrong place. There is no kind of symbolic agreement, such as that which

Marimekko and Vuokko had in order to make their design-labels originate from nature, which provides them with values of naturality and nationality. It can turn into a risky business for fashionable clothes to be depicted in an unsuitable location. Fashion promotion can turn against the whole idea of fashion itself.

What is interesting in this risky conflict is the idea of a *contrast* between the garment and the location. Since the radical upheavals that also affected fashion photography in the 1960s, there have been recurring attempts to play with the idea of putting fashion in a wrong place. I propose that we call this a *controversial* approach.

There are at least three different ways to create a conflict between garment and location. The first is a *functional contrast*. A good example of this features in a fashion story in a magazine. It tells of a young woman, an apparent sleepwalker, who awakens wearing merely a nightgown or underwear in different public places [like a bank and a tram], always surrounded by curious male onlookers. The very private garment, the nightgown or the underwear, has been exhibited in the most public of places. The result is surprise and shame, expressed by the pose and the gestures of the model.[21]

The second conflict is a *social contrast*. An extreme example would be *haute couture* fashion photographed in a slum. In the 1990s there was an international trend in fashion photography that used messy, suburban flats and dirty, public spaces as platforms for label garments. This new kind of 'realism' flourished especially in the British-style magazines.[22] My interpretation of these pictures and their ambivalent and probably ironical message is that they say: this is how life is, see, it is hard and grim. But there may still be pieces of clothing that have at least some *attitude* – the contemporary aura of fashion. The use of social contrast may be a form of irony as well, based on both paradox and distancing. The distance between the poor surroundings and the expensive fashionable clothes seems to pose a question about the place of the fashion in general.

Even further goes the *political contrast*, which depicts fashion in connection with the big global problems. An early [1974] Finnish example of this is C. G. Hagström's[23] fashion image in which the models are replaced by mannequins that are wearing fur coats in front of a projection depicting heaps of car wrecks [see Fig. 3]. This is not an outdoors location in a traditional sense of the word, but I have included it here because it has an open political message. Here we have open criticism of fashion, luxury

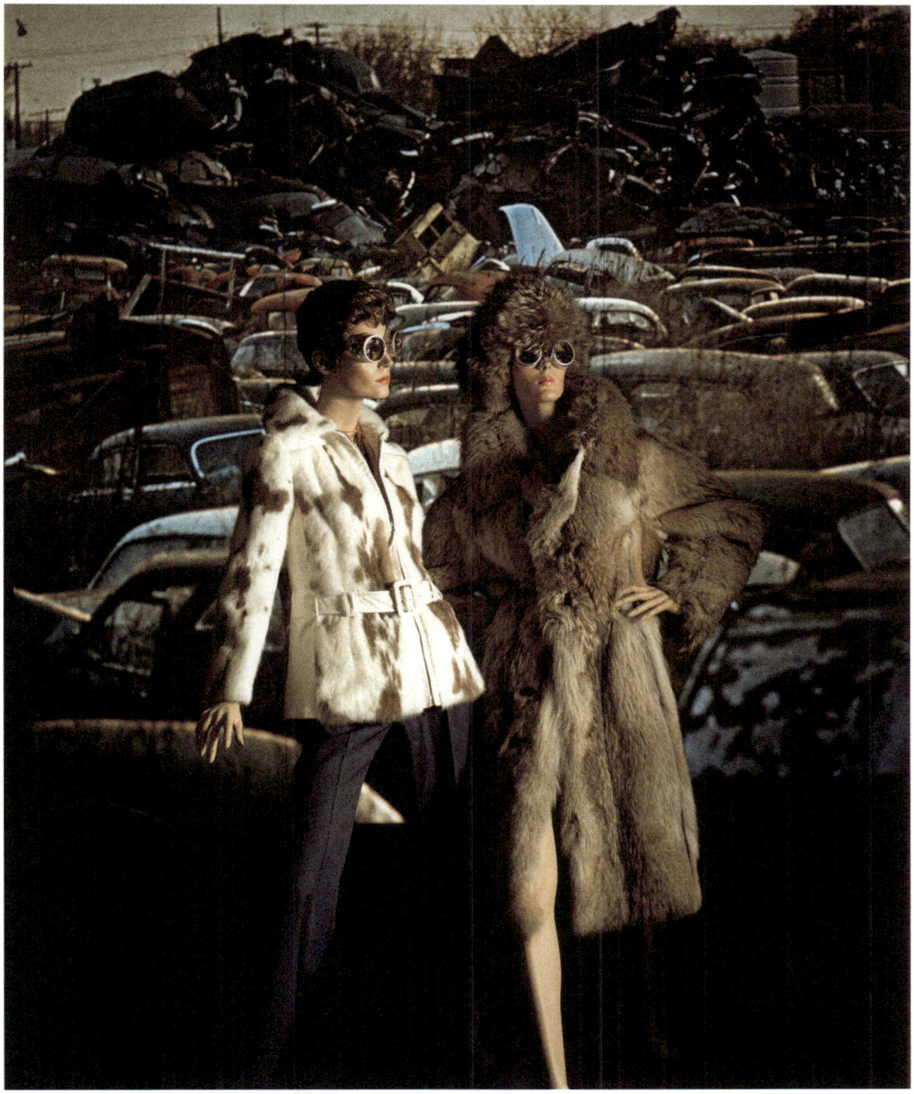

Fig.3:
Suomen Kuvalehti 1974
C. G. Hagström
[Image courtesy of
Suomen Kuvapalvelu]

and consumption in general.

Fashion photography may not be the best and most effective platform for political comment or social realism, and most fashion assignments do not ask for that kind of controversial content. But there is definitely something that can be derived from the controversial use of location: a sense of irony, a cool and detached attitude towards both fashion and the world. Irony may provide a means of dealing with the contrast. Detached irony lets us smile at both fashion and the world without really questioning and criticising the value of either.

This discussion has defined three different ways of using location in fashion photography and the Finnish examples have shown that all three can be used as vehicles for different values and assumptions. Functional settings represent fashion in its proper place and emphasise the practical uses of fashion. Symbolic locations can carry ideological connotations of modernity and even nationalism. In Finland, wild nature has been a location with strong symbolic connotations and could be one of the themes that deserve international comparison and further research. Controversial locations may look like mistakes and can make the fashion itself look ridiculous, but they may be an expression of a highly ironical, post-modern attitude as well.

ENDNOTES

1 P. Lappalainen and M. Almay, *Kansakunnan vaatettajat* [Porvoo: WSOY, 1996].

2 M. Salo, *Muodin Ikuistajat. Muotivalokuvaus Suomessa* [Helsinki: Taideteollinen korkeakoulu, 2005]. The freely translated title is *Eternalising Fashion. Fashion Photography in Finland.* The book is in Finnish, but has an English summary.

3 'Rhetoric' implies a wish to convince. How would choice of location work towards convincing people to buy the clothes depicted?

4 N. Rosenblum, *A World History of Photography* [New York: Abbeville Press, 1984], pp. 495–508.

5 M. Harrison, *Appearances: Fashion Photography since 1945* [London: Jonathan Cape, 1991], p. 21.

6 N. Hall-Duncan, *The History of Fashion Photography* [New York: Alpine Books, 1979], pp. 68–83; Harrison, *Appearances: Fashion Photography since 1945*, pp. 10–11; Rosenblum, *A World History of Photography*, p. 498.

7 Salo, *Muodin Ikuistajat*, pp. 36–7.

8 See figs 35, 47 and 51 in Salo, *Muodin Ikuistajat*, p. 31, pp. 36–7.

9 See figs 152, 153, 168, 169 and 178 in Salo, *Muodin Ikuistajat*, pp. 110–11, pp. 122–3, p. 131.

10 A Finnish example is fig. 240 in Salo, *Muodin Ikuistajat*, pp. 176–7.

11 Despite the industrial development, almost eighty per cent of the country today is still forested while ten per cent is water, mainly lakes.

12 Marimekko was founded in 1951 by Armi Ratia, who ran it until her death in 1979. Vuokko Nurmesniemi joined Marimekko in 1953 as a designer and founded her own label, Vuokko, in 1960, after leaving Marimekko. For more about Marimekko see: http://www.marimekko.fi/eng/marimekkocorporation/history/1950.

13 Max Petrelius [b. 1940] started his career as a fashion photographer in 1961 and soon became the main photographer for Vuokko. Movement and graphic clarity were the main stylistic features of his pictures.

14 M. Fried, *Why Photography Matters as Art as Never Before* [London and New Haven: Yale University Press, 2008], p. 34, p. 111.

15 See fig. 156 in Salo, *Muodin Ikuistajat*, p. 112.

16 Interview with Vuokko Nurmesniemi, 11 August 2004, in Salo, *Muodin Ikuistajat*, p. 113.

17 Salo, *Muodin Ikuistajat*, p. 113, p. 242.

18 M. Aav [ed.], *Marimekko: Fabrics, Fashion, Architecture* [New Haven and London: Yale University Press, 2003], and M. Heikkilä-Rastas, *Muodin vai muodon vuoksi?* [Helsinki: University of Art and Design, 2003].

19 Salo, *Muodin Ikuistajat*, pp. 110–14.

20 R. Barthes, 'Myth Today', in S. Sontag, *A Barthes Reader* [New York: Hill and Wang, 1982], p. 116.

21 Salo, *Muodin Ikuistajat*, p. 158.

22 V. Williams, *Look at Me. Fashion and Photography in Britain 1960 to the Present* [London: The British Council, 1998], p. 70, pp. 74–5. See also C. Nickerson, *Fashion – Photography of the Nineties* [Zürich: Scalo, 1996]; and C. Chermayeff, *Fashion Photography Now* [New York: Harry N. Abrams, 2000].

23 C. G. [Carl-Gustav] Hagström [b. 1940] studied photography at Fotoskolan in Stockholm from 1961 to 1963 and worked as a photojournalist for Finnish magazines before specialising in fashion. He preferred small-format cameras and wide-angle lenses that produced strong, dramatic compositions.

BIBLIOGRAPHY

Aav, M. [ed.], *Marimekko: Fabrics, Fashion, Architecture* [New Haven and London: Yale University Press, 2003].

Barthes, R., 'Myth Today', in S. Sontag, *A Barthes Reader* [New York: Hill and Wang, 1982].

Chermayeff, C., *Fashion Photography Now* [New York: Harry N. Abrams, 2000].

Fried, M., *Why Photography Matters as Art as Never Before* [London and New Haven: Yale University Press, 2008].

Hall-Duncan, N., *The History of Fashion Photography* [New York: Alpine Books, 1979].

Harrison, M., *Appearances: Fashion Photography since 1945* [London: Jonathan Cape, 1991].

Heikkilä-Rastas, M., *Muodin vai muodon vuoksi?* [Helsinki: University of Art and Design, 2003].

Lappalainen, P. and M. Almay, *Kansakunnan vaatettajat* [Porvoo: WSOY, 1996].

Nickerson, C., *Fashion – Photography of the Nineties* [Zürich: Scalo, 1996].

Rosenblum, N., *A World History of Photography* [New York: Abbeville Press, 1984, first edition].

Salo, M., *Muodin Ikuist ajat. Muotivalokuvaus Suomessa* [Helsinki: Taideteollinen korkeakoulu, 2005].

Williams, V., *Look at Me. Fashion and Photography in Britain 1960 to the Present* [London: The British Council, 1998].

Making Clothes Desirable in Norway
Images from Sohlberg Foto in the late 1960s

TONE RASCH

During the 1960s Sohlberg Foto was one of the leading photo studios producing fashion and advertising images in Norway. The studio was established by Jan Fredrik Sohlberg [1916–1979] a businessman and amateur photographer who had turned his hobby into a career working as a professional photographer.[1] The photographers Per Christoffersen, Peder Austrud and Tore Hvass also worked there. A primary task of the studio was taking fashion photos for magazines published by Ernest G. Mortensen. One of these was *Det Nye* [Novelty].[2] It was the first teen magazine in Norway and featured pop music, Hollywood movies and fashion as well as articles about pop stars or other people suitable for a teen audience.

Through an acquisition from a private collector, the Sohlberg Foto archive is now part of a larger collection held at the Norwegian Museum of Science and Technology.[3] The archive consists of about fifty thousand photos stemming from different photo sessions undertaken for magazines and advertising agencies. No paper records accompany the photos, but sometimes information about which magazine and volume the photo appeared in is attached. These notes confirm that many of the images were published in *Det Nye*. However, in the beginning of the 1960s many of Sohlberg's photographs were published in another of Mortensen's magazines, *Norsk Dameblad* [The Norwegian Magazine for Women] which was aimed at an older demographic.[4] As one might imagine, the pictures as well as the magazine were elegant and more suited to an older, and perhaps more traditional, readership. Everyday clothes and formal wear were featured and accessories such as bags, hats and glasses were emphasised as key fashion markers. An obvious difference between the photos for the two magazines is that the *Dameblad* pictures were black and white negative film while the pictures taken for *Det Nye* were mostly colour slides, 120 film 6x6 format. It is possible to suggest that this reflects innovations within photography and printing technology.[5] Many professionals changed from black and white film to colour during the 1960s, including Sohlberg Foto. The style of the photos changed as well.[6]

Fashion photography within Norwegian photo history

Commercial photography, such as product promotion and fashion photographs, have received little attention in Norwegian photographic history. None of the most recent major studies in this field contain any information about Sohlberg Foto. Peter Larsen and Sigrid Lien's *Norsk fotohistorie. Fra daguerreotypi til digitalisering* [Norwegian photo history. From daguerreotype to digitalisation], published in 2007, does not deal with advertising and promotional product photography from the period after World War II at all, which is interesting as this is the period in which it boomed. The 2008 exhibition *80 millioner bilder* [80 million pictures] included some fashion and promotional photography as a genre, but it was limited, i.e. pictures of shoes made for The Norwegian Shoe Council taken by the photographers Ragge Strand and Per Alfsen in 1962–1964.[7] The accompanying text noted that commercial photos, although numerous, were a rarely discussed genre within photographic history in Norway. Ekeberg and Østgaard Lund suggest that this might be because the mimetic character of these photographs was considered too naturalistic. There might be other reasons as well. Indeed, it is difficult to look at promotional photos as sheer visual expression, or as an art form, primarily because the commercial contexts of the pictures are fundamental and so dominant. However, economic and market issues are parts of twentieth-century history in the same way promotion is a part of visual culture, and this in itself this is a clear indicator for the necessity for further study. Therefore, the Sohlberg Foto collection offers an unexplored archive of commercial photography that has the potential to offer socio-cultural commentary as well as an aesthetic appreciation of the context in which the photos were taken and positioned.

For the purposes of this discussion, archival material will be contextualised within the Norwegian ready-to-wear industry for whom the images were commissioned. Likewise, as fashion is not merely production, but also consumption, the placement of said photographs within the magazine/s will also be fundamental to this discussion. As the first magazine specifically for teenagers it is reasonable to assume that *Det Nye* contributed to the introduction of pop culture to Norwegian weekly magazine readers. How did the pictures represent the new tendencies that we today understand as typical fashion of the 1960s? And how did the clothing industry respond to teenage fashion?

During the period, almost all clothes consumed in Norway were made domestically, either at home or by the Norwegian ready-to-wear industry. But the trade feared increasing imports. Fashion was one way to make Norwegian-made clothes attractive for both the producers and consumers. This investigation will focus on the extent to which the fashion photographer contributed to this new approach to trends adopted by the domestic fashion industry. Indeed, it is my opinion that the magazine, the ready-to-wear industry and the photographer each had a contributory role necessary to understand the deeper sub-text and meaning of the images. With this in mind, the promotional pictures should not be seen as isolated objects, but contextualised within the commercial sphere they depict, as well as acknowledging their purpose; publication in a magazine whose readership expected to be presented with fashionable clothing made in Norway.

The selected photos for further examination are from five fashion spreads published in *Det Nye* in 1968 and 1969. Both these and non-published pictures from same location will be examined. The examples represent different strategies to fashion within the clothing trade. The first is typical of the representation of fashion in the magazine. The clothes were made by the domestic industry, but neither the producers nor the designers were mentioned. The second, however, shows clothing that was referred to as *high quality*, a term solidified by an award from the textile trade organisation. The third and fourth articles deal with the ready-to-wear industry and the use of designers who, for the first time, were mentioned by name in the late 1960s. The final piece aims to exemplify the attempts made by the Norwegian fashion industry to create a 'Norwegian Fashion'.

Based on domestic ready-to-wear production, it is possible to understand the role of the fashion photographer seen from the producer's side. Primarily this is possible because the photographer was not entirely in control of the aesthetic production. The magazine had its own agenda and, as a contributor to a growing teenage popular culture, it took readers' preferences seriously. The meaning of the magazine, therefore, brings a new appreciation and itinerary to the presentation of the clothing within its pages.

Summer dresses on a polar vessel

The headline *Fram for norsk sommermote* [Norwegian summer fashion forward], published in May 1968, is a play on words in Norwegian.[8] The meaning of *forward* is the same as the name of the polar vessel *Fram*, built in 1892 and sailed by two of the most famous Norwegian polar explorers, Fridtjof Nansen and Roald Amundsen. The fashion spread was shot at the museum where the vessel is exhibited, a popular tourist attraction and familiar to readers of the magazine, thus suggesting Norway was leading the way in fashion too [see Fig. 1].

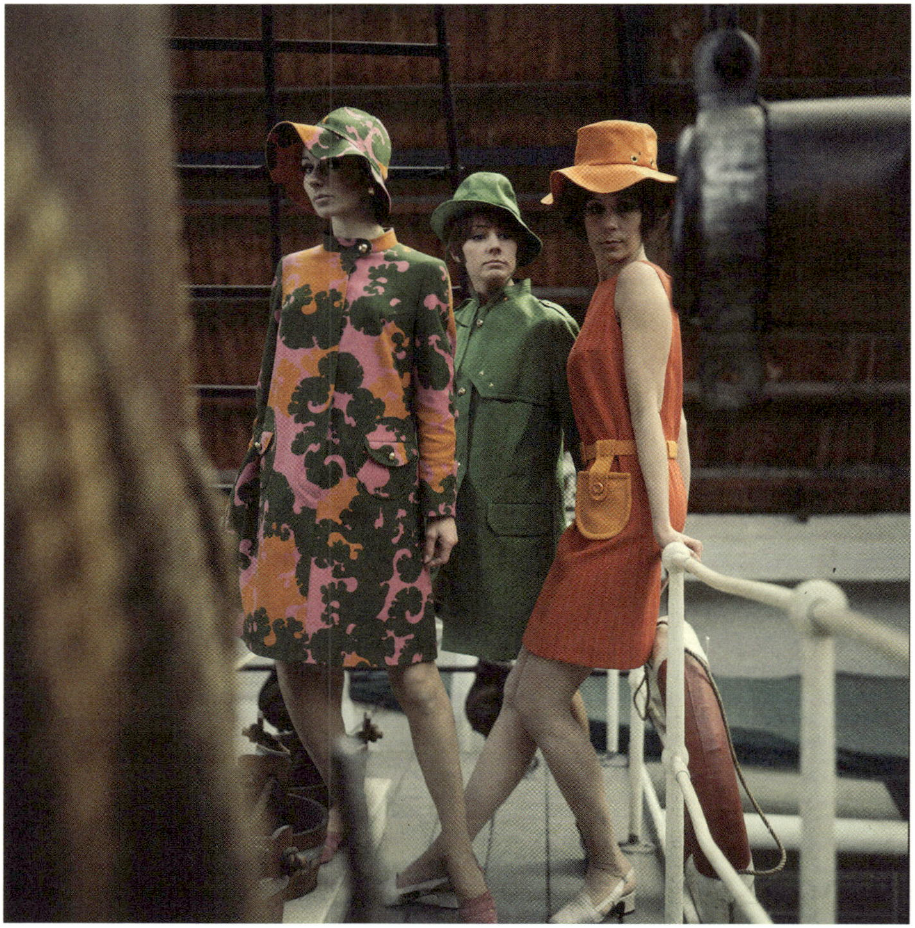

Fig.1:
Summer dresses with hats photographed at the polar vessel *'Fram'* 1968
Sohlberg Foto
[Image courtesy of DEXTRA PHOTO]

The photographs accompanying this feature showed short, tight summer dresses in bright and pastel colours, indicative of the iconic and youthful miniskirt fashionable during the period. The accompanying text emphasised the visual aspects closely connected to fashion. One dress was described: 'This model shows the romantic tendency of the season with puffed sleeves'. Another was described as 'tasteful'. Descriptions emphasised the femininity and delicacy of the clothes displayed. In visualising the fashionability of the clothes, the pictures naturally played a more important role than the short texts. Interestingly, no designers' or producers' names were mentioned, implying Norway and Norwegian-produced were enough to establish a concept of the brand.

The journalist mentioned that a dress in 1920s style was influenced by the BBC TV series *The Forsyte Saga*, based on John Galsworthy's novel trilogy. The series became very popular when it was shown on Norwegian television in 1967–68.[9] The story took place in an upper-middle-class British family at the beginning of the twentieth century, with an unhappy love story as the focal point.[10] The inspiration for fashion from such popular TV series was characteristic of the 1960s.[11] Regular TV broadcasting started as late as 1960 in Norway, and it is quite conceivable that the effect was especially strong on the as yet curious Norwegian audience. But not only *The Forsyte Saga* expressed romantic and retrospective tendencies apparent in the dress. Also the choice of scenery emphasised a romantic nostalgia. The *Fram*'s symbolic meaning was important, the explorers were national heroes, and the *Fram* museum gave the clothing a national identity, a sense of progressive exploration or the avant-garde, to Norwegian-produced clothes made in an international style.

The Norwegian Fashion Council and the Style-award

The fashion articles in the magazines from the 1960s show that the textile industry and clothing trade had 'fashion' on the agenda. For the industry, the fashion agenda was initiated by the establishment of The Norwegian Ladies Fashion Council [Norsk Damemoteråd] by retailers and merchants in 1967.[12] Together with the Council for Men's Wear [Rådet for herreklær] and the Shoe Council [Skorådet] it worked towards promoting a higher consciousness among producers, as well as consumers, about fashion and quality. An important part of the Fashion Council's work was to co-ordinate design issues and to inform said groups about forthcoming trends and production processes. By the end of the 1960s the Council's two representatives travelled to Paris four times a year, and occasionally to Great Britain and Italy, where they kept abreast of the latest developments. The

Council was heavily orientated towards international fashion organisations and was a part of the European Fashion Council, headquartered in Paris, where Norway represented the Scandinavian countries. After the annual meetings of the European Fashion Council, the trends were presented to the textile trade, from which the Norwegian Council attempted to align the collections made by different producers. The Council also co-operated with the International Wool Secretariat [IWS] which created the famous 'Woolmark' guaranteeing the use of high-quality wool. The Norwegian Fashion Council used pictures from the IWS in their promotion towards Norwegian clothing dealers.[13]

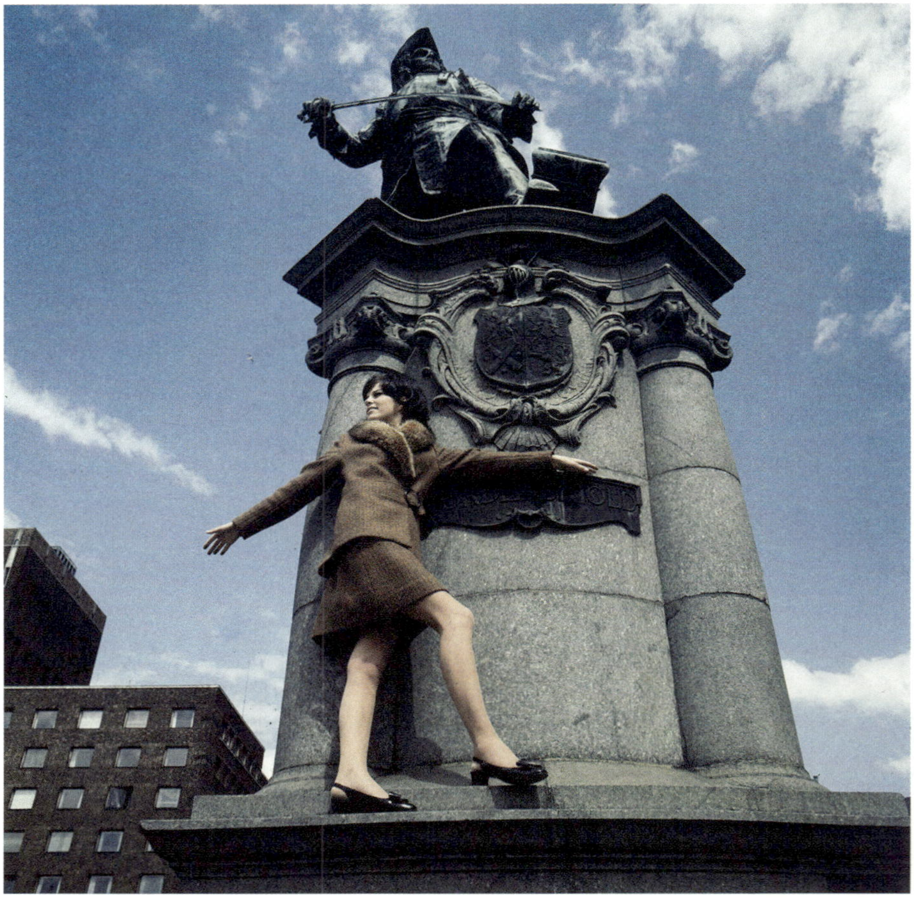

Fig.2:
Suit photographed at Tordenskiold monument in front of Oslo Townhall, 1968
Sohlberg Foto/Per Christoffersen
[Image courtesy of DEXTRA PHOTO]

The Style-award [Stil-merke] was established in 1968 and intended to promote Norwegian-made clothing. A panel of representatives from the Council and six fashion journalists made these awards, which were shown at the yearly fashion fairs in Oslo. The presence of the journalists on the award committee offered a great deal of publicity to the winners. The report *Norsk kunst laget av metal, stoff og sten* [Norwegian art made by metal, fabrics and stone] published in *Det Nye* in September 1968,[14] can be seen as a part of the endeavour to promote the Council's work. The headline referred to the location of the photos. Models wearing elegant, Norwegian-produced clothes posed with easily recognisable sculptures within the cityscape of Oslo [see Fig. 2].

Made from costly woollen fabrics, many of the featured garments were labelled 'Stil-68', emphasising that they were of the moment. The prices of the photographed clothes seem today to have been a bit too high for the average teenage girl, who was the presumed reader of the magazine.[15] Both price and style were intended for more mature and financially solvent customers. It appears, therefore, that the photograph fails to meet its intended demographic. Yet the high price indicates a level of attainment; these are styles to work towards or save for, whilst perhaps offering access to fashion to older potential customers. These subtle motives were also at play within the feature. Fashion theorist Elizabeth Wilson has pointed out that there has been a shift in the task of women's magazines: once they were informational, but in recent years that task has moved towards mirroring a way of being.[16] The Sohlberg photos were taken during the transition between these two tasks. The presentation of the Fashion Council's award-winning clothing may not have been intended as a realistic option or an attractive lifestyle for the teen readers. But the photographs were taken, and the clothes produced, in a period of change when fashion disseminated into everyday clothes for teenagers as well as the prosperous, grown-up women. Without doubt the readers of the magazine were the upcoming, new wave of consumers. With this in mind, one can see the importance of market targeting and the clothing trade establishing good taste among young girls at an early stage.

The Council's use of fashion designers

In a 1969 interview with the women's magazine *KK* [abbreviation for *Kvinner og klær*, meaning 'Women and Clothes'] the Council's representative Idunn Finckenhagen said that some Norwegian fashion designers based in Paris had been contacted to work for the ready-to-wear industry.[17] It was not said who they were or why these designers were chosen instead of fashion designers working in Norway, but their connection to Paris intended to emphasise the Fashion Council's international orientation and desire to add fashion credibility to these clothes. Two reports in *Det Nye* from 1969 featured coats made by Norwegian designers living in Paris.

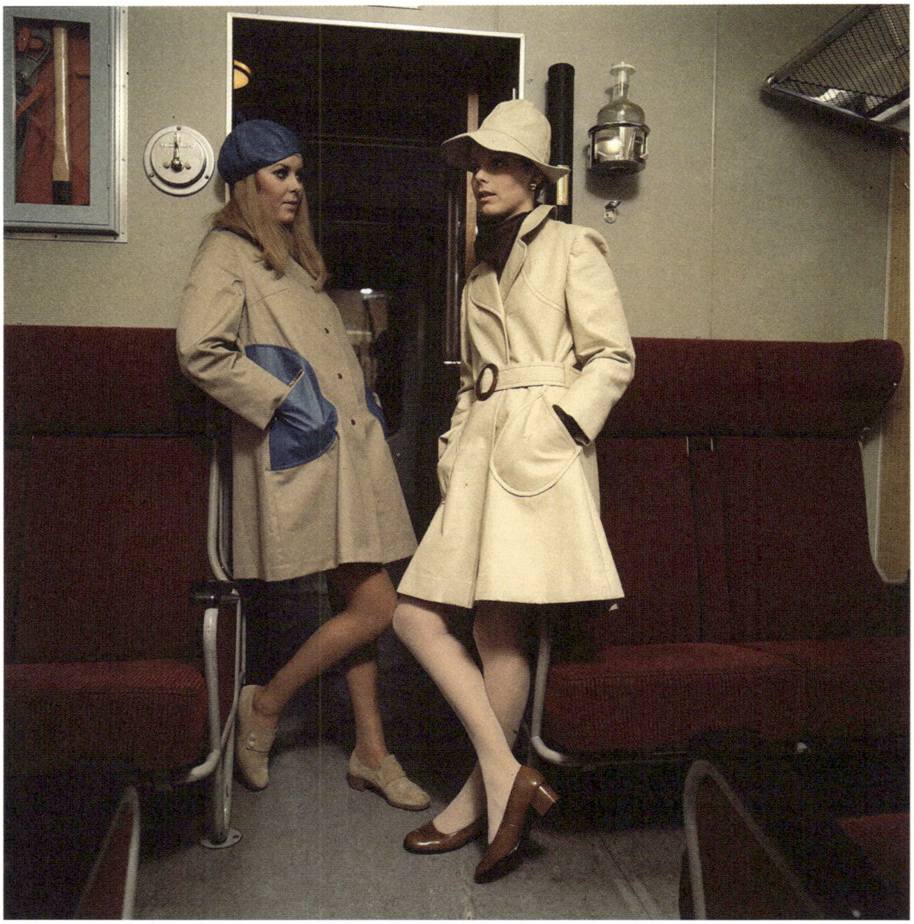

Fig.3:
Two coats from the co-operation between three Norwegian designers and the ready-to-wear industry, 1969
Sohlberg Foto/Per Christoffersen
[Image courtesy of DEXTRA PHOTO]

Med toget [By train] was published in March 1969[18] and the photographer was Per Christoffersen [Fig. 3]. Three designers were mentioned in the text: Per Spook, Thor Dahl and Øivind Bergerud. All worked within the French fashion industry.[19] They were young and had all been educated at the National Academy of Design in Oslo. Per Spook was the most famous of the three at the end of the decade and remains so today. He went to Paris in 1959, was an apprentice at Dior and Yves Saint-Laurent and studied at the Chambre Syndicales.[20] In 1962 he was employed by Louis Féraud, as the head of the design team, where he stayed until he opened his own fashion house in 1977. During the 1960s he also worked for the Norwegian textile and clothing industry designing women's wear.[21] Spook also wrote fashion reports for women's magazines and was frequently interviewed about new trends, as he was the first Norwegian fashion designer to become successful in Paris.[22] Consequently, it seems that he played a special role in linking Parisian high fashion and the domestic interest in the production of elegant and fashionable clothes.

Another set of coats that could be from the same co-operation between the designers and the industry was published in the report *Kåper i høst* [Coats this autumn] in *Det Nye* in the autumn of 1969.[23] The photos were taken by Jan Fredrik Sohlberg and, unlike earlier collaborations, designers Thor Dahl and Aage Høygaard. Høygaard had no connection to Paris, graduating from the National Academy of Design in Oslo in the spring of 1969. It is reported that at the fashion students' degree show garments designed by him were also modelled by him.[24] In this example, the designer becomes both subject and object, producer of and vehicle for his wares, noting a shift from *haute couture* to a more democratic style.

Ready-made clothes should be fashionable, but functional and easily maintained. But still the Norwegian ready-made industry and the journalists in the weekly magazines were most influenced by Parisian fashion. In that way their attitudes seemed quite conservative.

'Fjord Look'

The four extracts that have been examined show clothes that fitted the miniskirt fashion of the time. The clothes had no clear national identity. This was not the case in the fashion spread *Norsk industri satser på fjord og fjell* [Norwegian factories aim for fjords and mountains] from October 1968.[25] Per Christoffersen was the photographer.

These clothes stood out in many ways from the other examples. Firstly, the colours were different. The palette utilised secondary colours like turquoise, orange and green, all of which symbolically connected with national identity associated with Norwegian nature: the blue-green 'Fjord', turquoise 'Glacier', red 'Trout', orange 'Autumn' and green 'Moss'. The semiotic emphasis on the fashionable as 'naturally' Norwegian was further demonstrated by the reference to folklore as design inspiration, with ribbons trimming the dresses and jackets, and pewter buttons reminiscent of Norwegian national dress.

The style emphasised outdoor clothing associated with typically Norwegian pastimes. The models wore breeches like the cross-country skiers did in the 1960s. Still, the style was more romantic than sporty. The models posed in a meadow with ponies as if in a fairy tale, drawing from the iconography and iconology of Norwegian mythology, firmly situating the garments and a notion of fashionability within a nationalistic context. The use of coloured tights and the models' loose hair made the clothes appear more youthful, whilst referencing symbols of newness indicative of the age.

This national style was familiar and visible on many levels. The most obvious was the symbiosis of the 'Fjord Look' and the palette used by the Norwegian tourist board in its marketing of Norwegian nature. Following this genre, the 'Fjord Look' was staged within the landscape. The 'Fjord Look' was really an attempt to create a special Norwegian style that fitted the natural identity of Norway as a sparsely populated country on the margins of Europe with an overwhelming landscape.[26]

The Norwegian Textile Manufacturers' Association [NTMA] stood behind the concept of the 'Fjord Look'. Spinning and weaving mills, as well as knitwear companies, were members of the organisation. Like the Fashion Council, the NTMA worked to increase the sale of clothes, emphasising 'fashion' as the primary selling point. A key initiative was to give the clothing design a special Norwegian touch that would make it more desirable for both domestic consumers and the export market. But the reception of the 'Fjord Look' in 1968 was mixed. The press were mostly positive about the fashion venture as such, but the project was criticised for its references to folklore, i.e. the use of ribbons and dense woollen fabrics.[27] The concept was also discussed by the organisation Norsk Design Centrum [The Norwegian Centre of Design]. The NTMA had applied for the Norwegian design award 'Merket for god Norsk design' ['The award for good Norwegian design'] which resulted in a written commentary about the collection by the art historian Alf Bøe [head of the Centre] and the designer Roar Høyland. It concluded that it was impossible to judge the collection as *design* because of 'the irrational elements connected to the product's aesthetic form and its symbolic values'.[28] This foray into a *national* fashion was obviously a step too far, and one that the world was not yet ready for.

The agenda of the ready-to-wear industry

The examined reports show that different players within the Norwegian textile industry and trade worked towards a refreshing of domestic ready-to-wear production. We know in retrospect that the textile and clothes industry was in serious trouble during the 1970s and 1980s and much of the industry had to close down. In the 1960s there was still optimism. Both the Fashion Council and NTMA considered fashion and style to be an important selling argument. The merchants preferred a global style closely connected to that of the fashion centres, especially Paris. The factories, desperate to continue production, tried to develop a style based on national preferences and the 'Fjord Look' proved a somewhat unsuccessful – as it turned out – attempt to embrace a fashionability and aesthetic that was distinctly Norwegian. The weekly magazines co-operated with the domestic industry, profiling their wares. And fashion photography played an important role in this marketing.

Much of our knowledge about the fashion of the 1960s is based on fashion photography and publications. The clothes have often disappeared.

The fashion reports in the magazine show a contrast between a global and a national focus, i.e. the Norwegian ready-to-wear industry was inspired by *haute couture* and, according to the Norwegian textile trade, Paris was still *the* main fashion centre. Paris was fashion, and this needed to be fused with understandings of the domestic industry and market.

Norwegian-ness was expressed on different levels. The 'Fjord Look' was the most evident Norwegian design with naturalistic and folklore-inspired colours, cuts and decoration. But national identity and values were expressed in more subtle ways: the predominance of nature and the Norwegian landscape as a backdrop, the reference to the polar vessel and 'Stil'-award pictures, along with composition akin to that produced by the Norwegian Tourist Board, all added a sense of the local. On one level, one might conclude that the co-operation with designers living in Paris was a reminder that being in Paris was not enough. A Norwegian origin and cultural understanding was equally important. Indeed, clothing manufacturers favoured photography that emphasised this strong national iconography.

The photographer's role

To a large extent Sohlberg Foto depicted the clothes as the ready-to-wear industry wished. The garments were shown on young, attractive models and many of the photographs were shot outdoors in spectacular surroundings. The settings gave the clothes further meaning through contemporary urban environments or by recreating the romantic nationalism of the countryside. Traditional qualities of exclusivity and culture can be said to have given the ready-made clothes an extra value, one that would have been understood by consumers. The dresses and coats became something more than just garments. As Roland Barthes would suggest, this is the creation of a mythology of fashion, a garment and an idea, as the actual clothing did not have this kind of added value as a mere product in a production chain.

But there are other tendencies in the examined photographs. The model and the location are as important as the garment for fashion photography's visual expression. According to the models, they were often serious looking. But at the end of the 1960s they became less formal, emphasising a stylistic trend towards the action shot and movement indicative of the mood of the times. A clear example of this can be seen in unpublished

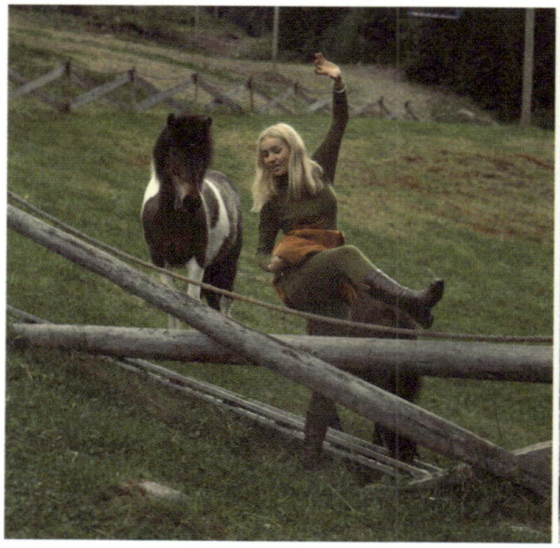

Fig.4:
Girl in *Fjord Look* costume with an Icelandic horse, 1968
Sohlberg Foto/Per Christoffersen
[Image courtesy of DEXTRA PHOTO]

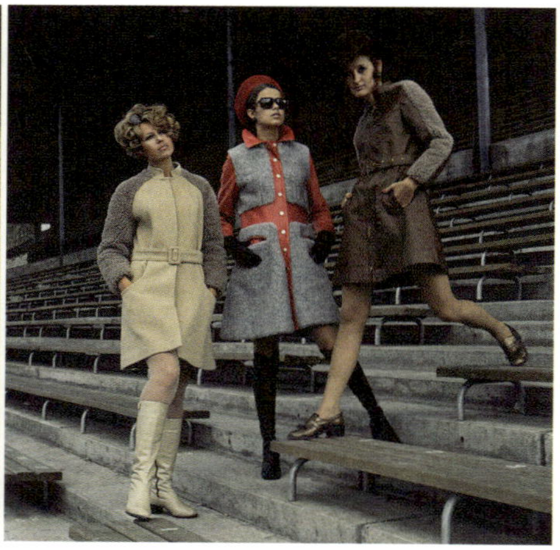

Fig.5:
Three coats designed by Aage Høigaard, 1969
Sohlberg Foto/Jan Fredrik Sohlberg
[Image courtesy of DEXTRA PHOTO]

photographs taken for the 'Fjord Look' campaign, in which one of the models was captured jumping over a fence [Fig. 4]. The focus on the model's long legs is characteristic both of the fashion in the 1960s and Sohlberg's photographs. Together with the often-outstretched arms, the models look as if they are embracing life. Similarly, locations were not always spectacular; for example, one shoot took place at a sports ground with simple wooden benches rather than a prestigious stadium [Fig. 5]. Nonetheless, the concept and ideology remained the same; fashion is a race in which everyone can compete. It doesn't matter what you look like, just what clothes you wear. This is available to all Norwegians, thus completing the democratisation of fashion.

The democratisation of fashion marked a move away from the hierarchy of *haute couture* as a model. Trends now came from further afield and traditional Parisian fashion was no longer *de rigueur*, with designs coming from London and a burgeoning youth culture. In Norway, the ready-to-wear industry was too indoctrinated by Paris to respond. The style of the Solberg photos was inspired by this emergent pop culture. And that might explain why the photographs fitted the expectations of the magazine's readers better than the dresses that were featured.

ENDNOTES

1 T. Hvass and P. Christoffersen, 'Jan Fr. Sohlberg', *Norsk Fotografisk Tidsskrift*, 6 [1979], p. 20.

2 The magazine was established in 1957 and is still being published.

3 The Dextra Photo collection was bought from Arne Knudsen/Knudsens Fotosenter by Sparebankstiftelsen DnB NOR in 2008 and placed in the Norwegian Museum of Science and Technology. Together with the Archeology of Photography Foundation in Warsaw, an internet exhibition about the Norwegian studio and a Polish fashion photographer will be launched during spring 2011.

4 The journal ceased publication in 1965.

5 H. Wilhelm, *The Permanence and Care of Color Photographs* [Grinnell: Preservation Publishing Company, 1993], p. 18.

6 V. Mendes and A. de la Haye, *Twentieth Century Fashion* [London: Thames & Hudson, 1999], pp. 179–80.

7 J. Ekeberg and H. Østgaard Lund [eds.], *80 millioner bilder. Norsk kulturhistorisk fotografi 185–2005* [Oslo: Forlaget Press, 2008], pp. 358–63.

8 'Fram for norsk sommermote!', *Det Nye*, 18 [1968], pp. 34–7.

9 http://www.snl.no/fjernsyn/En_del_kjente_fjernsynsserier, retrieved 27 June 2010.

10 http://en.wikipedia.org/wiki/John_Galsworthy, retrieved 30 May 2010.

11 Mendes and de la Haye, *Twentieth Century Fashion*, p. 181.

12 June, 'De er norsk Damemoteråd', *KK*, 26 [1969], pp. 14–15.

13 I. Finckenhagen, 'Haute Couture sommerkolleksjon. Februar 1968', *Manufaktur*, 5 [1968], pp. 225–30.

14 Gerd, 'Norsk kunst i metall, stoff og sten', *Det Nye*, 39 [1968].

15 One of the most expensive coats cost 740 NOK; in 2008 that would have been about 5700 NOK [about 710 Euro]. But the prices varied down to 200 NOK. See SSB website http://www.ssb.no/vis/kpi/kpiregn.html, retrieved 20 May 2010.

16 E. Wilson, *Adorned in Dreams: Fashion and Modernity* [London: Virago, 1985], p. 157, cited in C. Breward, *The Culture of Fashion* [Manchester: Manchester University Press, 1995], p. 197.

17 June, 'De er norsk Damemoteråd'.

18 'Med toget', *Det Nye*, 13 [1969], pp. 40–2.

19 A. Kjellberg, *Mote: Trender og designere, Oslo 1900–2000* [Oslo: Huitfeldt forl., 2000], p. 61.

20 A. Kjellberg, *Per Spook. Norsk motedesigner i Paris. Norwegian Fashion Designer in Paris*, Exhibition Catalogue [Oslo: Nasjonalmuseet, 2006], pp. 11–14.

21 One of his projects lead by the Norwegian textile industry was Elegant Fritid [Elegant Leisure Time] promoting a Norwegian-made synthetic fibre in 1966. Fashionable casual clothes were intended to increase the sale of the yarn. T. Rasch, 'Mote på norsk', *Kunst og kultur*, 4 [2006], p. 256.

22 Spook also wrote fashion reports for women's magazines and was frequently interviewed about new trends. 'Per Spook sier', *Det Nye*, 5 [1966], pp. 30–1: 'Per Spook har vårfornemmelser', *Det Nye*, 20 [1968]: 'Jovisst er det Per Spook', *Det Nye*, 4 [1970].

23 'Kåper i høst', *Det Nye*, 38 [1969].

24 Toril, 'Klær for enhver', *Det Nye*, 29 [1969], pp. 26–7.

25 'Norske fabrikker satser på fjord og fjell', *Det Nye*, 43 [1968].

26 A report in the textile trade journal in the winter of 1968 told how the clothes

were designed. Three Norwegian designers, names not mentioned, but two of them settled in Paris and one in London, were invited to go to the region of Romsdal in the northwest of Norway to be independently inspired by the nature as well as the culture. The designers' sketches were distributed to the producers, who derived some inspiration, but nonetheless made their own designs. It seems to have been important for the textile organisation that the industry was involved in all parts of the design process and in that way able to use the factories' own machinery and know-how. 'Lovende lansering av "Fjord Look"', *Manufaktur*, 5 [1968], pp. 237–8.

27 '"Fjord Look 70" – markert utvikling til det bedre', *Manufaktur*, 4 [1969], pp. 228–34: Gerd, 'Fjord Look enda bedre!' *KK*, 48 [1969], pp. 24–7.

28 Trygve Ask, *God norsk design: Konstitueringen av industridesign som profesjon i Norge* [Oslo: Dr.ing.avh. AiO, 2004], cited in Rasch, 'Mote på norsk', p. 258.

Fashioning Identity

These papers consider the photographic image as a constructor, a mediator of coveted identities as well as a neutraliser or domesticator of whatever personal characteristics are regarded as unaccustomed or dangerous. That clothes make the man is a truism which has stood the test of time, to which we then might add that fixing and promoting a particular identity, image or brand has always been one of the more important aspects of the photographer's role, and indeed, of photography as such. This has been done through conscious fabrication and promotion of an aspired image – constructing a photographic reality that, as such, corresponded to a reality made 'real' through the assumed documented objective authenticity of the frozen-in-time actuality of the photo. Choosing the right aesthetics – as in a Polaroid – one could neutralise or obliterate all the visual makers, figures of speech, or tropes which always have been part and parcel of assuming or creating an identity, so as to call forth an identity which – like a Polaroid – was so true to life as to render it a whole new 'identity-fashion'.

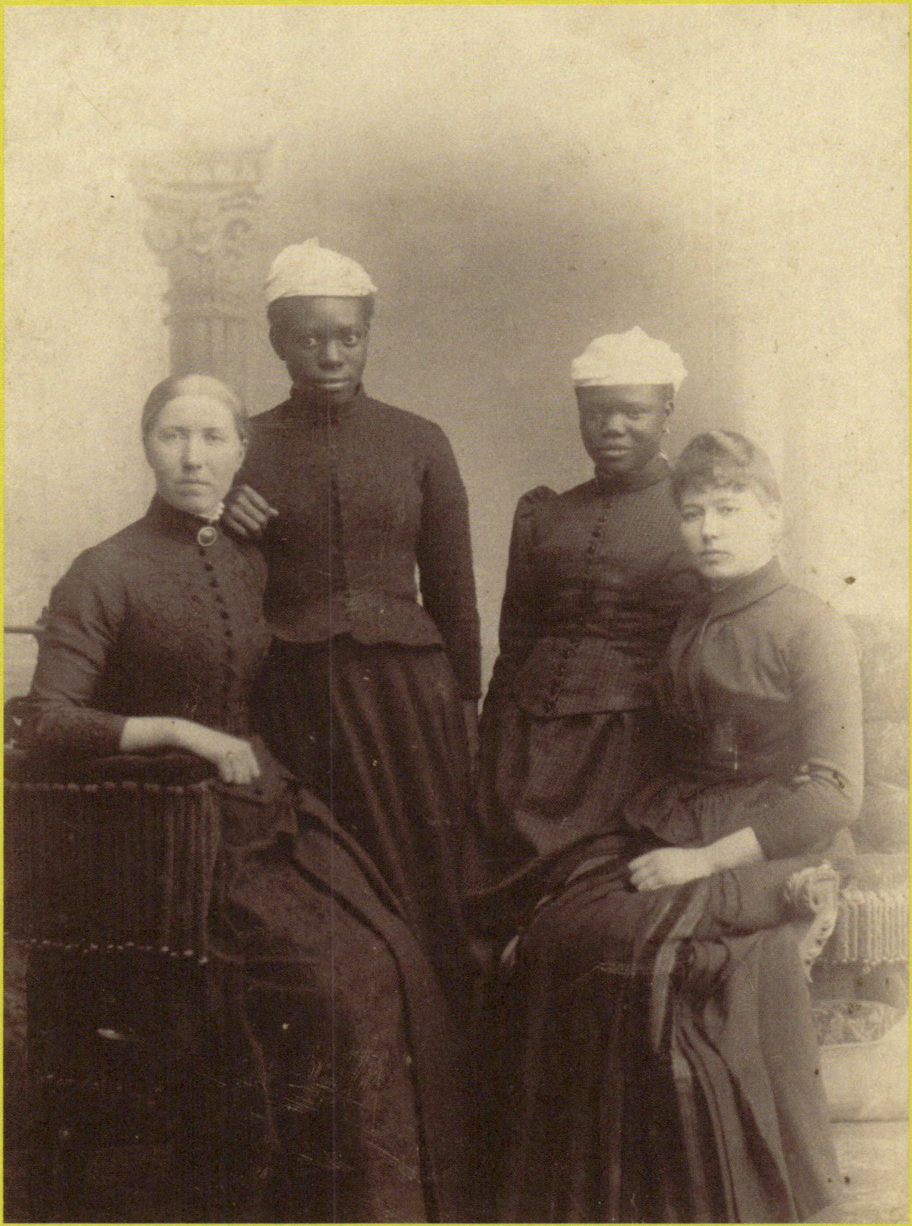

Fig.1:
Four unidentified women, Assens, Denmark, beginning of the 1890s. The two white ladies are most likely Mrs Emmy Andersen [1846–1893] and her adopted daughter, Mrs Christine Knudsen [1864–1893]. Mrs Andersen arrived at Assens in August 1891 with her husband Peter Andersen who after a long career in the Danish West Indies had been appointed mayor of Assens. Mrs Knudsen may have arrived with her parents and must have left the town no later than December 1892 to return to St Croix, Danish West Indies, where she died in January 1893. The two younger women are most likely from the Danish West Indies – note the characteristic headscarfs. All four persons are fashionably dressed. *Private owner.*

Dressing for Europe
Studies in the photographic image of black Danes

PER NIELSEN

During the summer of 2009, the local museum in the town of Assens, Denmark, published a photograph in *Fyens Stiftstidende* [a national newspaper published locally on the island of Funen].[1] The public were asked to help identify the individuals in the picture, which shows four women posing for the photographer [Fig. 1]. Two are sitting and two standing, the latter are quite young, probably teenagers. All are dressed in dark clothes, well dressed, and the two younger women have a sort of cap on their heads.

No one who sees the photo can miss the significance of the fact that the two ladies sitting are of European background while the two younger who are standing bear witness of an African past in their families.

This photograph is a valuable addition to the research material of an ongoing study initiated by the National Museum in Copenhagen about Danish West Indians of African background visiting or living in Denmark 1880–1920. The results of this project will be published from 2011 onwards.

In this paper I shall present some aspects of the research project by bringing up two occasions within the chosen period in which special attention seems to have been paid to the dress of Danish West Indians. Then I will point out some individuals and organisations in Danish society that may have had a special interest in showing the Danish West Indians in a certain way, including their dress. The focus will be on Danish West Indian fashion 1880–1917 in the West Indies and how that correlates with the way West Indians in Denmark dressed. The main discussion will be of the emphasis on skin colour and other physical features, heritage, folklore and fashion, and who would have had an interest in displaying and creating a stereotype image of Danish West Indians.

It will be argued that West Indian clothing had an important role in the intended creation of a feeling of national unity that was to include the mother country as well as the overseas possessions during the period 1880–1917. Furthermore that the experience of cultural diversity to the advocates of this national unity proved the strength of the Kingdom and gave credit to everyone's contribution to the whole. The use of photography in relation hereto will be highlighted.

A small selection of photographs in private and public collections will illustrate different aspects of working with the topic, such as the dating of photographs, interpreting fashion, using oral history and archival sources, and understanding the information in a broader political and socio-economic frame.

In the mentioned photograph there is an obvious intimacy between the two young women standing and the two ladies sitting. The tallest of the girls has one hand on the shoulder of the older woman in front of her, and it seems like the latter has her left arm around the younger person's waist. Their dresses touch. A similar contact is seen between the two other individuals.

The staff at the Assens Museum and Archives in Denmark have no information about the identity of these four persons, or of the date when the photograph was taken. The photo is glued onto a card on which is printed Atelier du Nord and an address in Assens. This implies that the photo was most likely taken in Assens, but we cannot know for sure. Although there is an indicated location on the photo card, the negative or the photo itself could have been brought to Assens from somewhere else. But family members of the person who owns the photo and who had asked the museum for more information about the individuals did have origins in Assens, and the owner knew for sure that none of the women were members of her own family. She had no information about who they were or when the picture was taken.

Denmark isn't widely known for having an imperialistic past, yet the country did participate in the European expansion of the seventeenth century and established a plantation colony on the island of St Thomas in the West Indies. This settlement was extended by the addition of the islands of St John and St Croix in the first decades of the eighteenth century. The colonisers brought enslaved Africans to these islands to work the land and so, by the time of emancipation in 1848, there were about forty thousand Danish subjects of African descent. Now, did the four women, the two younger as well as the older, have connections to the Danish West Indies, the three islands which in 1917 were sold and transferred to the United States and renamed the US Virgin Islands? The answer is most likely yes, and further comments on the matter will be given at the end of this paper.

The Danish West Indies produced tropical products, mainly sugar, and the African plantation workers are in old drawings and paintings from the days of slavery seen wearing very simple clothes which seem only to have had the role of covering the most intimate parts of the body. Through the nineteenth century this changed fundamentally, and field workers in the post-emancipation society of the latter part of the century are seen in photographs wearing clothes which are obviously influenced by the European and North American dress code of the day. On photographs from around the year 1900 the men usually wore light linen trousers and a white shirt along with a hat of some kind while the women wore a skirt, often in a light colour, a shirt or blouse in a similar colour and something to cover the head. For the workers in the port of St Thomas we see similar clothing. White skirts and white blouses seem to be very common among the many female coal carriers of this port town. On each woman's head is a headscarf and above this a piece of cloth twisted to make a so-called *cata*, a headpiece which would ease the pressure of the basket full of coal which was carried on the head.[2]

Pictures from the same period show people leaving church on Sunday morning; for example a picture of one of the Moravian churches, where most likely all of the members were of African descent, shows many of the men in dark jackets and trousers and with a hat to go with these. Some men would be in white trousers, a white shirt and a dark jacket. The women were almost all dressed in white. Their hats or other head coverings might be in colours and possibly with patterns.

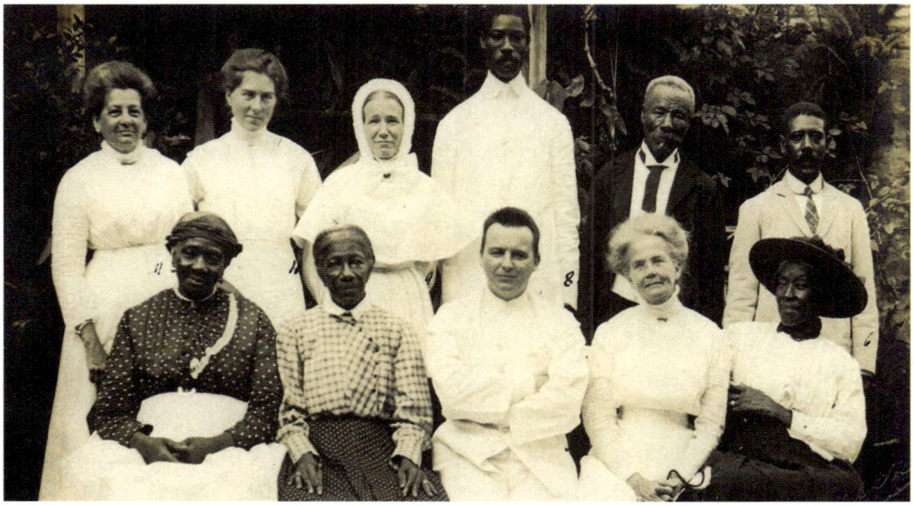

Fig.2:
Church Council of the Lord God of Sabaoth Lutheran Church in Christiansted, St Croix, Danish West Indies, 1913.
In the front left side sits Mrs Ann Eliza Williams, a member of the upper-middle-class. She wears a Madras headscarf. White clothes are commonly used by the council members, though several black members also wear darker colours.
Photograph in the National Museum, Copenhagen.

On a photo of the members of the Lutheran Church Council in Christiansted on St Croix, 1913 [Fig. 2], we see that white clothes are common for men and women alike as well as for black and white persons. The three individuals who have come to the island from Denmark, including the pastor, are all dressed in white, which underlined the idea of what Europeans considered suitable for the tropics. Some of the local council members, however, follow a more European dress code with darker colours. One lady wears a hat of European style while another has on a scarf with a chequered pattern. It is folded and bound to cover only the top of her head and leaves most of her ears visible. This is Mrs Ann Eliza Williams, widow of the engineer James Williams. She owned the house in which she lived and a couple of other houses in town. As the photo shows, she is a lady of African background.[3] Covering the head in the way Mrs Williams has done at this occasion is seen among women of all classes of black Danish West Indians, workers and professionals alike. The material used for such scarves is the so-called Madras of Indian origin, a fabric with a characteristic chequered pattern.

The two occasions in question are the *Nordic Exhibition of Industry, Agriculture and Art* [Den nordiske Industri-, Landbrugs- og Kunstudstilling] and the *Exhibition for the Colonies, Iceland and the Faroe Islands* [Dansk Koloni Udstilling samt Udstilling fra Island og Færøerne] which took place in Copenhagen in 1888 and 1905 respectively. The exhibitions should be seen in the light of the general interest in exhibiting products and innovations usually associated with the World Exhibitions beginning with the grand event in London in 1851 and followed up frequently during the following decades. Presenting a certain aspect of the arts came to play a role in these and in local exhibitions as well. The Swedish sections at the World Exhibitions are considered to be the first to include folk culture through traditional costumes, household utensils and buildings, usually from the Swedish countryside. This set a new trend as many countries took up this way of presenting national characteristics. Collecting material related to local folk culture became a movement in Europe and new museums had a focus on contemporary history as a result of the interest in folk culture. Each country or nation had something of its own, each region and local community something unique in the way the peasants used to dress or maybe still did dress on certain occasions.

At the *Nordic Exhibition* in Copenhagen in 1888 a committee was set up with the intention of establishing a Danish West Indian section to present

Caribbean produce. It was only natural to seek to give an impression of the climate and culture of the location where the produce originated, and sugar cane, palm leaves, corals etc. were used to help set the scene. At an early stage the committee suggested to the representatives in the West Indies that a family be found in the islands that could travel to Europe and represent the Danish West Indies, just like, for example, Russians would be representing their country and presenting its local products to the public. It was clearly pointed out that it should be a black family and a married couple, preferably with children.

In the West Indies the suggestion of sending a local family to the exhibition was not taken seriously. The committee in Copenhagen nevertheless insisted and added that they should have all expenses paid but no other payment as they should participate for their own pleasure. The committee was well aware that what made such a family interesting to the Danish public, namely having a different physical appearance and skin colour, might become a problem for the family. Therefore the ability to carry out some kind of craft would be important so that the intense attention of the public would be reduced and instead focus on the activity of making something for the entertainment of the viewing public.[4]

The Bundorph family of Frederiksted, St Croix, eventually travelled to Copenhagen. Mr Charles Bundorph spent the summer in Europe with his wife and their daughter Elizabeth and they were present at the exhibition every day. On the day of their arrival they had dinner at the house of one of the committee members, Mr Moses Melchior, and in his diary he writes on the third day of their stay: 'Bought clothes for the Negro couple.'[5]

Only one photograph of the Bundorph family is known. In it all three family members are well dressed [Fig. 3]. Mrs Bundorph is wearing a dark skirt and a dark tight jacket. On her head she has a chequered scarf, bound in about the same way as seen on Mrs Williams in the photo from 1913. This is the only detail in their clothing which associates the family with the West Indies. The photo must have been taken at the beginning of the stay as the image is included in a poster which advertised the exhibition.[6] It seems likely that most of the clothes which the three individuals are wearing were bought in Copenhagen. From the picture we get the impression of a very decent and ordinary family, people just like everyone else, and this seems to have been exactly the intention of Mr Melchior: to show that the Danish West Indies were a natural part of the Kingdom, distinct in their own way as far as produce and the origin of its people

Fig.3:
The Bundorph family of Frederiksted, St Croix, Danish West Indies, standing in front of the West Indian building at the *Nordic Exhibition of Industry, Agriculture and Art,* Copenhagen 1888.
Mrs Maria Louise Bundorph is fashionably dressed, most likely in clothes bought for her in Copenhagen. The Madras scarf is the only element of her clothing that identifies her with the West Indies.
Photograph in the Museum of the City of Copenhagen.

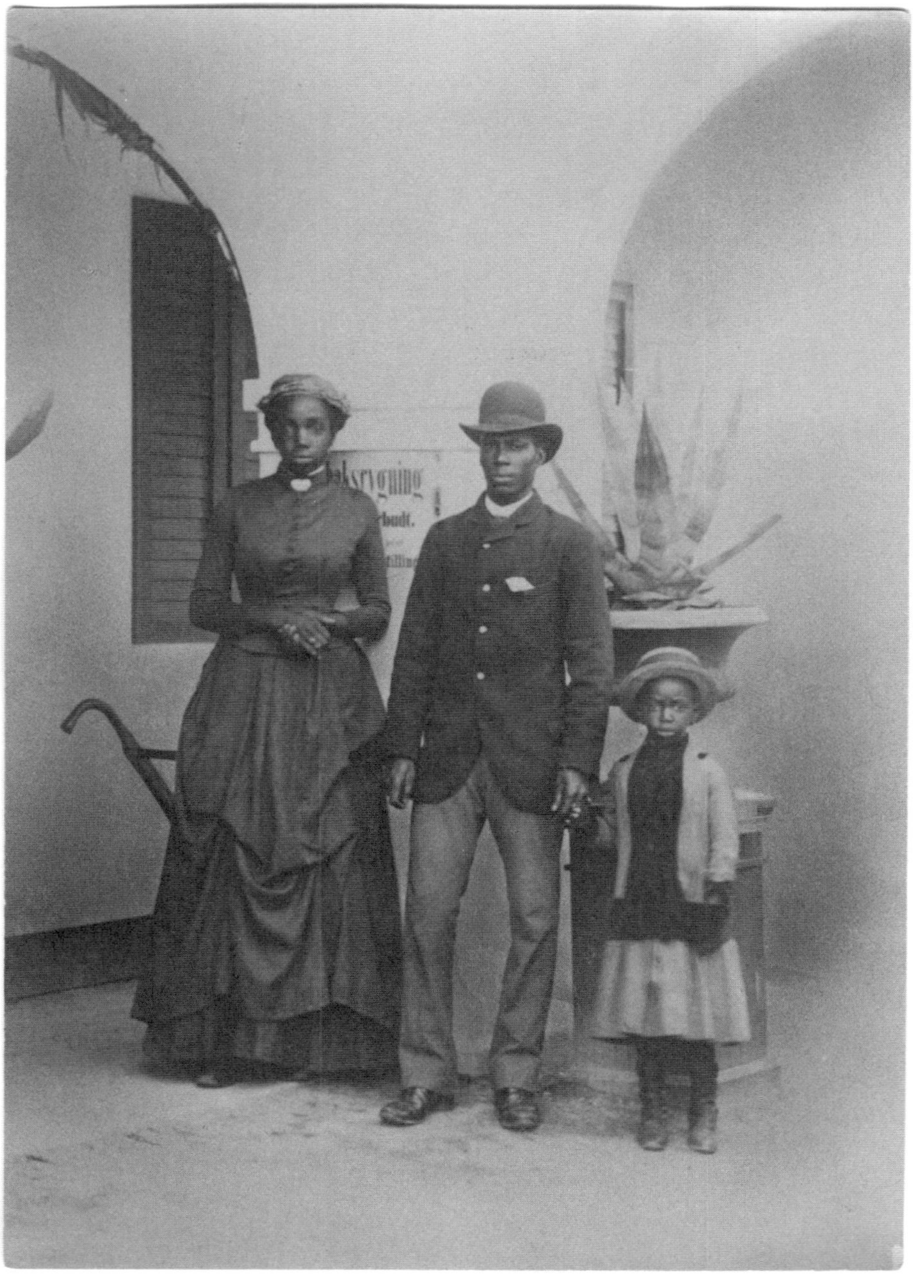

went, but equal to other parts of the country in the importance and the dignity of the population.

The so-called *Colonial Exhibition* in 1905, known officially as the *Exhibition for the Colonies, Iceland and the Faroe Islands,* was initiated by the author and women's rights advocate, Mrs Emma Gad. The president of the committee which took responsibility to organise the exhibition was the same businessman, Mr Moses Melchior, who was involved in 1888. The Crown Princess [from 1906 Queen] Louise was patron.

At the beginning of 1904 an exhibition of Danish West Indian produce had taken place in Copenhagen at the initiative of local businessmen with economic interests in the West Indies. An organisation named The Danish Atlantic Islands [De danske Atlanterhavsøer] with focus on the economic development, culture and research potential of the overseas possessions including Iceland, the Faroe Islands, Greenland and the Danish West Indies, had been established just prior to the exhibition and can be seen as part of a movement to try to maintain the small Danish empire united.[7] Mrs Gad had visited the exhibition and was impressed by the needlecraft made by West Indian ladies and now presented to the Danish public. She was not a member of The Danish Atlantic Islands, yet she shared its ideals and she decided right away that two of the West Indian women who had made the exhibited items should be invited to a summer programme for teachers of needlework along with participants from Schleswig, Iceland and the Faroe Islands. The programme was organised annually by the Organisation of Fine Crafts [Dansk Kunstflidsforening] of which Mrs Gad was president. Two West Indians arrived in 1904 to take part in the course, all expenses paid, and Mrs Gad was by then developing her next ambition to promote the idea of bringing the overseas possessions closer to the mother country. The exhibition of 1905 was already in place in her mind.[8]

This time the focus on presenting the cultural differences was itself a motive along with the commercial interests. Danish West Indians, Greenlanders, Icelanders and Faroe Islanders were to represent their lands, demonstrate local trades, crafts or other talents, all dressed in local costumes and in a setting that gave an impression of the unique nature and climate of the arctic world, the tropics etc.

To Mrs Gad the cultural differences were an important inspiration. No one was superior to the other. As far as the West Indian participants in the summer programme for teachers went, it was their talent in the field of the so-called 'Spanish work', a type of embroidery, which drew her attention and inspired her vision that these women had something valuable to contribute and that they too would benefit from inspiration from the nationals of the other parts of the Kingdom. This course had already, by 1904, been developed into much more than learning weaving and sewing. It was an introduction of each individual to the others and to the culture of the capital where visits were paid to theatres, museums, exhibitions, the Tivoli gardens and to dinner parties at private homes such as that of the Admiral Gad and his wife. This was a small part of Mrs Gad's effort to emancipate women, now including West Indians of African background. It was with great national pride that the Organisation of Fine Crafts was able to announce the presence of King Christian IX at the opening of its annual exhibition at the end of the summer programme for 1904. The Crown Princess handed out prizes for the best products, and the overseas participants were dressed in local costumes. In the years to come the women from the West Indies were usually in white skirts and white blouses decorated with, for instance, Spanish work. This came to be considered their local costume as a parallel to the old traditional costumes of individual localities in northern Europe despite the fact that Spanish work was a southern European traditional embroidery type and that the white dress was a modern fashion in the West Indies and not unknown in Denmark in the summertime.[9]

Mrs Gad and the committee that was to set up the exhibition in 1905 did not succeed in bringing a Danish West Indian family to Copenhagen. A man from St Thomas came with his mules and black pigs, which were to be exhibited in the West Indian section to give it a local flavour. Mr William Smith arrived with the animals a week after the opening of the exhibition. The two photographs which are preserved of Mr Smith in the scrapbook of the organisation show a man all dressed in white. Some weeks later two children from St Croix arrived to represent the islands together with Mr Williams. The children are likewise seen in white clothes on several photographs, though not in all cases.[10]

On the day of the opening of the 1905 exhibition when the Royal Family and the press were present, only one Danish West Indian of African background was there. Mrs Henriette Jensen had lived in Copenhagen since 1896 and was married to carpenter Peter Jensen. She had been hired for the occasion to serve in the restaurant. She appears in the photographs to be of all African background, but she spoke Danish [unlike most of the population in the Danish West Indies, who spoke English] and she already knew the city, and all the journalists as well as the King showed her great interest at the opening as well as later on that summer while the exhibition took place. On several photographs Mrs Jensen is dressed in white and in all but one picture she has a chequered scarf on her head [Fig. 4], bound

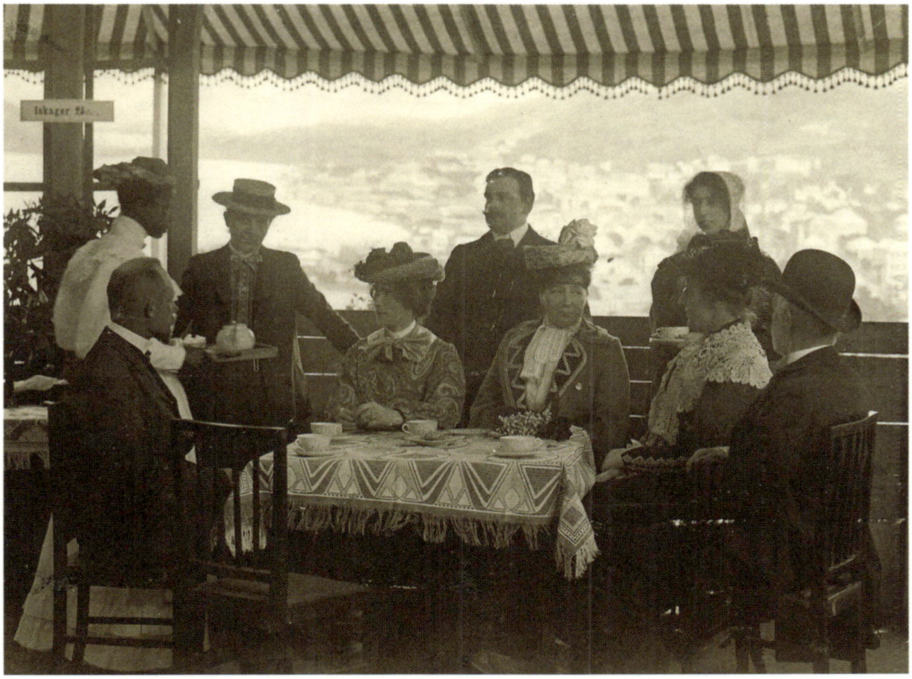

Fig.4:
Mrs Henriette Jensen and an unknown woman serve tea for a party at the Colonial Exhibition, Copenhagen 1905.
Mrs Jensen is dressed in white and wears a Madras scarf on her head while the unknown woman wears a traditional costume from Denmark. Seated to the right are Mrs Emma and Admiral Urban Gad. As president of the Organisation of Fine Crafts and initiator of the *Colonial Exhibition* Mrs Gad from 1904 until 1916 played a central role in presenting the West Indians as dignified members of Danish society.
Photograph in the National Museum, Copenhagen.

in the same way as seen in the photos of Mrs Bundorph 1888 and Mrs Williams 1913. Whether Mrs Jensen, ten years after leaving her native St Croix, was in possession of a white dress or was equipped with this by Mrs Gad and the committee is not known, but full attention was ensured – she was black, her dress was white and she wore a Madras chequered scarf.

Two photographs which must have been taken on one of the very first days of the exhibition show Mrs Jensen dressed in white and wearing the scarf. She is serving at a table together with a young woman in a Danish traditional countryside costume. One of these photos was published a few days later in the official booklet presenting the exhibition.[11]

We have seen how photographs in 1888 and 1905 were used to present an image of the black Danish West Indians. The individuals are very well dressed. In 1888 only the chequered headscarf adds a local West Indian cultural touch to the clothes of the Bundorph family, while in 1905 Mr Smith from St Thomas, the two children from St Croix and Mrs Jensen from Copenhagen are all dressed in white as a characteristic of West Indian fashion. In 1905 the white clothes have become a parallel to the traditional costume of other parts of the Kingdom which may well reflect the intention of Mrs Gad and others in favour of strengthening the ties between the mother country and the overseas possessions. Even though the Madras headscarf and the white clothes had been in use for some decades, it was a much shorter period than the European folk costumes. Thus the West Indian clothing can be described as modern rather than traditional.

As for the photograph of the four women presented at the beginning of this paper, the local museum staff have compared the studio background of this photo, as well as the furniture shown in the picture, to that of many others from the Atelier du Nord in Assens and are convinced that it must have been taken in Assens. The photographic studio, the Atelier du Nord, began business in 1891. Certain details of the dresses and the hairstyles, in particular of the younger of the white ladies, point to the early 1890s as the time when the photo was taken, presumably very close to 1890.

My own attention was drawn to the picture of the women because of the two younger individuals, who it has so far not been possible to identify. The older, the two white ladies sitting, on the other hand, would most likely be Mrs Andersen and Mrs Knudsen, a mother and her adopted, married daughter; both had for a long period previous to the time when the photograph was taken been living in the West Indies.

Mrs Emmy Andersen and her husband Peter Andersen were both born in Denmark though she grew up in St Croix. They got married in 1866, a few years after he had started his career as a lawyer in the Danish West Indies. The couple adopted Christine who was born in St Thomas in 1864 and at the age of about twenty-three she married a young lawyer, Otto Knudsen, who had arrived in the colonies from Denmark. In 1891 Mr Andersen was appointed mayor in the town of Assens and took up the office upon his and his wife's arrival there by the end of August of that year. Prior to their arrival the local newspaper had announced that Mr and Mrs Andersen left St Croix on the first of July, 'a mass of people was present to part with him, from the Governor to the poor who had benefitted from his and his wife's charity'.[12]

In 1889 Mrs Knudsen gave birth to a daughter in St Croix, and in 1891 she gave birth to another daughter in Assens. The Knudsen family must have returned to the West Indies not too long after the second child's birth, as Mrs Knudsen died in St Croix on 2 January 1893. So based on the existing information the date of the photo has to be between August 1891 and December 1892.

Neither in the local newspapers in Assens nor in the books where arriving and departing travellers were registered has any sign of two visiting young West Indian women been found. The intimacy between the persons in the photo does not point to a relationship as employer and servant. More likely, Mrs Andersen has brought the young, nicely dressed women to Europe to learn something, whether it be housekeeping, cooking, sewing, teaching or something else. Their very fashionable clothing could have been made in the West Indies as well as in Denmark. If Mrs Andersen plays a role in dressing the young women she surely must have intended to present them as very decent members of Danish society and the use of the scarf adds a little local cultural touch suitable for Europe during the late nineteenth century.

With the increased interest in specific local cultural characteristics in every corner of Europe in the last decades of the nineteenth century, dress and fashion became important to characterise more than being a nanny. In Denmark the right clothes became a way of placing the West Indian Danes in the Kingdom or for many conservatives simply in the constructed Danish nationality where the Icelandic, the Greenlandic and the West Indian subjects were looked upon as equal members but each with their particular cultural characteristics.

Race is not an issue that is emphasised, most likely because it is associated with prejudices and therefore not useful for uniting. Cultural diversity, however, was considered to be a strength. Cultural differences existed within little Denmark itself and were therefore fully acceptable. Everyone should, according to the organization The Danish Atlantic Islands, for example, be proud of the diversity, and the white dress became the local costume of the Danish West Indies and is no less interesting than any other costume found in the European parts of the Kingdom. And this is the case even though the white clothing is an expression of fashion common at the time while the local costumes in different parts of Iceland, the Faroe Islands and Denmark often had been traced with great efforts to secure their survival as symbols of the local traditional culture.

In the long run this national construction, or this imagined community – to use the well-known term from the professor of international studies Benedict Anderson's influential book *Imagined Communities* from 1983 – was only shared by a limited part of the Danish population. Before long history would show that the concept of a common nation was not strong enough to keep either the Danish West Indies or Iceland within the Monarchy – one was sold, and the other withdrew.

Photographic images had played their roles, but they did not prove to be sufficient to unite the black and white Danes. It was only a small segment of the Danish population who considered the Danish West Indians to be real Danes, real and equal citizens, and about two thirds of the voters in December 1916 voted in favour of selling and transferring the islands and their population to the United States. Those against were the majority of the voters in the Faroe Islands, maybe as an expression of solidarity with the West Indians, a majority in the northern part of Jutland where influential members of the church had spoken against the transfer of Danish citizens and a conservative group all around the country, but with most of its members in the capital, who either saw a commercial interest in keeping up an outpost in the Americas or felt their national pride was shaken if the Kingdom's territory was diminished. Despite the use of clothing and photography the prosperous merchant, Mr Melchior, and the women's rights advocate, Mrs Gad, united with the Royal Family and a few more, were not successful in creating a sustainable image of the dignified and equal West Indian citizens.

ENDNOTES

1 *Fyens Stiftstidende* 13 August and 3 September 2009.

2 Fine examples of photographs from the Danish West Indies are published in: Elizabeth Rezende and Anne Walbom, *St Croix. Historic Photos 1860–1917* [Copenhagen 2009]. Per Nielsen, 'Opfattelser af race og klasse i Dansk Vestindien. Udsendte danskeres syn på vestindiske kularbejdere 1890–1917' [Conceptions of race and class in the Danish West Indies. West Indian coal workers as seen by European Danes 1890-1917], *Nationalmuseets Arbejdsmark* [Annual Journal of the National Museum] 2004, pp. 209–229.

3 Photograph in Nationalmuseet. Afd. for Nyere Tid. [National Museum, Copenhagen, Modern Section.] No. 2020/1970: Per Helweg-Larsens postkortsamling. The lady on the back of the photo is identified as Mrs Williams and can be found in censuses: Rigsarkivet [Danish National Archives]. Folketælling [Census] Christiansted 1880 Kongensgade 16, 1890, 1901 and 1911 Østergade 37, 1911 Strandgade 23.

4 Rigsarkivet. Vestindiske lokalarkiver [West Indian local archives]. 11.53.258. St Thomas og St Jan guvernement. Vedr. udstillingerne i Kbh. 1872 & 1888.

5 Erhvervsarkivet. [Danish National Archives. Business Section.] Moses & Søn G. Melchior, København. Privatarkiv II. Handelsdagbog okt. 1887–nov. 1889.

6 The photograph and a copy of the poster are at the Museum of the City of Copenhagen [Københavns Museum].

7 *Atlanten. Medlemsblad for Foreningen 'De danske Atlanterhavsøer'.* [The organisation's journal.] Copenhagen 1904–1917.

8 *St Croix Avis* 9.7.1904. – Landsarkivet for Sjælland. [Danish National Archives. District of Sjælland.] Ergoterapeutskolen i København [herunder Dansk Kunstflidsforening]. Pk. 2. Protokol: Udstillinger m.m. 1900–11.

9 Photographs of participants are published in: *Husmoderens Blad* 9. Aarg. [1904] Nr. 34, p. 269. *Dansk Vestindisk Selskabs medlemsblad* [Journal of the Danish West Indian Society] 2001. Nr. 3, pp. 22–24, and 2007, Nr. 4, p. 7.

10 The photographs of Smith and the children are in: Nationalmuseet. Afd. for Nyere Tid. No. 6/1984. Dansk Kunstflidsforenings scrapbog *Dansk Koloniudstilling samt Udstilling fra Island og Færøerne 1905.*

11 Andreas Bruun: *Illustreret Vejledning over Dansk Koloniudstilling (Grønland og Dansk Vestindien) samt Udstilling fra Island og Færøerne.* [Illustrated Guide to the Colonial Exhibition.] Copenhagen 1905, s. 32.

12 A. Falk-Jensen og H. Hjorth-Nielsen: *Candidati og Examinati Juris 1736–1936.* Copenhagen 1954–1959. Assens newspapers: Information provided by Mr Tim Grejsen, Assens Museum and Archives.

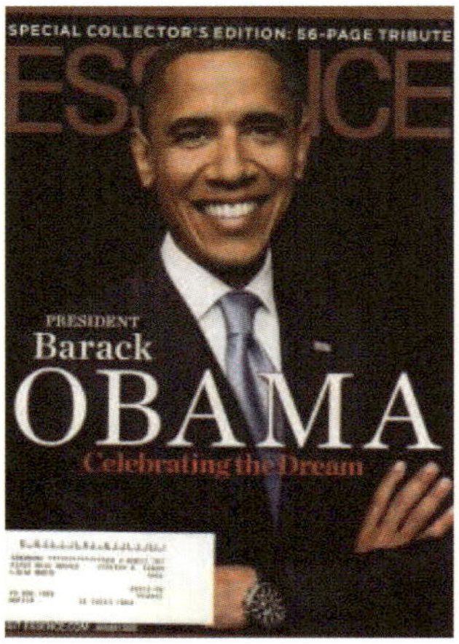

Fig.1

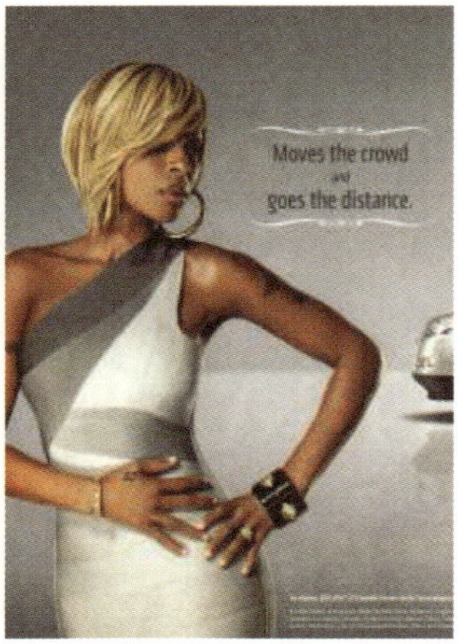

Fig.2

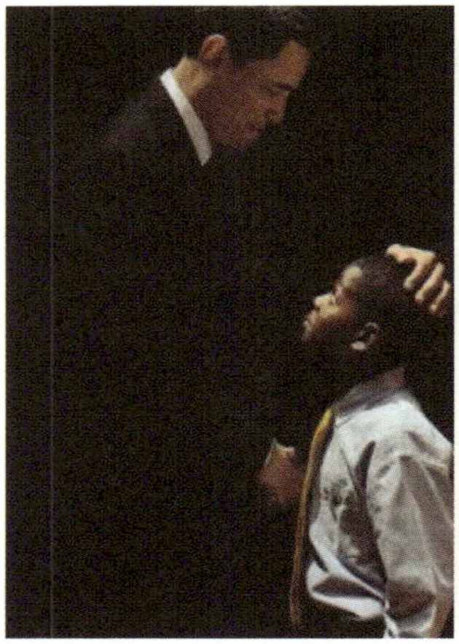

Fig.3

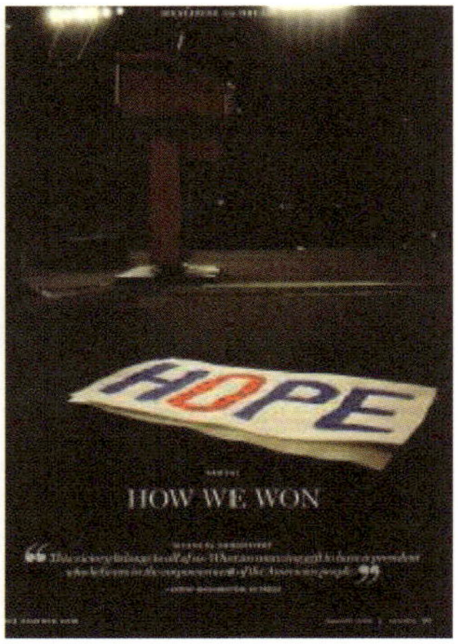

Fig.4

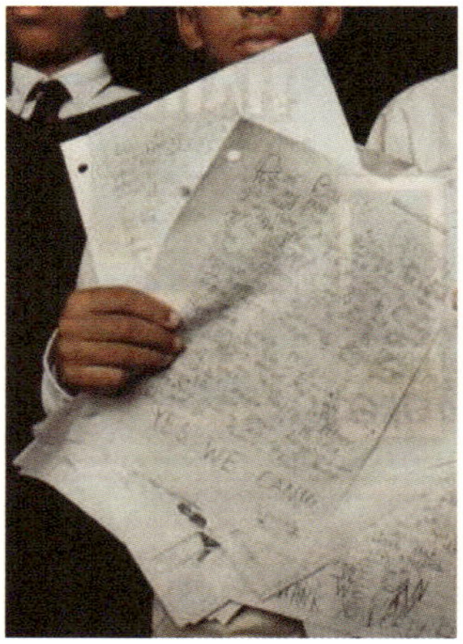

Fig.5

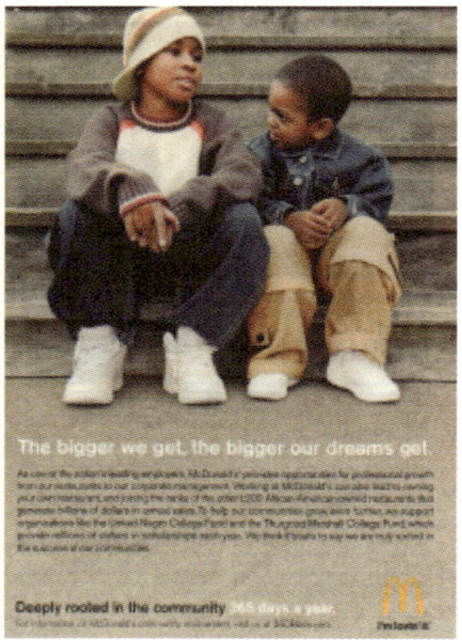

Fig.6

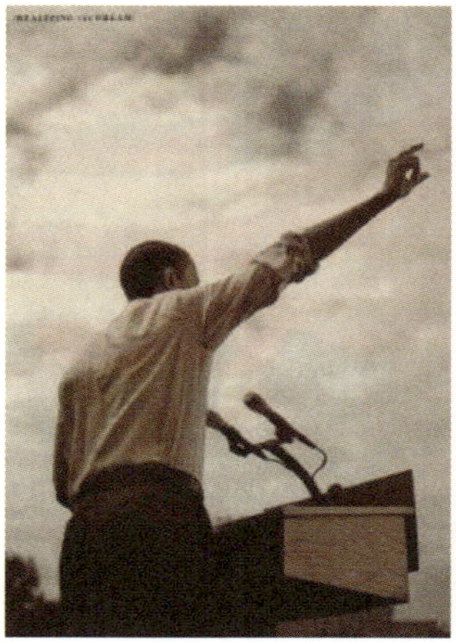

Fig.7

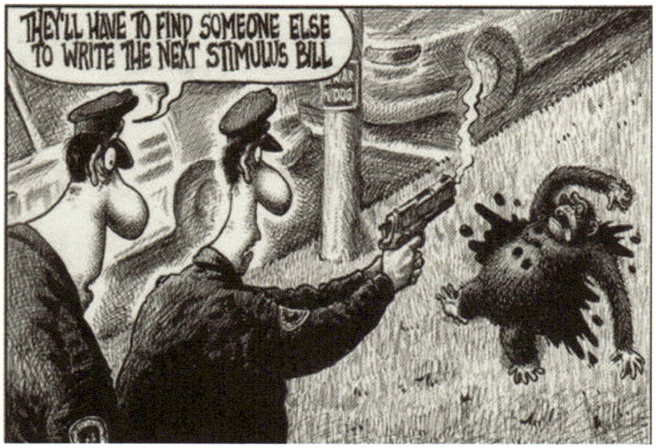

Fig.8

Domesticating Blackness
Decoding US racial politics in targeted advertising

LIDIA MARTE

The question of 'who is an "American"?' keeps recurring in US history, with answers ranging from educational qualifications, to gender, race and to place of birth.[1] The many images that circulated of candidate, and now US President, Barack Obama, seem to offer a historically specific answer, coinciding with the hasty announcement of a 'post-racial' era.[2] These images seem to suggest that the dream of equality has been achieved, a Black man elected to the White House proves, somehow, racism in America is a thing of the past and racial inequality no longer warrants discussion. Readings of Obama's image against the discourses of a 'colour-blind' America could help us question generalised conceptions of the African-American population as unified, thus hindering an investigation of disparity, one of intersecting identities and interlocking forms of oppression.[3]

This investigation will explore how the re-production of certain representations of Blackness 'domesticates', is made palatable, safe, and controlled for public 'consumption' focusing on images of Barack Obama. Without the re-production of Obama's image as a happily married, heterosexual, middle-class, elegant, measured, professional and eloquent male to embody an acceptable 'black respectability'[4] would there have been an election victory?

This paper intends to assess the ways in which 'Blackness', as demonstrated in representations of Obama, constitute notions of domestication and by association contribute to an understanding of racial politics in the contemporary USA.

'Domesticating' is a term that is redolent of the first colonial 'seasonings' in the Americas; the forced enculturation of racial regimes through slavery. *Domesticating* refers also to socialisation practices that attempt to 'normalise' a White, middle-class, Christian, heterosexual trope as the image-path to become a mainstream 'American'. This Anglo-conformity assimilation model prescribes ways in law and institutional practices for how diverse racial-ethnic groups become incorporated into a nation.[5] In this sense domesticating points to processes through which the 'image' of a US nation is periodically renegotiated through struggles for

Acknowledgements
I am grateful to the solidarity of those that helped to make this paper coherent and readable. Thanks to Brian Stross for suggestions, and support with grammar and organisation. Thanks to Michael A. Langkjær and Æsa Sigurjónsdóttir for their helpful editing suggestions and for their patience. Special thanks to Michael, for his trust in the potential of this piece from its early stages.

inclusion of marginalised 'others'. National inclusion implicates not only labour and citizenship rights, but also how these 'others' are inscribed into mainstream memory-history archives through which boundaries of belonging are also policed and negotiated.

Blackness is widely recognised among African Diaspora and Critical Race Theory scholars as a social construction; a contested space which could range from an assigned or self-claimed racial category, to a situational space of individual performativity, to a political positioning.[6] 'Domesticating Blackness' in the context of this paper refers to the micro-politics through which practices and visual notions of difference – in this case of race – are accommodated, resisted and/or re-signified through changing contexts.[7]

Using images from *Essence*'s fiftieth anniversary collector's volume [*President Obama: Celebrating the Dream*, January 2009] in which a host of prominent African-Americans were asked to respond to their experiences being 'witness to history', with testimony interspersed with images from the Presidential campaign trail, this segment will serve as a practical exercise in 'ethnographic semiotics'. By juxtaposing pairs of reportage and advertising images [see figure page] analysis will decode the visual tensions and coincidences that reveal aspects of the production of domesticated Blackness in relation to current racial politics in the US.

Situated perspectives: The production of *Essence*

Essence is a commercial publication for popular readership. Published in a US standard magazine format it has a visually busy cover; usually a centered Black individual portrait and multiple headings for articles [many of which are a few paragraphs long]. Since the essays are so brief, it appears that 'real' Black men and women interviewed and photographed are featured to show that apparently they can afford to consume the products advertised in the other pages. The estimated circulation is over one million subscribers; ninety-one per cent of readers are Black, and sixty-seven per cent are Black women between the ages of eighteen and forty-nine.[8] First published in 1970, it is considered the oldest magazine targeted to and predominantly read by African-American women. Research on *Essence* foregrounds how the magazine offers a space for 'Black women to construct themselves in public media', yet reproduces some male elite gaze.[9] According to one study, in this publication there is a reproduction of normative models of race and gender/sexuality that might be considered stereotypes; yet positive representations of African-Americans are most common, which is still rare in other mainstream media.[10]

The proposition that *Essence* is a Black women's publication is immediately problematic. The many photographic advertisements for luxury items, financial services and expensive cars suggest arrived and aspiring Black middle-class readers with disposable incomes as the target audience – potential consumers of products advertised in the numerous pages [roughly half of the magazine's content is taken up by ads]. The magazine reads almost like a catalogue of products and ideals of middle-class lifestyle and role models. As Lutz and Collins proposed in their analysis of *National Geographic* magazine, representing others is a way of representing ourselves, which is another way of assigning accountability for partial perspectives.[11] In this sense, rather than simply representing 'African-Americans', magazines such as *Essence* appear to offer a specifically situated narrative of their own economic projects and aspirations as a successful entrepreneurial group within the African-American population.

Examination of the political-economy of *Essence*'s images is needed before asking who is shaping these images of domesticated Blackness. Whoever controls the means of media production will shape, or at least influence, the kinds of representations privileged in them. Rushing to conclusions based on the magazine itself as product, or based on the images, leaves out the organisational power structures, micro-politics of editorial decisions and even labour practices.[12]

How are these images visually and ideologically produced? What political 'work' are they made to perform *inside* the space of the magazine and *outside*, within the social context that shaped them?

Inside the frame: *Essence* and the public production of Black masculinities

The most visually striking aspect of *Essence* magazine's special issue was the shades of Blackness, healthy-looking Blackness, amidst a forest of advertising in which a counterpoint narration – contradictory and productive – emerges from the space of the page and within the subtle relation among the pages. The carefully controlled relations among ads and photo-images speak uneasily to each other, and the text/image dialogue questions whose dream is potentially being fulfilled.

The portraits of Obama that appeared in the reportage pages of *Essence* offer dignified portraits of a Black masculinity [in contrast to rap, hip-hop vocabulary, mural art once seen as graffiti, gangster, criminal or sports figure] reproducing familiar genres of Black males shown in mainstream US media. In spite of the well-orchestrated safety of Obama's image, there seems to be also a fear of contagion and danger; his suspicious cosmopolitanism, the politics that this campaign helped bring forth – juxtaposed with the *You Tube* posting of erotic videos featuring multi-coloured sexual fantasy-pieces using Obama's image. This was indeed a dangerously racialised desire – that public media in the US tries so hard to keep invisible and segregated – and is indeed an intriguing element; how many times had voters had the luxury of fantasising about a political candidate?

Yet this grand, dignified testimony is simultaneously presented with ads for McDonalds recruiting its Black workforce, or hair relaxers to emulate beauty standards of hegemonic others. Piercing the dream-imaged narratives of an inclusive class mobility among African-Americans suggested by the Obama images, these ads, in apparent contradiction, echo beyond the frame to illustrate the growing gap in wealth between White elites and Black and other 'minority' groups, but also point to a growing Black middle and upper class.[13]

In Figures 1 and 2 [cover and back cover], the cover of *Essence* features a centred, formal portrait of Obama, dark colours predominating, calling attention to his picture-perfect white teeth and broad smile. In the inside cover, silver and white predominate in the dress of a woman in the foreground and a car in the background. The dark woman in the car advertisement, resembling some famous celebrity dancer-singer, appears self-assured but also dangerously paired to the car as another object. Yet the strap-line 'Moves the crowds and goes the distance' anchors her looks of empowerment and pride in the luxury items – jewellery and car, which starts at $39,810, which one presumes someone who looks like her is now able to afford.

In Figure 3 a profile view of Obama greets a Black boy with a handshake and a supportive touch on the head. The caption reads: 'Democratic nominee Obama looks into the eyes of America's future after a town hall meeting in Greensboro North Carolina, in March 2008.' Obama's attractiveness might have awakened dormant desires in adult US voters, but his youth, warmth and eloquence also made an impression on young children, especially on Black boys. The trope of respectability is still there – through the formal clothing and the low-key treatment of contrast – but what makes this image so powerful is what is *not* there; the many American descendants of African slaves and the struggles they had to endure to make this moment possible. The yellow tie on the boy, the low-key mood of the photo, all enhance the 'tear-jerking' potential of this representation, regardless of how posed or genuine the actual moment was. The image is created in a way that makes us imagine some sort of healing is going on with that boy's self-image related to readers through a process of self-identification.

In Figure 4 [features: *witness to history* page, 'Hope'] the large typography and colours of the word are anchored immediately with Obama's campaign slogan 'hope we can believe in' as an obvious reference. But there is more to this image; the visual angle, the view of a post-speech emptiness and the quote below – by Kerry Washington[14] – about the work of a presumed national unity and a majority mandate. At the top again, reads the phrase 'Realizing the Dream' [the class mobility dream?], below, 'How we Won: this victory belongs to all of us ...'. The echo of this 'we' keeps recurring, but who is this 'we'? All we know for a fact is that Obama and the particular sectors that supported him have won a chance at state power.

When text and image are taken together, the text subtly tells us how to interpret the image, and sometimes it is the reverse; usually it is both. The tensions among the photographs become visible when we focus on some elements, for example choice of clothing, camera angles and key words from the captions, that anchor the signification. Some of these images appear already suspiciously close to one another, such as in Figures 5 and 6. Both pages portray young Black males. Two formally dressed boys from a charter school in New York City appear in Figure 5, and in Figure 6 two kids dressed 'hood-style' lounge on steps of a nondescript place. Figure 6's caption reads: 'The bigger we get the bigger our dreams get', an ad for management and ownership of McDonalds restaurants, which claims to be 'deeply rooted in the community' [which assumes there exists *one* homogeneous Black community, but also proposes a communal *we* that includes African-Americans and McDonalds corporation].

The way these boys are dressed suggests an urban neighbourhood, as do the kinds of cement steps. They are not playing with a dog on a manicured lawn, nor riding bikes on clean streets. Is McDonalds recruiting for the future working class? In the smaller-type caption McDonalds also claims to support Black colleges, funds and scholarships, establishing the 'future-president' contradictions that help us jump to Figure 5. 'We know how to dress and consume and we know how to write', the charter schoolboys seem to say in Figure 5. This is a photo from reportage of one of Obama's campaign trails. In this close-up portrait we don't see the background, and the two Black boys are dressed in formal clothing, in contrast to the casual dress in the McDonalds ad. The boys – one assumes in a classroom – hold hand-written letters, addressing the President, and we can read some lines, including 'yes we can'. [But who can? Are the McDonalds boys also invited?] Even though these two images are within the same space-time of the magazine representationally, they seem to inhabit different worlds. Are two separate paths to the 'American dream' being promoted; one to the presidency and another to managing a McDonalds franchise?

A suspicious 'we' keeps reappearing in the documentary and the advertising images, which makes us question and suspect different answers, just as the who is an 'American' question will continue to exist in a contested multiplicity. The dialectical counterpoints of image/text, through 'anchoring and relevance',[15] take turns in the attention of the readers. The text limits or narrows to a set of propositions the interpretive meanings the reader could make, according to the purpose of the image in question. But the image, as well, limits how far we can interpret the textual elements – or caption – given the case. The task of a critical analysis is precisely to question and infer from such limits the kinds of boundaries and tensions proposed by the representation. I believe, however, that without going outside of the image frame, this task could not be completed. The texts in the layout of these images are very productive, and appear almost self-explanatory, yet they function in this context as the main 'punctum' of the image[16] as well as the anchors of outside-the-frame meanings and realities.

This forced dialogue between these images helps us to recognise some brief moments of tension in the uneven narration of the American dream. When pairing these images, the ads bring out the dissonance, the stone inside the shoe. While the reportage shows engaged Black people, celebrities and a Black president, the McDonalds ad reminds us, 'Wait, not all at once, someone has to work, we still need local managers and cheap labour for our restaurants!' Another example, in Figure 7, a sepia portrait of Obama during a speech with the phrase 'realizing the dream' at the top of the layout, makes us question 'whose dream?' Is this the same as Martin Luther King Jr's dream [equality for all] or the classic American dream [individual financial success]? Are these two the same, are there other dreams? A space of ambiguity is left there, which risks taking over the heroic aspect of Obama's gesture.

Both the photojournalistic reportage and the advertising photographs are composed pages; constructed, planned and revised layouts to achieve certain effects using a documentary-like, almost infomercial strategy. For example, in Figure 6, notice the candid casualness of those young Black boys on the steps, dreaming away their American dreams: and in contrast, in Figure 5, notice how the adolescent Black males in the charter school image seem staged, controlled, deliberate, already successful and domesticated. It is almost as if, in the sharing of tropes and genre strategies, these images were mocking each other.

Returning to the text/image counterpoints, it is important to remember that Obama's image as candidate included also celebrated oral and written speeches; it was this outside-the-image, 'founding father', literary evocation and deliberate resemblance of Obama's political persona to past presidents, such as Roosevelt or Lincoln, that made him remarkable and refreshing to many voters, and perhaps with such displays he alienated many others. The respectability trope of Obama's visual image could not have worked well without this particular charisma of 'looking presidential', accomplished through historical awareness and eloquence. Emphasis on these talents might have been needed, perhaps, to claim adherence to the most fundamental proof of belonging and upholding of national traditions.

Outside of the frame: A safe Blackness; respectability and conditions on the ground

Obama's public biography – of a biracial child with alleged Scottish, English and Cherokee ancestry, born in Hawaii, who experienced multiple migrations, public service in Chicago and becoming a senator and outstanding orator – had the makings of a culture hero's story[17] and serves as an exemplar of difference. A thinly racially mixed man, not an image of someone perceived as potentially dangerous. Obama's benevolent facial expressions gave him an aura of reconciliation, not only domestically, but to a global audience – especially in the Global South – that might have interpreted it as a promising softening of US foreign policy. Obama has the type of Blackness, with Apollonic features, preferred by elites of all stripes, closer to Whiteness, just tanned enough to be exotic. The well-orchestrated performance illustrating a caring, thoughtful, intelligent and well-domesticated individual, who happens to be socially constructed as

Black [despite recognition that he is half White], hides the problematic aspects of his domestication.

The need to manufacture a safe image stems, in part, from a US national narrative of White nation under a Christian god, ideological means through which populations of colour have been subjected to an eternal foreignness. The diverse aspirations of a 'house Negro' versus a 'field Negro' as metaphors of the diverse experiences of oppression that African-Americans experienced during slavery keep returning in debates among Black scholars and activists,[18] referring to issues of image and respectability.[19] What becomes a legitimised, naturalised, domesticated Blackness could close doors to more radical movements, especially if the apparatus of the State is left intact no matter how black, blue, or female candidates are; access to electoral politics is not necessarily a sign of real power to change social structures once the candidate becomes the President.

Domestication can be understood as a dialectical process of simultaneous resistance and accommodation according to one's own situated life projects. Ideological domestication – which has been the focus of this discussion – through the work of public narratives attempts to de-historicise and de-politicise the present. From a Black entrepreneurial perspective *Essence* magazine is creating 'necessary-for-racial-uplifting' positive representations of Black people, as their focus on celebrities and great African-American achievers reveals. African-Americans – in common with other Afro-diasporic populations in the Americas – were exposed to, and produced different responses to, structural violence and historical inequalities.[20] There is a further erasure of marginalisation when complex processes of social mobility and ideological divergences among African-American groups are dismissed – a case in point being a growing upper class of Black Republicans.

For many Blacks in the US, respectability as image and as lifestyle is neither a choice, nor in some cases an option. In the history of US 'racial formations'[21] respectability and citizenship have gone hand in hand as many generations of minority women and men put their suspected foreignness to the test of the nation. Black masculinity and femininity, class, ethnicity, age and even region come into play when locating acceptable, domesticated models of Blackness.[22] This image was needed to achieve basic citizenship rights and to tame down the aspects of 'difference' feared by some sectors of the US demographic, helping to construct a collective image of rational decent people, since wider support from the whole civil society was then needed.

Representational practices – besides communicative and expressive functions – are used frequently to do the ideological work of justifying institutions and people's social actions.[23]

As asserted by Thaggert, Black males continue to be represented as public entertainers – athletes and musicians – but increasingly urban, working-class Blacks became the stereotype; pathologically violent, lazy but crime prone, and untrainable educationally, dangerous Black men: whilst Black women were stereotyped as poor by choice and behaviourally deviant in family and gender practices.

During the two Bush administrations, and more visibly after Obama's election, active attacks on multiculturalism and diversity have appeared – such as the omission of civil rights leaders in public school textbooks as proposed by the Texas Board of Education – and overt expressions of racism in public discourse have become more common and acceptable. The resurgence of fundamentalist movements and White supremacist militias in the US is not absent from the plethora of image responses to this 'historical moment' of Obama's presidency. The disturbing political cartoon in Figure 8 was published in the *New York Post* in February 2009, just a few months after Obama's presidential victory. The image seems to be expressing opposition to Obama's policies [caricatures of two White men shooting a chimpanzee; the speech bubble reads: 'They will have to find someone else to write the next stimulus bill']. There seems be a smoking gun in one of the men's hand, and a chest-wounded chimpanzee dying. The interplay of text and image reveals very concrete referents not only to ideological opposition by the Christian right, but it also anchors *unambiguously* – as cartoons tend to do – an alarming display of racism. It seems that not even a well-domesticated, respectable Blackness can be considered 'safe' to certain sectors of US society. In comparison with Figure 7, the sepia portrait of Obama, the multiple, contested proposals of Blackness are evidenced and negotiated, demonstrating ruptures and opposition from constituents with a different 'racial' and economic project for the nation.

Fast food semiotics: Images, technologies and domestication

The 'production of history' – in Trouillot's sense – is not primarily about veracity or even authority, but about the concrete power of inscriptions in built environments and institutions, about access to the means of production of representations.[24] The power not of photographs, but of 'photographic-ness' [since the material substratum has changed], this look of crisp ultra-realism is an effect that could ironically come as easily from a heavily controlled setting in an advertising photo studio in New York City as from a scene of Obama shaking hands with voters on a street in Memphis. Between the documentary or reportage images of Obama and the ads as graphic, commercial art there is a narrow line of separation, yet only if we read inside, outside, through and beyond the frame.

The election of a Black president in the US of 2008 responded, of course, to more concrete factors than merely a successful image-branding campaign. It is obvious that the images were more outcomes than causes, but they were made to perform political work effectively, taking advantage of a media-saturated US public sphere. Moreover, Obama and his supporters did tremendous grassroots work of mobilisation among diverse communities and across generations, and they understood and used the power of images and media. In this sense, *Essence* portraits of Obama might have been part of this wider project.

The symbolic act of getting elected seems plenty for now, considering the exclusionary racial national imaginaries in the US. It is important to acknowledge the right of people who have been mis- and under-represented to use images strategically, not only to acquire individual and group power, but also as a legacy and attempt to join mainstream historical archives of a nation that, until recently, excluded their experiences and contributions. The victory and so many new media archives guarantee Obama's future memorialisation and vignettes in textbooks that might resonate with Black kids – or not – in the future, for managing to inscribe one more landmark on the changing narratives of the US nation.

ENDNOTES

1 L. Ling, 'Who is an American?', *International Political Sociology*, 4 [2010], p. 99–103.

2 D. Thomas and J. Jackson Jr, 'Racialized publics', *Transforming Anthropology* [Special issue on race and the public sphere], 17:2 [Berkeley: University of California Press, 2009], pp. 74–8.

3 P. Hill-Collins, *Black Sexual Politics: African-Americans, gender and the new racism* [Chicago: Routledge, 2004], p. 67.

4 S. Reid-Brinkley, 'The *Essence* of res[ex]pectability: Black women's

negotiation of Black femininity', *Meridians*, 8:1 [2007], pp. 236–60.

5 J. Howard, 'Gendered interventions: American protestant evangelism under Japanese-American internment', *Transforming Anthropology*, 14 [2006], pp. 31–4.

6 S. Hall, 'What is this *Black* in Black popular culture?', in E. Smith [ed.], *Representing Blackness: Issues in Film* [New Brunswick, New Jersey: Rutgers University Press, 1997], pp. 123–34.

7 A previous usage of this term refers to the re-commodification of Black women through becoming 'refined' consumers, reproducing White middle-class lifestyles, and emulating ideals of womanhood in the US in the nineteenth to twentieth centuries. L. Merish, 'Domesticating "blackness": Harriet Jacob, Sojourner Truth, and the de-commodification of the Black female body', in L. Merish, *Sentimental Materialism: Gender, Commodity Culture, and Nineteenth-Century American Literature* [Durham: Duke University Press, 2000], pp. 191–228.

8 J. Woodard and T. Mastin, 'Black womanhood: *Essence* and its treatment of stereotypical images of Black women', *Journal of Black Studies*, 40:2 [2009] pp. 215–37.

9 T. Mastin, A. Coe, S. Hamilton and S. T. Howard, 'Product purchase decision-making behavior and gender role stereotypes: A content analysis of advertisements in *Essence* and *Ladies' Home Journal* 1990–1999', *Journal of Communications*, 15:4 [2004], p. 233.

10 B. Donald, *Toms, Coons, Mulattoes, Mammies, and Bucks: An Interpretive History of Blacks in American Films*, [New York: Viking, 1973]. See also T. Lott, *The Invention of Race: Black Culture and the Politics of Representation* [Maldon, Massachusetts: Blackwell, 1999], pp. 23–7.

11 C. Lutz and K. Collins, *Reading National Geographic*, [Chicago: University of Chicago Press, 1983].

12 For example, Susan L. Taylor, owner of a small cosmetics business, was the Black woman executive who worked for Essence Communications Partners since the founding of the magazine in 1970, and was editor-in-chief from 1981–2000. Taylor later became the magazine's publication director and author of a column, but left her position in 2007. Time Inc. [owned by Time

Warner] bought forty-nine per cent in 2000 and the remaining fifty-one percent of Essence Communications Partners in 2007, which means that the publication no longer had a Black ownership or editorial direction at the time of publication of the special Obama election issue in 2008. T. Arango, 'Taylor leaves *Essence*', *New York Times*, [28 December 2007]: on line, retrieved November 2010, http://www.nytimes.com/2007/12/28/business/media/28mag.html

13 *Essence* has indeed published reports on wealthy Black Republicans [among whom Condoleeza Rice and Colin Powell are the most prominent examples].

14 Kerry Washington is an African-American actress.

15 R. Barthes, *La Chambre claire: Note sur la photographie* [Paris: Cahiers du Cinema, Gallimard, Seuil, 1980], p. 22. See also R. Barthes, *Mythologies*, trans. Annette Lavers [France: Les Lettres nouvelles, 1957], p. 26.

16 This term was used by Barthes in *Camera Lucida*, as I understand it, it is not only a *piercing* which makes a photo-image memorable, in the visual and affective sense, but it also creates another sort of anchoring, it seems like a precondition to jump out of the frame, to the 'studium' – context – and to be able to identify tensions and meanings in the image as representation, but also in the image as site of contested political claims.

17 Besides multiple news and popular media summaries, there are official versions of Obama's biography in two of his books, *The Audacity of Hope: Thoughts on Reclaiming the American Dream* [New York: Three Rivers Press/Random House, 2006] and *Dreams of my Father: A Story of Race and Inheritance* [New York: Three Rivers Press/Random House, 1995].

18 M. Marable, 'Racializing Obama', The Free Press, published 16 April 2008, http://www.freepress.org/columns/display/4/2008/1647. Retrieved August 2009.

19 S. Jhally, *Enlightened Racism: The Cosby Show, Audiences and the Myth of the American Dream* [Boulder: Westview Press, 1992].

20 Hill-Collins, *Black Sexual Politics*, p. 94.

21 M. Omi and H. Winant, *Racial Formations in the United States: From the 1960s to the 1990s* [New York and London: Routledge, 1994], pp. 145–59. Omi and Winant's interdisciplinary concept of 'racial formations' encompasses not only historical, geo-political, economic, legal and ideological conditions of emergence and institutionalisation of racial categories, but also the

representational public realms through which such practices are made common sense through unequal power negotiations in a particular society. For example, Brazil and the US have different racial formations but intersect at certain axes within the global racial formations that arose from 1490s colonisation of the New World. *Colourism* – shifting racial meaning of skin colour according to situational contexts – is, for example, prevalent in Brazil, while in the US a more stark Black and White opposition exists. This does not mean, however, that racism does not exist in Brazil. Colourism responds more directly to the preferred Latin American assimilation model of *mestizaje* – racial mixture – used by elites as a racially neutral ground from where to build national unity out of diverse populations.

22 As suggested by Patricia Hill-Collins's analysis of Black sexual politics. Sojourner Truth and Frederick Douglass [both 1800s ex-slaves who contributed to the immediate freedom of many, and later to the abolition of slavery] still represented, for example, risky radical versions of Black agency; by the 1940s to 1950s a kind of Martin Luther King image – sharply dressed, well-educated, Black Christian male – became the norm, a respectability that cost blood in many cases.

23 From the 1970s to 1990s – a period that corresponds to the emergence of neo-liberal restructuring in the US, including outsourcing of jobs and a shift from industrial production to the service sector – a dismantling of the civil rights movement was under way and a longer vision of integration and equality was fading. S. Hall, *Representation: Cultural Representations and Signifying Practices* [London: Sage Publications/Open University, 1997]. I use in this paper Stuart Hall's conceptualisation of representation as practice and product embedded in wider political-economic and discursive formations, but also actively doing some of the work of ideology, usually as an image-saturation strategy to justify social inequalities. In this sense, stereotypes do have a material effect on people's lives. Public Representations are main sites of socialisation and of informal education for a nation and in our days, for the world. Black public images, although by-products of state policy since the era of slavery in the US, became also reproducers of racial ideologies and therefore are implicated in systemic discriminatory practices. Two other important points are useful [his emphasis on reception, and the contested meaning as decoded in between sender-receiver], that gap, that space of negotiation, is in a sense the 'ground' or the social context within which situated experiences shape particular ways of consuming and interpreting media.

24 M. R. Trouillot, *Silencing the Past: Power and the Production of History* [Massachusetts: Beacon Press, 1995], p. 34.

BIBLIOGRAPHY

Citrin, J., B. Reingold, and D. P. Green, 'American identity and the politics of ethnic change', *The Journal of Politics*, 52 [1990].

Donald, B., *Toms, Coons, Mulattoes, Mammies, and Bucks: An interpretive history of Blacks in American films* [New York: Viking, 1973].

Gilroy, P., 'Sounds authentic: Black music, ethnicity, and the challenge of a changing same', in C. Potash [ed.], *The Jimi Hendrix Companion: Three decades of Commentary* [London: Omnibus, 1996].

Hall, S., 'What is this *Black* in Black popular culture?', in E. Smith [ed.], *Representing Blackness: Issues in Film* [New Brunswick, New Jersey: Rutgers University Press, 1997].

Hazell, V. and J. Clarke, 'Race and gender in the media: A content analysis of advertisements in two mainstream Black magazines', *Journal of Black Studies*, 39:1 [2008].

Hooks, B., *Reel to Real: Race, Sex and Class at the Movies* [London: Routledge, 2008].

Jhally, S., *Enlightened racism: The Cosby Show, Audiences and the Myth of the American Dream* [Boulder: Westview Press, 1992].

Ling L., 'Who is an American?', *International Political Sociology*, 4 [2010].

Lott T., *The Invention of Race: Black Culture and the Politics of Representation* [Malden, Massachusetts: Blackwell, 1999].

Lutz, C. and J. Collins, 'Conclusion', in *Reading National Geographic* [Chicago: University of Chicago Press, 1983].

Marable, M., 'Racializing Obama', The Free Press, published 16 April 2008, http://www.freepress.org/columns/display/4/2008/1647. Retrieved August 2009.

Mastin T., A. Coe, S. Hamilton and S. T. Howard, 'Product purchase decision-making behavior and gender role stereotypes: A content analysis of advertisements in *Essence* and *Ladies' Home Journal* 1990–1999', *Journal of Communications*, 15:4 [2004].

Merish L., 'Domesticating "blackness": Harriet Jacob, Sojourner Truth, and the de-commodification of the Black female body', in L. Merish, *Sentimental Materialism: Gender, Commodity Culture, and Nineteenth-Century American Literature* [Durham: Duke University Press, 2000].

Obama, B., *The Audacity of Hope: Thoughts on Reclaiming the American Dream* [New York: Three Rivers Press/Random House, 2006].

Obama, B., *Dreams of my Father: A Story of Race and Inheritance* [New York: Three Rivers Press/Random House, 1995].

Omi, M. and H. Winant, *Racial Formations in the United States: From the 1960s to the 1990s* [New York and London: Routledge, 1994].

Reid-Brinkley, S., 'The essence of res[ex]pectability: Black women's negotiation of Black femininity in rap music and music video', *Meridians*, 8:1 [2007].

The African-American Mosaic: A Library of Congress Resource Guide for the Study of Black History and Culture, retrieved April 2009, http://www.loc.gov/exhibits/african/intro.html

The Atlantic Slave Trade and Slave Life in the Americas: A Visual Record, The New York Library Digital Collection, retrieved November 2008, http://digital.nypl.org/schomburg/images_aa19

Thaggert M., 'Stand by your man: Richard Wright, lynch pedagogy, and rethinking Black male agency', in Marcellus Blount and George Cunningham [eds.], *Representing Black Men* [New York: Routledge, 1996].

Thomas, C., 'Race movies as voices of the Black bourgeoisie: The scar of shame', in Valerie Smith [ed.], *Representing Blackness: Issues in film and video* [New Jersey: Rutgers University Press, 1997].

Trouillot, M. R., *Silencing the Past: Power and the Production of History* [Massachusetts: Beacon Press, 1995].

Westerbeck C., 'Frederick Douglass chooses his moment', in Susan F. Rosen [ed.], *African Americans in Art: Selections from the Art Institute of Chicago* [Chicago: Art Institute of Chicago, 1999].

Woodard J. and T. Mastin, 'Black womanhood: *Essence* and its treatment of stereotypical images of Black women', *Journal of Black Studies*, 4:2 [2009].

Fashion's Other Images
Casting photographs and the production of a professional vision

STEPHANIE SADRE–ORAFAI

Upon entering the offices of LVX, a leading fashion casting agency in New York City, the first thing you notice is the large display of Polaroids that line nearly half the length of the agency's floor-through loft space.[1] Neatly butted end to end, the photos are uniform in composition: each a tightly-cropped headshot with the model's name and agency scrawled in thick black letters on the photo's stiff white border. The repetition and volume of images is striking. As traces of tens of thousands of fleeting encounters that have occurred, and continue to occur, in the space of the agency, the portraits are a visual census of New York's emerging and working editorial models and the agencies that represent them. However, to discuss only their symbolic or representational features would be incomplete. Their very materiality – inalterable, one-off analogue images in a digital world – is crucial for understanding not only the reasons for their collection and display, but also how casting agents frame their professional vision and the broader epistemological project of casting itself.[2]

While popular and scholarly critiques have analysed the semiotic messages and ideological effects of fashion's fantastic and frequently controversial iconography, few have attended to the documentary practices that precede it. In this essay I analyse fashion's *other* images – casting photographs – and the practices behind their production. Drawing on eleven months of ethnographic fieldwork at LVX, this essay examines the material and visual practices of a group of four casting professionals, focusing on the kinds of documents and images they create to organise and evaluate models. Exploring the broader visual economy of casting, I interrogate the discourses of objectivity and 'realness' casting professionals centralise as they produce, rank, and assess forms of evidence in their practice. From the experiential to the analogue and the digital, what different ways of seeing do they employ and how do they use these to craft a professional vision? I begin with an overview of casting in the New York fashion industry, including its development and central characteristics. I then describe the structure of a typical casting encounter, showing how agents at LVX process and place these images within a broader visual economy, moving from casting encounter to casting archive. I conclude by arguing that an ethnographic analysis of fashion's other images complicates our assumptions about the inevitability of the casting process and demonstrates instead the motivations and constraints that structure the process, ultimately enriching our understanding of published fashion images.

From aesthetic to information industry: Casting in the New York fashion industry

Although casting has always been a part of producing fashion images, its status as a legitimate and separate profession is relatively recent. While the convergence of consumer culture and the development of photography laid the groundwork for the professionalisation of modelling in the mid-twentieth century, casting's specialisation began only in the late 1980s and early 1990s.[3] Due in part to the exponential rise in the number of modelling agencies, schools, and scouting networks, and the globalisation, multiplication, and fragmentation of design practices, independent casting agencies arose as a response to the sheer volume of models that flooded the market. Whereas previously the work of casting was typically done 'in house' by photographers, designers, or art directors, independent casting agencies, like LVX, are now commissioned to do this work on a much larger scale, and, increasingly, to find 'real people', or non-professional models, as part of this task. Functioning as intermediaries or brokers between modelling agencies and the clients that hire them, casting agents handle the logistical details of scheduling models' time and negotiating their rates, as well as providing an aesthetic direction and range of options within a client's requested specifications, typically described in terms of both 'strength' and 'diversity'.[4]

While casting is undoubtedly an aesthetic industry, it is also organised as a knowledge or information industry. Categories and 'types' are central and practical everyday concerns for both casting and modelling agents.[5] From breakdowns [terse descriptions of desired or required features for prospective models written by the casting agent or provided by the client for each job] to the management of large volumes of mostly visual material generated in the casting process itself, casting agents work with various kinds of images, documents, and retrieval systems. These 'doings with documents', while mainly performed by apprentice casting assistants, freelance employees, and unpaid interns, for whom they serve as primary vectors for socialisation and professionalisation into the field, are integral components of the aesthetic decisions made by the industry's top-tier practitioners.[6] Indeed, despite popular representations of casting as performed by singular individuals [*the* casting director] who make a series of aesthetic deliberations – or better yet deliver definitive and instantaneous 'I know it when I see it' snap judgments – with equally discriminating and singular clients [*the* designer, *the* photographer] there is a large supporting workforce burdened with the technical and mechanical tasks of producing, sorting and organising visual and other kinds of documents to facilitate these decisions.

The work of casting agents then, while motivated by aesthetic and market-oriented ends, is not reducible to them. Through their photographic practices, casting agents explicitly differentiate themselves from their advertising and editorial clients. Their documentary style produces bodily knowledge about models that is both diagnostic and predictive, used to assess models' suitability for other photographic contexts, but ultimately requiring their expertise to read the images. To understand how they achieve this, we must further explore their image production process. We begin with the initial casting encounter.

Casting encounters, casting archives

While casting interactions may appear spontaneous, they are routine and structured with regular activities and stages. Typically occurring in the agency workspace, they begin with agents greeting models and directing them to sit, fill out a casting information sheet, and wait to be seen. On these forms, models must provide their name, date of birth and contact information, along with their height and clothing size, hobbies, occupation, and response to the purposely vague question 'Where are you from?' Next, agents introduce themselves, collect the completed information sheets, and make small talk. They do this to gather information and put models at ease so that they will be relaxed for their photos, the next activity. Finally, agents take the casting pictures, which during my fieldwork at LVX included a Polaroid and series of digital images of four standard casting poses: headshot, profile, torso, and full-body. They then clip the Polaroid to the casting sheet so that the digital images can be identified later, place it in a wire basket, thank the model for coming, and then the interaction is complete.

Depending on the number of active jobs, agents at LVX saw between ten and two hundred models per day. On average, each meeting took less than five minutes and, because of the agency's open layout, these interactions were observable to all employees. While seeing models interrupted agents' other work, it was almost never delegated to freelance workers or unpaid interns. The experiential dimensions of meeting a model face to face were critical in later editing practices.

After the casting encounters, assistants processed the digital images into 'layouts', or standardised visual casting documents, using an agency-designed template in Photoshop. This had four boxes for each of the standard casting poses and fields for the model's name and height, along with the month and year the layout was created. One layout was created for every model seen at the agency and was then used to organise, archive and present models to clients. Making layouts was tedious and time-consuming and typically performed by lower-level casting assistants, freelance workers and interns. When I learned how to do layouts, agents emphasised the importance of the document representing 'how the person really looks'. Since days could pass before layouts were completed, and often the assistants who created them had neither met nor seen the models in person, they had to make these judgments based on the attached Polaroid, purposefully taken at close range, tightly cropped at the shoulders with the model's face filling as much of the frame as possible to show what he or she 'really looked like'. Agents prized the formal qualities of the Polaroid – immediacy and inalterability – for capturing this kind of evidence.

In addition to choosing the most representative pictures, assistants also had to resize, crop, and lightly retouch each image to remove red-eye and lighten the overall picture so that it was clear and bright. The process took between seven and ten minutes. Once saved, each layout was printed and inserted into clear plastic sheet protectors with the casting information form on the reverse. These were then sorted and filed into the agency archive, which consisted of nearly two hundred four-inch-thick black binders. More than just a reference of what each model looked like, though that was important, the files represented the fact that someone at the agency had met this person and could draw on their remembered impressions in the editing process.

Importantly, no images, shot or layouts created in the agency were ever discarded. Instead, each model's file grew thick with time as their relationship with the agency deepened. Also, despite the kinds of judgements and evaluations agents routinely made of models they met, both in reference to specific jobs and in absolute terms, they made no written notations on the files. For each new job, they would either physically go through the binders to find models to propose, call in 'packages' [suggestions of models who were appropriate and available for a particular job] from agencies, or use their own remembered impressions of which models they had seen that might fit the casting brief. This meant that all writing on an individual's layout was self-reported. The resistance to both discarding images and annotating files suggest two things. First, the documents they created were not meant to be prototypes of what models could look like, but rather proof of what they had looked like. In this way they were backward-looking documents that then required agents to animate them to create forward-looking potentialities. Second, while the lack of annotation can be explained, perhaps, by the volume of models seen making such an endeavour impractical or inefficient, looking at how agents actually used the files suggests instead that, while their work is deeply subjective, they valued the objective images they produced precisely because they are more flexible kinds of documents that allow multiple interpretations.

Indeed, despite the importance of creating these objective images, agents at LVX repeatedly said that images alone were insufficient and required narration and framing. Rather than a binding representation of a model, the casting images were starting points, or tools agents used in conjunction with stories, to try to recreate the multi-sensory dimensions of a casting interaction. As Hank, a casting assistant, explained:

I think for us, visually … we do a really good job … to present an objective image, where it's like you really see what the shape of their face is and what their body looks like … It's really to be a physical representation of what this person looks like … [Then when we meet with the client], that's when it's our job to talk about these people and sort of impose upon these physical images … moods and emotions and feelings that the client thinks that they're looking for.[7]

The stories casting agents tell their clients could be pieces of biographical details they collected during the casting interactions or looser interpretations based on their own aesthetic read of a model. For example, Liz, a senior casting associate, described the kind of pitch she made for a designer looking for an edgy cast for his runway presentation:

I'll be like, she's cool. She doesn't have a great walk, but she's definitely like a tough, fucked-up schoolgirl, you know? So you kind of help guide them into that vision. Yeah, sometimes you will say something about their personal life, like she's been horseback riding for ten years, or she's a cool surfer. You definitely say something.[8]

In this way, casting agents positioned the objectivity of the images they created as enabling their subjective practices. To fully appreciate why they would need to do this, it is necessary to have a sense of the larger visual economy in which these images circulate.

Creativity and the visual economy of casting

Modelling agents produce several kinds of promotional images that casting agents also employ in their presentations and editing process. These include *portfolios*, physical and digital collections of models' published and unpublished work; *composite cards*, double-sided cards bearing models' images, measurements, and agency contact information; and *Polaroid or digital sheets*, which most closely resemble casting photos, used to show the most recent pictures of the model. While these promotional images vary in their levels of similitude, casting agents at LVX framed them all as untrustworthy representations doctored by model agents to present their models in the most flattering way. Rather than a paranoid delusion, this stance was roundly confirmed throughout the industry. Indeed, casting agents accepted and expected digitally altered images from model agencies. In their photographic practices, casting agents emphasised a distinction between 'actual' and 'flattering' images, with the sign of a truly beautiful or good model being the ability to 'come through' his or her casting photo. They stressed the need for their imaging practices, for creating 'objective' and seemingly authorless images with standard poses, focal lengths, backgrounds and lighting, so that models might be evenly evaluated and judged. Unsurprisingly, model agents universally detested casting images, with one agent I worked with going so far to call them 'mug shots', complaining, 'They're just such ugly pictures.'

This apparent lack of 'artistry', however, fulfilled a specific aesthetic goal for casting agents and simultaneously positioned them within a wider field of cultural production. This positioning indexed an industry-specific theory of creativity, which posited creativity as essentially an act of transformation requiring raw materials devoid of traces of others' creativity.

Importantly, this material must not only be raw but also able to reflect and channel external and internal forms of affective work and creativity. Standard industry practices enacted this conceptualisation, wherein those clients considered to be the most creative, such as top photographers and designers, typically wanted to see models without any promotional images, thus in a raw state, while advertising clients, considered to be more conservative and less willing to take creative risks, required a barrage of both promotional and casting images before hiring a model.

Clients sometimes transgressed this idealised division, and when this happened agents at LVX complained in ways that reinforced and highlighted their own tacit expectations of 'client'. For example, while working on a resort campaign for an Italian designer, agents scoffed at the photographer's request to see images of the models from the designer's show alongside the standard casting layouts. Liz, who had previous experience working with the photographer, explained that he disliked their photos and wanted to see the models closer to the style of the shoot. Exasperated, one of the casting assistants exclaimed, 'I'm sorry, but this is what these girls *actually* look like. Without lighting! Without makeup or styling!'

In addition to structuring casting practices, this theory of creativity also shaped how models were socialised into the industry. Model agents routinely used the phrase 'coming through', as a way of measuring a model's affective and professional potential, referencing not only their ability to connect through photographic media, but also their sincerity or believability to become something besides themselves. It is important to note how this particular theory of creativity places the burden of an unsuccessful image on the model, while its rewards are attributed to the photographer or other primary creative actor. Casting photographic practices reinforce this.

Conclusion

Casting is about heightening, animating, and eventually restaging face-to-face interactions with models. As such these images are never meant to replace this in-person assessment.[9] Instead, casting agents use layouts, with their stark documentary aesthetic, as a tool to present clients with a greater range and number of models than they can see directly. Their framing techniques emphasise the objective and subjunctive dimensions of casting as a professional vision, relying on talk to frame what a model could look like in particular contexts working with a particular set of creative professionals. Casting agents marked this type of figurative transformation, which they do verbally, from the material transformations their clients produce with models. Through an ethnographic analysis of fashion's *other* images, this essay has shown the importance of attending not only to these documentary photographs, but also the processes of their production.

ENDNOTES

1 LVX, like all other names used in this essay, is a pseudonym. My fieldwork at LVX was part of a larger ethnographic research project I conducted over four years [2003–2007], which also included participant observation at a high-end women's modelling agency, a mid-range men and women's modelling agency, editorial offices of two fashion magazines, and a photo production agency, all in New York City. This research was funded in part by the Wenner-Gren Foundation for Anthropological Research [Grant no. 7493], the Ford Foundation, and the Graduate School of the Arts and Sciences at New York University.

2 C. Goodwin, 'Professional vision', *American Anthropologist*, 96:3 [1994], pp. 606–33.

3 H. Koda and K. Yohannan, *The Model as Muse: Embodying Fashion* [New Haven: Yale, University Press, 2009]; E. Wissinger, 'The value of attention: affective labor in the fashion modeling industry', [PHD dissertation, City University of New York, 2004].

4 Alongside the growth of this profession, modelling agencies, too, have become more established corporate entities connected to various scouting networks and feeder agencies around the world as the pace and search for new faces in both emerging and developing markets intensifies. It should be noted, too, that 'diversity' in this context may mean ethnic or racial diversity, but more often refers to a range of 'types' that could include categories such as 'classic' and 'edgy', or 'blondes', 'brunettes' and 'redheads'.

5 S. Sadre-Orafai, 'Developing images: race, language and perception in fashion-model casting', in E. Shinkle [ed.], *Fashion as Photograph: Viewing and Reviewing Images of Fashion* [London: I. B. Tauris, 2008], pp. 141–53.

6 R. H. R. Harper, *Inside the IMF: an ethnography of documents, technology and organizational action* [San Diego: Academic Press, 1998]; cf. H. S. Becker, *Art Worlds* [Berkeley: University of California Press, 1984].

7 Hank, November 30, 2007, interview with the author, New York, NY.

8 Liz, September 7, 2007, interview with the author, New York, NY.

9 Indeed, except in rare cases where a model is so well known and the quality and predictability of her appearance and professionalism undoubted, most models are rarely 'direct booked', or hired based on their photographs alone.

Framing Modernity

Framing and modernity would seem a contradiction in terms, seeing as 'framing' connotes freezing and delimiting, as in the framed photo, whereas modernity signifies flux and open-ended change. Yet, even modernity can be pinned down, framed, and delimited as 'that which now is modern', particularly through the social media of blogger 'look books'. However, the very framing – its ubiquity and variety of frozen images or icons – constitutes an in-and-of-itself experience of modernity, because it is precisely the jostling and ever-changing offers of new looks, new fashions, and new faces of the global internet village [or to stay within the historical framework of modernity: the global virtual hyper-city]. By thus framing the changeable, ever mutable and *per se* ephemeral, it turns out we are also re-affirming that uniformity of expression and environmental rationalised sameness which belonged to modernisation – recalling Benedict Anderson – from the onset. At the same time, there seems to be nothing as quaint, as gauche and *altmodisch* as the framing of a previously experienced modernity [as in a snapshot of an individual in the newest fashions] which, again, just confirms the experience of modernity as an unrelieved existential fact.

Fig.1:
Pick of the Bunch exhibition,
Fashion Museum,
Bath, UK, July 2007.
Photo: author's own.

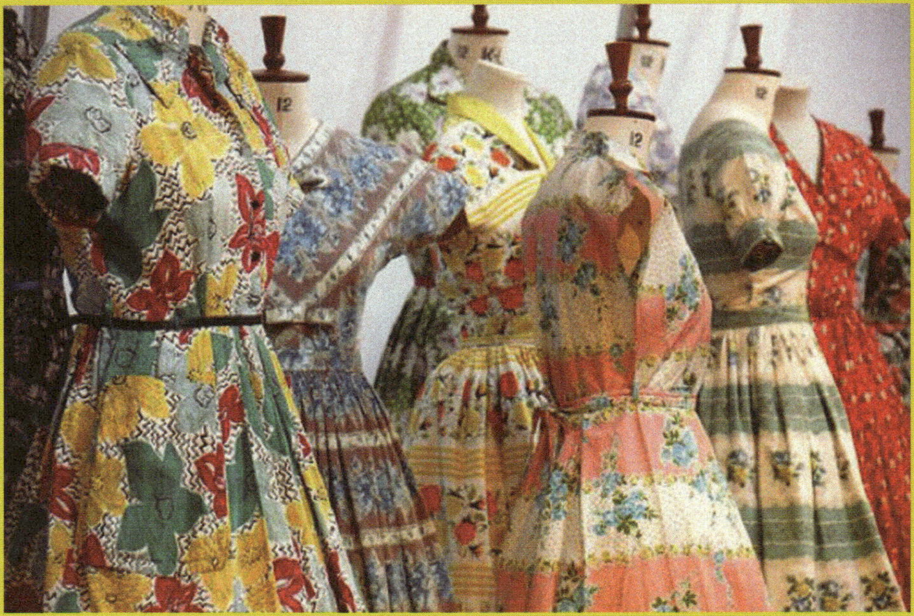

In the Picture
The photograph as 'evidence' in fashion research and display

JO TURNEY

Introduction

In 2004, Bath Spa University and the Fashion Museum, Bath, engaged in a collaborative research project that aimed to address mutually held concerns relating to the display and critique of everyday dress that would also demonstrate the interplay between fabric and form in garment construction. The premise of the project was to address and investigate the relationship between fashion and textiles from a material culture perspective in order to question traditional methods of display and established discourses in fashion and textiles history. This approach intended to move away from designer-led display, which frequently discounts the significance of textile design, everyday dress and the experience of wearing clothing. In order to assess these aims and to fulfil the Museum's policy of inclusivity, the subject for investigation had to realise the following criteria: a] exhibit a familiarity that could be understood as 'ordinary'; b] demonstrate a relationship between textile and garment; c] demonstrate the dissemination of and changes in fashion in order to utilise the Museum's collection and mission; and d] address and/or challenge 'accepted' fashion and dress theories. The focus became floral printed dresses, as most women [and some men] have at some time worn one, fabric enhances or detracts from form, and the genre is continually 'in fashion', and therefore subject to the dynamics of change, and is understood as an unproblematic representation of femininity and its associated ideals. The result of this project culminated in an exhibition,[1] book[2] and interactive website[3] which aimed to highlight the significance of the floral printed dress in the twentieth century.

This discussion is a reflection of the Floral Frocks project from which two main themes emerge; the significance of visual and primarily photographic material in stimulating the memory of experience [the wearing of clothing] and methods of analysing and interpreting the resultant ethnographic fieldwork.

Fundamental to this project were the relationships between people and their things, to engage the audience with museum collections, and consequently to use visual and material artefacts to stimulate memory and heighten experience.[4]

In 'The photograph and the mental image', a paper presented at Harvard in 1912, George Santayana emphasised the role of the photograph as an *aide-mémoir*; a means of establishing a linear and temporal continuum for life stories, a means of *remembering* in a time where events and occurrences exceed the brain's natural storage capacity. He commented:

Photography imitates memory, so that its product, the photograph, carries out the function imperfectly fulfilled by the mental image. The virtue of photography is to preserve the visible semblance of interesting things so that the memory of them may be fixed or accurately restored.[5]

Santayana's comments are somewhat problematic; photographs act as frames and therefore do not provide the 'whole picture'. Likewise, the recording of 'interesting' things could be interpreted as merely subjective, and in the case of much amateur photography, staged, and therefore 'un-real' and un-representative of 'natural' groups, things or situations. Nonetheless, amateur photography, particularly the snapshot as seen in family albums, offers an insight into norms of staging, posing and valorisation [worthy of photograph] that create a temporal genre associated with the 'styles' popular at the time of taking, availability of technology and the genre itself. Therefore, one can propose that collections of this type of photograph are familiar as well as familial, and could be utilised as an example of a 'common' visual culture.

Temporality is significant; memories, unlike photographs, are not static entities and are subject to change over time. The way/s in which the viewer addresses and understands a photograph, particularly as an extension or positioning of the self within its context, is largely dependent on socio-cultural, spatial and temporally specific norms, which Celia Lury defines as a 'prosthetic culture'. She acknowledged:

... vision and self-knowledge are inextricably and productively entwined in modern Euro-American societies; photography – itself not a static apparatus – thus offers one way into an exploration of the historically specific and dynamic relations between seeing and knowing ... the photographic image may have contributed to novel configurations of personhood, self-knowledge and truth.[6]

For Lury, the photograph is a means by which individuals take possession of, formulate and *own* their personal identity/ies.[7] This implies that identity, or self-realisation, can be assessed and developed in response to photography via a combination of factors working simultaneously [consciousness, memory and embodiment]. Therefore, by viewing photographs, subjects are able to reinhabit earlier images of themselves [or others] by applying acquired knowledge [post-image], memory [lived or imagined] and consciousness [an understanding of what or whom the respondent believes they are today]. As a result, the photograph becomes a fragment of life narratives that are reimagined, redressed and remembered at each viewing. To address the photograph in these terms offers the potential to develop insights into dress and experience in the past that fuse official with unofficial histories, utilising the snapshot as an expression of times, places, and attitudes toward dress and its performativity.[8] Consequently the aim of this paper is to demonstrate how the snapshot, combined with ethnographic research, can facilitate innovative and inclusive approaches to museum display that offer visitors a framework for interaction.

Displaying dress: Putting the 'life' back into clothes

In the introduction to *Adorned in Dreams*, Elizabeth Wilson romantically discussed the 'lifeless' display of dress in a museum context, noting that:

> These clothes are congealed memories of the daily life of times past. Once they inhabited the noisy streets, the crowded theatres, the glittering soirees of the social scene. Now, like souls in limbo, they wait poignantly for the music to begin again. Or perhaps theirs is a silence patient with vengefulness towards the living.[9]

The necessity to emphasise the experience of clothing through wearing, as outlined by Wilson, highlights the need to extend investigations and discussions, and perhaps catalogue the ways in which fashionable clothing informs and is performed in daily life and vice versa. This is particularly pertinent with regard to the display of fashionable dress in a museum context, in which garments are often displayed as disembodied objects, hanging lifelessly in cases, devoid of movement, alien from their intended function. Therefore visitors experience 'art' objects, and garments become artefacts, which by definition are distanced from the everyday experience of the viewer/wearer.

The aim of this project was to encourage audience engagement with the exhibition through the 're-embodiment' of garments, to breathe life into the static exhibits Wilson describes through experience, recollection and memory by drawing from ethnographic and photographic 'evidence'. The juxtaposition between visual and material data from the Museum's collection, the fashion media and the recorded experience of consuming [buying/wearing] floral dresses in everyday life, aimed to centralise the praxis at which official, designer-led histories merged with unofficial, experiential and visual testimony. In this respect, the memory of wearing specific garments became fundamental to the development, research and presentation of this project. Indeed, testimonies resulting from photographic evidence presented a rich diversity of experience and memory that otherwise would not have informed the project, which in turn contributed to the appearance of the resultant exhibition.[10]

Clothing, fashionability and life narratives

Clothing is inherently close to the wearer and therefore testimony and garment recollection is highly significant, but highly personalised. The memory of clothing is emotive, often sentimental and frequently representative of a linear life narrative as demonstrated in family photographs and so on.[11] Revisiting the clothes that we have worn, either through photographic evidence or through the garment itself, is a link with the past and our position within it.[12]

Likewise, history, although potentially considered as a linear narrative, or in the case of fashion, a hemline history, is really a multiplicity of voices and objects communicating simultaneously to an equally diverse range of audiences.[13] History, therefore, is about lived and remembered experience and is essentially the background noise to our everyday experience. In order to make sense amidst the din we select and reassemble specific thoughts, experiences and events, and remake them into personal narratives, which can be seen as the formation and formulation of memory. Indeed, we feel compelled to make what is essentially chaos, manageable, organised and ostensibly linear [one thing follows another] in order to make sense of what has happened, re-emphasising a significance to our own daily life and experience of the world and to any potential contribution to our future expectations and experiences. In this respect, the past must speak to the present and consequently is always under construction, narration and negotiation. Fashion, albeit somewhat dubiously, facilitates individuals to participate in the time in which they live; to perform modernity, and to situate themselves within specific timeframes.

As clothing is inherently close to the body it can, to a certain extent, be understood as a projection of personal identity.[14] This means that clothing, and particularly fashionable clothing, has the potential to communicate something significant about the wearer to those around them.[15] These acts of discursive display need not reflect the 'real' emotions or status of the wearer; they can be socially restricted through sartorial codes of appropriateness, or can be projections of aspiration, of how the wearer would like to be seen. This combination of intimacy and the outward presentation of the self within a specific temporality, establishes a highly personalised and emotional relationship between clothing and the wearer.[16]

The distinctly emotive relationship between clothing and the wearer enables garments to become significant objects;[17] meanings and values are attached[18] to seemingly innocuous garments, consequently rendering them part of the wearer's autobiography of objects. They become part of the wearer's memory and therefore become memorable.

As clothing remains 'fashionable' for such a short length of time, garments are rarely kept by wearers. Similarly, the wide availability of cheap and ready-to-wear clothing throughout the twentieth and twenty-first centuries, alongside ever-shorter fashion cycles, has established a culture of clothing obsolescence. With this in mind, finding respondents who were able to discuss existing items of their past clothing proved highly problematic. In lieu of actual garments to discuss, photographs of clothing [snapshots] offered the potential to provoke experiences of wearing.

Like clothing, snapshots are equally significant, transitory, and personally coded. Although garment and photograph are both objects, we do not see the actual photograph, merely what it depicts, and therefore a distinction can be made between object and representation of that object.[19] One might suggest that there is no substitute for the 'real' thing, the garment, but the photograph, through semiotic appraisal, allows and stimulates remembrance of times, places and people otherwise not depicted or forgotten. They help us make sense of our lives:[20]

Personal photographs are embedded in the lives of those who own or make use of them ... Personal pictures are made specifically to portray the individual or the group to which they belong as they would wish to be seen and as they have chosen to show themselves to one another ... the photographs that we keep for ourselves – not always in family albums – are treasured less for their quality than for their context and for the part they play in confirming and challenging the history of their users.[21]

Wells' observation is particularly pertinent in an assessment of the relationship between snapshots and clothing; both are the articulation of aspects of personal and *fantasy* narratives, coded, controlled and communicated to a particular audience at a particular time; the medium becomes the message. Similarly, both media are performative; parading in clothing and posing for a photo both exhibit a conscious staging of behaviour, appearance, socio-cultural awareness, and a clear understanding of forms of presentation and representation. Indeed, the clothing one remembers and the photographs one keeps are unlikely to be unfavourable or unflattering;[22] they show us in our 'best light', an image of ourselves as we would like to be remembered.

Nonetheless, whether snapshots are 'real' representations of those featured or not does not belie the significance of the object as an *aide mémoir*. Like fashion, photography exhibits modernity; it captures the moment [however staged] and locates the subject historically. Subjects become 'part of things', part of a wider world, of wider sensibilities, and the individual is able to inhabit his/her contemporaneity. The snapshot says 'I was there', but also demonstrates, through the clothing worn, ideals, aspirations, world-view, social role and identity not merely at the time of captured moment, but also its meaning and value in the present.[23]

From a psychoanalytical perspective, the formulation of self-identity is understood as an inherently modern construct, marking a move from a disciplined society to one dominated by self-gratification. In a society concerned with the pursuit of happiness, the cataloguing of 'happy' events [holidays, weddings, christenings, etc.] through photography enables the individual to identify personal pleasures, return to them via the snapshot, and redress them in a process of self-contemplation.[24] One might suggest that keeping ones clothes and/or photographs, is a form of self-appraisal, of life mapping through visual and material evidence, enabling the creation of linear histories of the self in an increasingly fragmented world.[25] They help us make sense of the distance we have travelled and enable us to predict the road ahead. Yet such appraisals are not static. They are revisited, revised and renegotiated; new narratives are created, new observations made. The object may stay the same, but its significance is subject to change.

In addition to the significance of memory as a means of negotiating one's route through the complexities of life and placing oneself historically, it equally demands remembrance. By keeping objects, snapshots or by telling stories or keeping a diary, memory becomes commemorated, recorded, repeatable or reproducible. To remember, therefore, can be seen as a means of not merely positioning oneself within temporal and spatially specific locations, but also of making and leaving one's mark. The 'I was here' becomes 'remember me'.

Floral Frocks: Methods of memory

With this in mind, the development and display of the Floral Frocks project involved the harvesting and stimulation of memories. Respondents were selected from a variety of sources; people who answered an advert in the *Bath Chronicle*, residents of a nursing home in Bath, and focus groups of much younger people originating from the whole UK, but now resident and working in London. All respondents and focus group members were women, lived in the UK, represented ages from sixteen to eighty-five, and had varying socio-cultural backgrounds. Observational fieldwork and interviews were conducted in several ways:

a) Respondents were asked to recall their experiences of wearing floral printed dresses whilst looking through their own photo albums in their own homes.
b) Focus groups were asked to respond to images from other people's family photo albums.
c) Focus groups were asked to respond to photographic images from the fashion media, from the 1920s to 2000.
d) Respondents were asked to comment and reflect on 'high fashion' floral printed dresses from the Fashion Museum's collection.
e) Respondents who had no experience of wearing a floral printed dress were asked to discuss why this might be.

The point of such questioning relied ultimately on the stimulation and simulation of memory, prompting memories through the use of visual and material objects [photographs and garments] and group discussion to provoke discussion, both of a personal and collective nature. Commentary was acquired regarding the nature of fashionability, its dissemination and the culturally symbolic associations with specific items of clothing, revealing the ways in which 'ordinary' people related to specific items of clothing through their representation in photographic, material, or discursive form. Likewise, assessing the meanings of floral printed dresses in relation to an established hierarchy of fashion intended to highlight the ways in which messages surrounding what it was to be fashionable, and indeed how the formation of the fashionable self was communicated, were reappraised in the here and now.

Visual ethnography: Testimonies, responses and recollections

The respondents who discussed their own snapshots were able to create narratives around each photograph that formulated an autobiography of fashion. One respondent, commenting on her youth in the 1950s, commented:

I would shop with my mother in department stores in London. She was a fashionable woman who had impeccable taste. She always chose my clothes, which were watered-down versions of her own; not quite so grown-up, girlish and floral.[26]

The testimony outlines the significant influence of one's mother on performing femininity during a transitional life phase. Clothing was selected on terms of suitability, which reflected age and experience, and the interviewee appeared happy to emulate her mother in terms of dress [she was 'fashionable' with good taste], and by aping her dress, albeit in a modest and understated way, the transition was seen to be eased. This was a recurrent theme in the testimonies of women over fifty. In what appeared to be a transitional life phase, access to the dynamic world of fashion presupposed a dynamic self, and its successful negotiation required tentative steps and the guidance of an older female relative. Here, clothing and the performance of a normative femininity embodied by mothers and aunts were pivotal in the development of the near-adult female self.

From these memories of personal development, the respondent continued by moving on to a photograph of herself wearing a floor-length, body-hugging and somewhat revealing black dress covered in large, bold, exotic flowers, some twenty years later. She said:

This dress was given to me by a male friend to wear to Glyndbourne. My divorce had just been finalised, and after a period of not knowing who I was, the dress enabled my transformation from the dowdy housewife to the centre of attention. This was the dress that enabled me to start afresh; emerge from the darkness and unhappiness as a butterfly. I moved on and became 'me'.[27]

The potential to understand fashion or dress as an indicator of life transition and transformation was a recurrent factor in many of the testimonies and responses. Clothing was seen to punctuate a visual autobiography, and many older interviewees expressed little sentiment when discussing photographs of their early adult lives. These times and the garments they wore seemed to represent a naivety and almost impossible romanticism that was lost; representative of a transitional life stage that was now gone.[28] The cynicism outlined in the testimonies bears witness to another age in terms of time, but also in relation to personal development, speaking of the unfulfilled expectation of romance and relationships,[29] of broken hopes, aspirations and desire to conform to unattainable ideals.[30] On speaking of her teenage years in the 1950s, a respondent commented on photographs of an earlier self:

I look at myself there and think of how silly I was. ... These days girls don't feel the need to get married, catch a husband. Everything was so formal, so fussy. People don't realise how many clothes that you had to wear or the dress codes that needed to be observed. We always wore a hat and gloves when we went out ... even if it was only for afternoon tea. Even in the height of summer.[31]

The sentiment expressed encapsulates the distance between the here and now and the there and then. Both society and the respondent had moved on; time had changed socio-cultural conventions and life expectations. Loss, in this testimony, exists not as nostalgia, but as a symptom of 'being born too early', having missed out on freedoms afforded to a younger generation. As Rebecca Arnold suggests, this emotional response to the past in relation to dress and a sense of self is not uncommon:

Fashion has a great resonance, acting as a collective memory; nostalgic styles are traces of the past, mapping individual and group experiences, recalling both reassuringly familiar and yet ... upsettingly clear evocations of earlier histories.[32]

One may assume therefore that such recollections, resulting from encounters with photography, elicit a dialogue with an earlier self, a less knowing entity, and recognise personal development as a move away from 'that' person [in the photograph] whilst simultaneously inhabiting it. Therefore the memory is distanced from the present, but is recalled as distance travelled from a younger, naive self to the knowing, present one.

For groups who commented on images from the fashion media, the responses were somewhat different. For this group the identification was aspirational, situating their memories in a collective understanding of what it was to be fashionable, as well as promoting a sense of individuality. A younger respondent on seeing a youthful model in a childlike, floral, printed dress noted:

OMG! I had a dress like that! I bought it when grunge was fashionable and I was madly in love with Kurt Cobain [in an attempt to be cool]. It was a long strappy summer dress with a floral print of red and pink roses featuring specks of light green foliage. It had side ties that I tied at the back, which gave it a nipped-in waist and the skirt was kind of A-line. I wore it teamed with a rather lovely army [sludge-coloured] green vest and DM [Doc Martens] boots – what an ensemble! I bought it in Top Shop and I think it cost between twenty and thirty pounds. I absolutely loved that dress and when I wore it I felt incredibly cool – the bee's knees – when in fact, on reflection, I probably looked a right idiot! I was trying to emulate the style of Alicia Silverstone in the Aerosmith videos of the time [I believe Crazy was one of them]. I think she wore a short, floral dress in one of the videos with a pair of scuffed DMs. I remember my mum commented that she liked the dress but wished I would wear it with a nice pair of sandals rather than 'those unflattering boots'. [33]

The rejection of the respondent's mother as a role model in favour of the then teen celebrity Alicia Silverstone, combined with a quest for coolness, highlights a transition from familial to collective role models based on age and peer group.[34] Indeed, the creation of cool was not merely a response to the dictates of the fashion industry, but a personal manipulation and interpretation of existing styles to create an individual whole.[35]

Somewhat conversely, the older respondents within this group referenced the significance of floral pattern in the creation of a sense of social propriety. They all mentioned the ways in which floral motifs appeared to be representative of a specific kind of respectability, which could be understood as the acknowledgement and display of the moral.[36] Indeed, the significance of specific motifs as communicators of morality is essential to an understanding of either the acceptance or rejection of the group mentality, in addition to a key component inherent in the language of clothes; the ability or possibility to both reveal and conceal. As this testimony of a youth lived in the 1950s describes:

The floral prints were natural and quite innocent. They were clean and crisp. Larger prints or brighter-coloured designs were worn by girls who were loud, easy, if you like. I would never have worn them.[37]

The intimation that boldness in design was synonymous with character seems rather far-fetched, yet morality and motif were alluded to in all the testimonies of the older women. The centrality of respectability appeared to pervade a sense of a fashionable femininity, whilst also reinforcing class distinction and stereotypes. The separation between them and us can be paralleled with good and bad taste, and to studies such as Clement Greenberg's essay on kitsch, which highlights the degenerative and subversive potential of popular culture.[38]

I remember one occasion and the embarrassment of having it [a brown floral dress] pulled up around my ears by my best friend when we were out in a busy pub. The next day I got her back when she wore the same dress and I pulled it up around her ears when we were out shopping on a busy high street. Why we always wore the dress I don't know ... [39]

The implications relating to the inherent properties of clothing to demonstrate social propriety and inclusion – fitting in or standing out and modesty or display – are obvious in this testimony. A desire to conform or to rebel appears significant through the experience of wearing a seemingly innocuous garment, and as such social discourse emerges between the wearer and the wider world as expressed by the interviewees.

For groups who viewed other people's family albums, responses were predominantly related to a personal memory of their relationships with their own family members. For example, a younger respondent remembered her grandmother's fondness for floral printed dresses after viewing an older woman:

> My grandma was a rather large woman with a big, round belly. The dress I'm thinking of stretched tightly across her belly and was in spring colours, actually quite citrus – pink, white and yellow flowers. The print was quite a big design. It came with a matching jacket and finished at her knees. I remember it being that viscose material – maybe a cotton mix – it wasn't a nice material to cuddle her in as it was a bit scratchy. I think she used to buy them from the catalogue. This memory is quite vague but it reminds me of Sunday lunchtimes in the garden waiting for the barbecue food and stuffing myself with crisps and dips when I was about eleven.[40]

The testimony reflects an understanding not only of family, but also of lineage, of times past and the distance between the here and now and the there and then. References to the fabric and colours of the large design as well as the mode of purchase situate the memory in time, but also seem to demonstrate a common recollection of what grannies wore. Tinged with nostalgia, the comments paid testimony to an understanding of not just family gatherings, but of how grandma felt when embraced, and intimates her position within the family, how she was perhaps larger than life, so much so that her clothes couldn't contain her. The recollection is also indicative of the relationship between floral motifs, generation and shopping habits; granny and her floral frocks became representative of an older generation, one that bought clothes, made from unpleasant fabrics, from catalogues and, by association, existed outside of the remits of the 'modern' world of fashion.

Conclusion

The paradox of the display of both photography and dress is that both are of the moment lost; simultaneously embracing both life and death. Neither, alone, can simulate or stimulate the experience of wearing the clothes or of having 'been there'.[41] Yet, when considered in conjunction with responses to images of floral printed dresses prior to the exhibition, new approaches and meanings became apparent.

Evocations of personal life experiences and re-evaluations of the self through personal appraisal or putting oneself 'in the picture' enabled the prioritisation of emotive thematic considerations over aesthetics or traditional fashion history. Issues such as 'coming of age', family, modernity, age, fun, shame, appropriateness, naivety, all became central to the photographic display. The personal became the public, and the memories of others were communicated to visitors in order to stimulate their own.

There can never be *one* fashion history; clothing plays a highly significant part in the formation of the self, and the use of snapshots mark life experiences and events that link the personal with the public, the private with the institutional. Revisiting the clothes that we have worn either through photographic evidence or through the garment itself is a link with the past and our position within it.[42] Although fashion is ephemeral by nature, for interviewees and visitors to the exhibition it became less so, marking not merely the 'style' of the era, but evidencing literal snapshots of life narratives, of times remembered or forgotten and re-remembered.

ENDNOTES

1 *Pick of the Bunch,* exhibition, Fashion Museum, Bath, July–August 2007.

2 R. Harden and J. Turney, *Floral Frocks* [Woodbridge: Antique Collector's Club, 2007].

3 www.floralfrocks.org

4 Part of this enquiry was to follow a method involving both objectification and identification, a process that psychoanalysts such as Jacques Lacan would describe as *desire,* but is essential to the museum experience, i.e. the visitor is in awe of that which is displayed, and can imagine themselves possessing and interacting with exhibits. This is a process of institutional valorisation and contextualisation; an expression of cultural capital, i.e. objects are valued because they are in a museum and therefore are worthy of desire.

5 George Santayana, 'The photograph and the mental image', in Vicki Goldberg, *Photography in Print: Writings from 1816 to the present* [Albuquerque: University of New Mexico Press, 1988], p. 260.

6 Celia Lury, *Prosthetic Culture: photography, memory and identity* [London: Routledge, 1998], p. 2.

7 The plural is used here as the concept of whom one 'is' and how the self is presented changes over time.

8 Y. Kawamura, *Fashion-ology* [Oxford: Berg, 2005], p. 5; T. Polhemus, *Street Style* [London: Thames and Hudson, 1994].

9 E. Wilson, *Adorned in Dreams: fashion and modernity* [London: I. B. Tauris, 1985], p. 1.

10 The choice of garments displayed reflected the most popular responses to the photographic evidence, whilst selected examples of snapshots were used as a filmic montage to stimulate the memory and experience of the visitor.

11 Peter Stallybrass, 'Worn worlds: clothes, mourning and the life of things', in Dan Ben-Amo and Liliane Weissberg [eds.], *Cultural Memory and the Construction of Identity* [Detroit: Wayne State University Press, 1999], p. 29.

12 L. Taylor, *The Study of Dress History* [Manchester: Manchester University Press, 2002], pp. 3–23; S. Kuchler and D. Miller [eds.], *Clothing as Material Culture* [Oxford: Berg, 2005], p. 1.

13 Eric Hobsbawm, quoted in Ben-Amo and Weissberg [eds.], *Cultural Memory and the Construction of Identity*, p. 8.

14 F. Davis, *Fashion, Culture and Identity* [Chicago: University of Chicago Press, 1994]; M. Barnard, *Fashion as Communication* [London: Routledge, 1996]; A. Lurie, *The Language of Clothes* [London: Hamlyn, 1983].

15 T. Dant, *Material Culture in the Social World* [Buckingham: Open University Press, 1999], pp. 89–91.

16 S. Woodward, *Why Women Wear What they Wear* [Oxford: Berg, 2008], offers a clear overview of this approach.

17 A. Appadurai, *The Social Life of Things: commodities in cultural perspective* [Cambridge: Cambridge University Press, 1986].

18 J. D. Prown, *Art as Evidence: writings on art and material culture* [New Haven: Yale University Press, 2001].

19 Lury, *Prosthetic Culture*, p. 2.

20 J. Tagg, *The Burden of Representation: essays on photographies and histories* [Basingstoke/New York: Palgrave Macmillan, 1988], p. 34.

21 L. Wells [ed.], *Photography: a critical introduction* [London/New York: Routledge, 2000], p. 121.

22 P. Bourdieu, *Photography: a middle-brow art* [Cambridge: Polity Press, 1990], p. 27.

23 *Ibid.*, p. 23.

24 Spence and Holland [1991], quoted in Wells [ed.], *Photography: a critical introduction*, p. 123.

25 Z. Bauman, *Life in Fragments: essays in post-modern morality* [Oxford: Blackwell, 1995]; Bourdieu, *Photography: a middle-brow art*, p. 14.

26 D. S., interviewed October 2004.

27 *Ibid.*

28 J. Attfield, *Wild Things* [Oxford: Berg, 2000].

29 Interviewees frequently referred to clothing as being part of another self; one during a failing marriage, another during a quest for a romance that failed to materialise, and several of hopefulness and a naive happiness that bore no relevance to their current lives.

30 P. Church-Gibson, '"No-one expects me anywhere": invisible women, ageing and the fashion industry', in S. Bruzzi and P. Church-Gibson [eds.], *Fashion Cultures: theories, explorations and analysis* [London: Routledge, 2000], pp. 79–89.

31 D. W., interviewed October, 2004.

32 R. Arnold, *Fashion, Desire and Anxiety* [London: I. B. Tauris, 2001], p. 7.

33 Z. K., interviewed October, 2004.

34 Lurie, *The Language of Clothes*, pp. 52–9; I. G. Klepp and A. Storm-Mathisen, 'Reading fashion as age: teenage girls' and grown women's accounts of clothing as body and social status', *Fashion Theory*, 9:3 [2005], pp. 323–42.

35 Davis, *Fashion, Culture and Identity*, pp. 183–8; A. McRobbie, *Zoot Suits and Second-Hand Dresses* [London: Hyman, 1989], pp. 23–49.

36 A. Ribeiro, *Dress and Morality* [London: B. T. Batsford, 1986], p. 12.

37 D. W., interviewed October, 2004.

38 C. Greenberg, 'The avant-garde and kitsch' in G. Dorfles [ed.], *Kitsch: the world of bad taste* [London: Studio Vista, 1969], pp. 116–26.

39 S. J., interviewed October, 2004.

40 N. J., interviewed October, 2004.

41 T. de Duve, 'Time exposure and snapshot: the photograph as paradox', in J. Elkins [ed.], *Photography Theory* [New York/Oxford: Routledge, 2007]. p. 109.

42 Taylor, *The Study of Dress History*; Kuchler and Miller [eds.], *Clothing as Material Culture*, p. 1.

BIBLIOGRAPHY

Appadurai, A., *The Social Life of Things: commodities in cultural perspective* [Cambridge: Cambridge University Press, 1986].

Arnold, R., *Fashion, Desire and Anxiety* [London: I. B. Tauris, 2002].

Attfield, J. and P. Kirkham [eds.], *A View from the Interior* [London: the Women's Press, 1995].

Attfield, J., *Wild Things: the material culture of everyday life* [Oxford: Berg, 2000].

Barnard, M., *Fashion as Communication* [London: Routledge, 1996].

Bauman, Z., *Life in Fragments: essays in postmodern morality* [Oxford: Blackwell, 1995].

Bourdieu, P., *Photography: a middle-brow art* [Cambridge: Polity Press, 1990].

Church-Gibson, P., '"No-one expects me anywhere": invisible women, ageing and the fashion industry', in S. Bruzzi and P. Church-Gibson [eds.], *Fashion Cultures: theories, explorations and analysis* [London: Routledge, 2000].

Clarke, A. and D. Miller, 'Fashion and anxiety', *Fashion Theory*, 6:2 [2002].

Dant, T., *Material Culture in the Social World* [Buckingham: Open University Press, 1999].

Davis, F., *Fashion, Culture and Identity* [Chicago: University of Chicago Press, 1994].

de Duve T., 'Time exposure and snapshot: the photograph as paradox', in J. Elkins [ed.], *Photography Theory* [New York/Oxford: Routledge, 2007].

Greenberg, C., 'The avant-garde and kitsch' in G. Dorfles [ed.], *Kitsch: the world of bad taste* [London: Studio Vista, 1969].

Gregson, N. and L. Crewe, *Second-Hand Cultures* [Oxford: Berg, 2003].

Guy, A. [ed.], *Through the Wardrobe* [Oxford: Berg, 2001].

Kawamura, Y., *Fashion-ology* [Oxford: Berg, 2005].

Kirkham, P. [ed.], *The Gendered Object* [Manchester: Manchester University Press, 1996].

Klepp, I. G. and A. Storm-Mathisen, 'Reading fashion as age: teenage girls' and grown women's accounts of clothing as body and social status', *Fashion Theory*, 9:3 [2005].

Kuchler, S. and D. Miller [eds.], *Clothing as Material Culture* [Oxford: Berg, 2005].

Lomas, C., '"I know nothing about fashion. There's no point in interviewing me": the use and value of oral history to the fashion historian', in S. Bruzzi and P. Church-Gibson [eds.], *Fashion Cultures: theories, explorations and analysis* [London: Routledge, 2000].

Lurie, A., *The Language of Clothes* [London: Hamlyn, 1983].

Lury, C., *Prosthetic Culture: photography, memory and identity* [London: Routledge, 1998].

McRobbie, A., *Zoot Suits and Second-Hand Dresses* [London: Hyman, 1989].

Miller, D., 'Reappropriating the state on the council estate', in T. Putnam and C. Newton [eds.], *Household Choices* [London: Future Publishing, 1990].

Miller, D., *A Theory of Shopping* [London: Polity, 1998].

Polhemus, T., *Street Style* [London: Thames and Hudson, 1994].

Powdermaker, H., *Stranger and Friend: the way of an anthropologist* [New York Norton, 1966].

Prown, J. D., *Art as Evidence: writings on art and material culture* [New Haven: Yale University Press, 2001].

Ribeiro, A., *Dress and Morality* [London: B. T. Batsford, 1986].

Roach, M. E. and J. B. Eicher, *The Visible Self: perspectives on dress* [New York: Prentice Hall, 1973].

Santayana, G., 'The photograph and the mental image', in V. Goldberg, *Photography in Print: Writings from 1816 to the present* [Albuquerque:

University of New Mexico Press, 1988].

Sparke, P., *As Long as it's Pink: the sexual politics of taste* [London: Pandora, 1995].

Stallybrass, P., 'Worn worlds: clothes, mourning and the life of things', in D. Ben-Amo and L. Weissberg [eds.], *Cultural Memory and the Construction of Identity* [Detroit: Wayne State University Press, 1999].

Tagg, J., *The Burden of Representation: essays on photographies and histories* [Basingstoke/New York: Palgrave Macmillan, 1988].

Taylor, L., *The Study of Dress History* [Manchester: Manchester University Press, 2002].

Thompson, P., 'The potential for oral history and life story research on the crafts movement', in T. Harrod [ed.], *Obscure Objects of Desire: Reviewing the crafts in the twentieth century* [London: Crafts Council, 1997].

Wilson, E., *Adorned in Dreams: fashion and modernity* [London: I. B. Tauris, 1985].

Wells, L. [ed.], *Photography: a critical introduction* [London/New York: Routledge, 2000].

Woodward, S., *Why Women Wear What they Wear* [Oxford: Berg, 2008].

On the Style Site*

Ephemeral images in time

CHARLOTTE BIK BANDLIEN

Introduction

The article has its point of departure in the Cand.polit. thesis 'Producing Scarcity – An Investigation of the Retro Market' [2004]. The thesis invites further investigation of social production of scarcity via 'style communities', where exclusive style [in the sense 'for the few'] functions as identification – however constantly in flux related to its ability to reflect social groups due to fashion mechanisms run riot. One possibility to pursue this is by looking at street-style weblogs like *Face Hunter* [Fig. 1] with a slightly 'alternative' image. Via mediated photographic representations of social groups with symbolic power and their 'personal style', such blogs contribute to the construction of transnational 'style communities' and the article suggests that the photographic style contributes to a neutral-urban, transnational, subcultural or nicheing unifying backdrop. The study of such blogs further touches upon distinctive strategies as well as relations between counter-culture [as imagined] and the commercial sphere.

An early draft of this article was presented at a conference held in May 2008 by the Norwegian Anthropological Association, coined 'Perceptions of communities', in the group session 'Reflexive field practices and imagined communities – examples from visual anthropology, art and material culture'. It was then reworked and presented again at the conference 'Images in Time: Flashing forward, backward, in front and behind photography in fashion, advertising and the press' in Reykjavik in November 2009, as part of the activities within the 'Wardrobe network'[1] organised by Copenhagen Business School. This article is an enhanced version of that paper.[2]

In this article I propose that the ephemeral images of street-style blogs such as *Face Hunter*[3] may prove to function as both nodes and prisms regarding today's fast-fashion mechanisms. I emphasise the term propose, as this article is more of a suggestion for future research than a presentation of results. My main focus is on the function of these images, rather than the images in themselves, leaving detailed image-analysis for another time. My focus is thus in line with Schroeder; 'to understand how visual images function within a cultural system of meaning influenced by advertising,

*This refers to the publication *On the Style Site. Art, Sociality and Media Culture* by art historian Ina Blom from 2007.

consumption, marketing and mass media.'[4] My postulation is that street-fashion blogs like *Face Hunter* affect and determine fashion, contribute to the construction of transnational 'style communities' through mediated photographic representations of social groups with symbolic power [their so-called 'personal style'] and that the photographic style offers a neutral-urban, transnational, subcultural or nicheing unifying backdrop. Theoretically, the article is based on a synthetisation of sociological perspectives [function/reception] and art historical perspectives [content/intent].

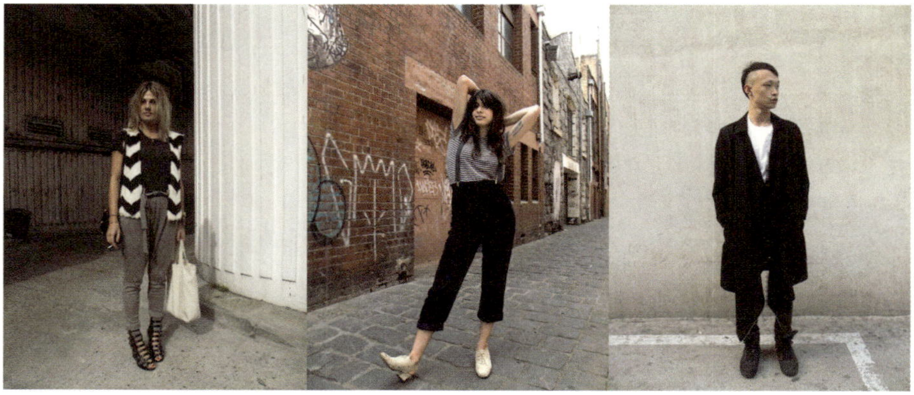

Fig.1: Typical images from the weblog *Face Hunter.*

Since the 1950s, the street has been the predominant backdrop for fashion photography in magazines and advertising. Through this association, fashion has become closely aligned with concepts of modernity as linked to the urban and the everyday, and as such fashion photography of the street can be said to offer an immediacy and realism that is contrasted with the fantasies and dreams of studio-based fashion images.[5] However, as noted by Gil Blank from *Influence* magazine, NYC, there can be no meaningful limit to the cross-contamination between notions of authenticity and supreme self-awareness. Photographs of street style are increasingly prevalent in contemporary culture, where weblogs such as *Face Hunter*[6] offer diverse fashion enthusiasts a chance to see what people are wearing from Buenos Aires to Cape Town, Tokyo to Oslo. The blogs cover both traditional fashion capitals and emerging fashion cities, in that a diverse array of people are represented, spanning different nationalities, although the coherence in age and socio-economic profile is quite consistent.[7] The blogs show photographs of people in various cities and how they are dressed; mainly outside on the street, often in connection to openings and events. The blogs are continuously updated, and linked together around the world.

This article offers an analysis of one of the dominant trends during the past twenty years: retro. More specifically, the study concerns the social construction of transnational symbolic value attached to material objects by aesthetically influential social groups – applying a theoretical approach based on anthropological consumption theory [in particular Miller, Appadurai, Bourdieu and Douglas and Isherwood]. What interested me within this rather vast phenomenon [the term has indeed come to be associated with quite opposite and conflicting things] was the ephemeral nature of socially constructed value. This particular study was done within the market in twentieth-century original designer furniture and involved customers, dealers and stylists from magazines such as *Wallpaper*; all active parties in constructing a symbolic value, separate from the so-called objective valuation inherent in design history – the verbalised cause of interest.

Photo analysis was part of the thesis and, analytically, Appadurai's term 'tournaments of value'[8] was applied to shed light upon the exchange and relationship between images of material objects, the objects themselves, and people. However, it was indeed a challenge to operationalise the huge number of contexts affecting the symbolic value in addition to the ones included in the thesis – and held together they form a more complete or informed platform for understanding how material objects are perceived, interpreted and eventually devaluated as symbols of social groups. Another challenge was operationalising the transnational aspects, and last but not least, capturing a field in flux ['cool is a shark' – if it stands still, it dies]. The thesis invites further investigation of social production of scarcity via 'style communities', where exclusive style [in the sense 'for the few'] functions as identification – however constantly in flux related to its ability to reflect social groups due to fashion mechanisms run riot. The street-style blog *Face Hunter* may prove to serve as both a node and a prism into this ephemeral sphere, and choosing such a blog as focus of inquiry may also solve the operationalising challenges of studying fashion mechanisms.

With anthropological consumption theory as the foundation, a renewed interest in phenomenology [as most researchers are interested in visual and material culture these days] and modest enthusiasm regarding mere semiotic directions, theories on contemporary art have gradually come into my focus – and certain challenging aspects started to come together after discovering art historian Ina Blom's book *On the Style Site* [2007]:

While the terminology of style has all but disappeared from recent art critical and art historical discourse, artistic practice in the last decades has increasingly focused on the stylistics of the social environment … Blom argues that this development calls for a new reading of the relationship between art and the 'question of style', one that approaches style not just as an art historical tool or method of explanation but as a social site in which the relations between appearance and social identity are negotiated … the negotiations of the contemporary style site are related to the significance of style in an information economy increasingly set on capturing the forces of life itself.[9]

I was initially theoretically inspired by the seminar 'Art/Anthropology – practices of difference and translation' held at the Museum of Cultural History in Oslo in November 2007 – an attempt to identify links between contemporary art and anthropology – and I would like to take the opportunity to present one of my favourite quotations, by Mary Douglas in the book *Thought Styles*, on why approaching the field of aesthetics as an anthropologist is not necessarily an altogether comfortable task: 'They [art historians] find us embarrassing, we, the anthropologists. They suspect that our crude imputations of motive do violence to the aesthetic issues.'[10] Well, yes and no. The analytical separation of aesthetic and symbolic value challenges both, as the integration of the two is what makes taste effective as social distinction.

I suggest treating *Face Hunter* as a 'style site'. The term is defined by Blom as follows, and synthesises both sociological and aesthetic dimensions:

The key issue here is how style is associated with the notion of appearance and how appearance in turn relates to processes of recognition and identification. The question of style then has to be thought in relation to the forms of social identity that arise from processes of recognition. It is this relation – the interaction between appearance, recognition, and social identity – that should be understood as a site.[11]

In fact, the term 'style site' is quite similar to an anthropological 'field', that is, a demarcation of focus of inquiry.

Regarding fashion mechanisms, clothing is an interesting surface as this domain of material culture is in fact one that no one can avoid. Style, as in how people construct their appearance, also represents an intriguing dualism in that it is both directly attached to people and the body, and simultaneously; neither the level of identification nor the mediation of style relies on direct social contact, or social interaction – and these blogs distribute style worldwide with a click.

Blom points out that our [the Western world] everyday life is characterised by being formed, designed and stylised:

> This focus on style, which has become more pointed since the early 1990s, … intervenes, more precisely, in a specific historical and cultural situation in which design and style issues have taken on an unprecedented significance – both in relation to economic 'production', in the traditional sense, and in relation to ideas about changes in the concept of production itself – changes brought on by the so-called information economy or attention economy.[12]

This emphasis on style and its relation to the concept of production in our time made me think of Daniel Miller's critique of Bourdieu's *Distinction* [1979/1984], presented in *Material Culture and Mass Consumption* regarding his gap between our dispositions and the material world:

> However welcome Bourdieu's analysis of consumers may be when contrasted to the more common attempt to explain the same material as simple expression of business interests, the book's impact is not enhanced by its entirely ignoring the sphere of production. Bourdieu's habitus does not spontaneously generate a world of goods, only a set of dispositions. To understand how the congruity between the two is achieved demands an investigation of marketing, designers [as by Forty 1986] and other distributive agencies. It is not sufficient merely to talk of the articulation of two independent spheres.[13]

These blogs represent a substantial stylistic distribution, and they affect the sphere of production due to the symbolic power of the people portrayed [and I should add, of the photographers].[14] The style captured on these blogs finds its high-street counterpart faster than you can say 'production'. The blogs thus certainly contribute to a movement in power, often stereotypically described as from trickle down towards trickle up [continuing the pioneering actions of the British magazine *i-D* showing people on the street[15] – a radical shift at that time] although I am not so sure about the validity of postulations of democratisation.[16] This shift is also reflected in the world of high-fashion/conceptual magazines, where the stylists putting together the looks are now much more powerful than they used to be, and according to Thom Murphy, a stylist who has contributed to *Another*, *i-D* and others, jobs and assignments are now often given directly to them instead of to the celebrity photographers as they were just a few years back. The semiotic reading of style puts the stylist at the top of the hierarchy, making the act of selection the most prestigious.

So why the term style and not fashion? The notion of style opens up to a somewhat different approach than is found in classic fashion theory; often more concerned with the designer sphere or merely the ideals produced as creative output from magazines, websites, shows etc., or the co-operation between magazines and buyers in distribution as such. The style term understood as such a site contributes with a starting point in real social life – or *in the wardrobe if you like* [17] – and these blogs invite this perspective *within* the 'fashion-ology' of Kawamura,[18] that is, the joint social construction of fashion separate from the materiality of it. Treating *Face Hunter* as a 'style site' is also an entry to everyday practices, without the usual link to what *most* people do – as, when focusing on such a broad stylistic level, the creative expression and interpretation seem to disappear in the stylistic diffusion process, causing a dilution of the symbols, a movement from content to empty surfaces of merely being 'in fashion'; causing symbolic inflation and consequently symbolic devaluation.

So who is portrayed on the *Face Hunter* blog? The realism that street-style blogs engage with can be seen to 're-socialise' fashion outside the fantasy narratives provided by consumer capitalism and this [at least geographic] decentralisation of fashion might be seen as an extension of fashion's democracy in contemporary culture.[19] However, it is quite clear that certain of these 'urban tribes'[20] portrayed in, for example, *Face Hunter* are in charge. It is indeed a challenge to abstract a proper term for this group of aesthetically influential people portrayed. On an emic level, or how people tend to refer to themselves, the term 'alternative' is frequently used, opposed to a perceived 'mainstream'. Empirically it could be described as people in so-called creative or intellectual occupations, and, on an etic or analytical level, Bourdieu's term cultural capital and symbolic power are obviously useful. Culture historian Frank Mort uses the term 'taste communities' in his *Cultures of Consumption* [1996][21] –

a mere descriptive solution I find somewhat lazy – however, swapping taste with style, I have come to find the term 'style communities' quite practical.

In the section 'Retro in a broader style context' in 'Producing Scarcity', the customers' styles were treated in terms of how they were subject to critical judgement related to whether or not they were perceived 'appropriate' customers or not; that is, style was seen as an indication of their perspective, of their motivation, their knowledge, their references – all relevant factors as the retro pieces were sought, kept or protected from 'outsiders'. This seemingly superficial judgement of style may be seen as somewhat more substantial, referring to a stylised presentation of self as a *causal consequence* of cultural capital – and thus not so freely chosen as it is often presented.

Even Blom conveys a strong Bourdieusian grounding in saying: 'Take the example of fashion: its never-ending changes in style camouflage the fact that a particular social order remains unchanged. But precisely because style is the locus of repression, it is also the place for the undoing of this repression.'[22]

Bourdieu, as we all know, saw taste as a hidden power, and key to social equality. A more modest ambition in claiming the importance of studying style is its relevance in understanding fashion mechanisms.

Just as the interest in retro was a strategy for creating an 'alternative' to the 'mainstream' as imagined, fashion blogs like *Face Hunter* have a reputation of representing an approach to clothing and style in opposition to dominant habits. Keywords would be: anti-fashion, subversive, used, quirky, individual, customised, etc. However, these blogs may just as well be said to function as an 'a-z in individual, alternative dressing this week' – variations of a theme. Now, nearly ten years after the early formation of my research interest, it is much easier to point out what has characterised the past twenty years of 'protest' against 'mainstream' style: retro, re-use, second-hand, third-hand, vintage, fusion, glocal [global + local], environmental, ethical, etc. However, the blogs certainly represent a selective embracement of both brands and designers, though mainly 'intellectual' or 'educated' designers such as the Belgian avant-garde known as the Antwerp Six, representing fashion as art, as comment, as subversive, as critique [other favourites would be Rei Kawakubo and Martin Margiela, etc.]. There are also more direct links between art and fashion, exemplified by a brand such as aNYthing [A New York Thing], a brand having its origins in the contemporary art scene on the Lower East Side; a Scandinavian counterpart is found in Håkki, a T-shirt/art project. It is no coincidence that these blogs often report from vernissages or art-school parties.

The style portrayed may be perceived as protest against fashion, trends and consumption, but due to the symbolic power held by these groupings they affect the sphere of production, the commercial structures, setting precedence for mainstream style after some time [seemingly even after days] – mass produced versions of the stylistic expressions available in high-street stores. This is a paradoxical consequence of 'counter-culture' in our time. As noted by Blom on rock as style site: 'The question is, then, how to understand or account for the collective formations produced in and through rock since it constitutes a social/aesthetic practice that permeates common culture at the same time as it continually produces new social surfaces.'[23]

Fast fashion eats blog images for breakfast

Eclecticism [or sampling culture; the quintessential post-modern term used in the fields of cultural production] is the obvious sociological reaction to the problem of diffusion of our time due to the speed of production and information flow. It is also the obvious ideological reflection of it. What we are dealing with, then, are style communities based on a common ability to interpret and compose complex or eclectic stylistic expressions, in the same way, at the same time; communities based on coinciding dynamic valuations, related to how Bourdieu presented prerequisites for [proper] understanding of a piece of art.[24] Thus the aesthetics or style portrayed is not meant to be recognisable by everybody. Being close to this field is of importance to grasp the nuances. Cultural capital and references are regulating access, both in terms of knowing what blogs to follow and being able to understand what is portrayed. The photographer's job is similar to the curator's; competent choosing and selection of eclectic styles, or, as Susan Sontag formulated it: 'An aptitude for discovering beauty in what everybody sees but neglects as too ordinary.'[25]

Alan Warde, who has been working on developing 'dimensions of a social theory of taste', says: 'Arguably, however, an omnivorous or eclectic orientation is in itself now the most prestigious of orientations to culture delivering distinction effectively in the way that Bourdieu imagined.'[26] Or as Yvan Rodic coined the style he captures: the 'New Creole Culture'.

While particular styles of fashion might be presented as unique by street-style blogs, the converse is true of their representation. Street-style blogs have absorbed the visual language of straight photography, characterised by a full-length, immediate portrait in street situ. The style of photography is used to render fashion capitals and non-fashion cities identical. The city as backdrop suggests a generalised metropolis rather than a distinctive geographic location. The recurring vistas of brick walls, concrete pavements and urban streetscapes that we see on so many of these sites provide a homogenous urban background to contemporary fashion. The street has become a site of uniformity constructed by the particular mode of straight-up photography that has emerged in these blogs.[27]

Straight-up photography provides a neutral background to observe and demarcate street-style fashion trends through a homogenous image of the city constructed through the uniformity of the photographic format. While the 'individual style' that is represented in these blogs might suggest a rebellion against global conformity, subcultural similarities across cultures are emphasised by the city acting as a unifying and uniform backdrop to these hybrid styles.[28]

This firm context is especially important given the extreme instability of the content, and this may be seen as related to establishing a unifying context to a content characterised by its ephemerality, thus aiding the establishment of a sense of a transnational style community.

Summarising remarks

Although it is now quite some time since art historian Bourriaud moved on from his famous term 'relational aesthetics' [as a relevant term for describing the contemporary art scene], this 'aesthetic theory consisting of judging the works of art based on the social interactional relations they portray and produce'[29] is a theoretical perspective of relevance with regards to grasping fashion mechanisms via style; judging style based on the social interactional relations it portrays and produces. The study of fashion blogs such as *Face Hunter* as 'style sites' then, answers to Miller's critique of Bourdieu [1979/1984][30] and incorporates an active role of appropriating and interpreting culture parallel to Bourriaud's other famous term 'semionauts', meaning 'one that discovers the path between signs'.[31]

In attempting to grasp today's fashion mechanisms, blogs such as *Face*

Hunter may prove to function as both nodes and prisms into style sites constructed by these ephemeral images in time.

ENDNOTES

1 http://uk.cbs.dk/research/departments_centres/projekter/wardrobe_network

2 The material was also presented at a conference in Oxford in 2010, Fashion – Exploring Critical Issues, and was published in an E-book in 2011 under the heading 'On the Style Site – Face Hunter as Node and Prism'.

3 Exactly which blogs hold this position is obviously in flux. Right now, or at least at the time this article was presented as a paper [2009], *Face Hunter* was a good example.

4 J. E. Schroeder, *Visual Consumption* [London: Routledge, 2002], p. 3.

5 J. Berry, 'Street-style: Fashion photography, weblogs and the urban image', draft paper from the conference Fashion: Exploring Critical Issues, Oxford, 2010.

6 http://facehunter.blogspot.com/

7 Twenties to thirties, upper-middle class.

8 A. Appadurai, 'Introduction: commodities and the politics of value', in A. Appadurai [ed.], *The Social Life of Things: Commodities in Cultural Perspective* [Cambridge: Cambridge University Press, 1986].

9 I. Blom, *On the Style Site: Art, Sociality and Media Culture* [New York: Sternberg Press, 2007], back-cover blurb.

10 M. Douglas, *Thought Styles: Critical Essays on Good Taste* [London: SAGE Publications, 1996], pp. 71–2.

11 I. Blom, *On the Style Site*, p. 16.

12 *Ibid.*, p. 12.

13 D. Miller, *Material Culture and Mass Consumption* [Oxford and New York: Basil Blackwell, 1987], p. 155.

14 Yvan Rodic, the man behind the blog, has become quite a character in the fashion world since he started blogging in 2006; front row seating for the most influential, a TV show, a weekly column in the *Observer*, a book published with a collection of his photographs, etc.

15 Precursors to the images of street-style blogs can be found in the 'Strictly' series of photographs styled by Simon Foxton and photographed by Jason Evans in 1991 for *i-D* magazine.

16 The democratisation is often said to be related to a general public being portrayed, however, this is not exactly the case even on anonymous blogs such as *Face Hunter* [as opposed to other influential blogs where people in the fashion business are openly sought out and named] – a quick flick-through of his photos from Oslo 2007 reveals a strong link to influential people in the Norwegian field of fashion.

17 The CBS-led Wardrobe network aims to develop new methodologies and perspectives of studying material culture under the Wardrobe heading.

18 Y. Kawamura, *Fashion-ology. An Introduction to Fashion Studies* [Oxford and New York: Berg, 2005].

19 Berry, 'Street-style: Fashion photography, weblogs and the urban image'.

20 www.exactitudes.com

21 F. Mort, *Cultures of Consumption. Masculinities and social space in late twentieth-century Britain* [London: Routledge, 1996].

22 Blom, *On the Style Site*.

23 *Ibid.*, p. 32.

24 P. Bourdieu, *Distinction: A Social Critique of the Judgement of Taste* [London: Routledge and Keegan Paul, 1986].

25 S. Sontag, *On Photography* [New York: Noon Day, 1977], p. 89.

26 A.Warde, 'Dimensions of a social theory of taste', in A. Warde [ed.], *Journal of Cultural Economy 1(3)* [London: Routledge, 2008].

27 Berry, 'Street-style: Fashion photography, weblogs and the urban image'.

28 *Ibid.*

29 N. Bourriaud, *Relasjonell estetikk* [Oslo: Pax, 1998/2007], p. 165.

30 Miller, *Material Culture and Mass Consumption*.

31 *Ibid.*

BIBLIOGRAPHY

Appadurai, A., 'Introduction: commodities and the politics of value', in A. Appadurai [ed.], *The Social Life of Things: Commodities in Cultural Perspective* [Cambridge: Cambridge University Press, 1986].

Bandlien, C. B., 'Producing Scarcity – An Investigation of the Retro Market', [Cand.polit. thesis, University of Oslo, 2004].

Berry, J., 'Street-style: Fashion photography, weblogs and the urban image', draft paper from the conference Fashion: Exploring Critical Issues, Oxford, 2010.

Blom, I., *On the Style Site Art, Sociality and Media Culture* [New York: Sternberg Press, 2007].

Bourdieu, P., *Distinction: A Social Critique of the Judgement of Taste* [London: Routledge and Keegan Paul, 1986].

Bourriaud, N., *Relasjonell estetikk* [Oslo: Pax, 1998/2007].

Douglas, M., *Thought Styles: Critical Essays on Good Taste* [London: SAGE Publications, 1996].

Douglas, M. and B. Isherwood, *The World of Goods: Towards an Anthropology of Consumption* [Harmondsworth: Penguin Books, 1979/1996].

'Exactitudes', online photoproject on urban tribes www.exactitudes.com

Kawamura, Y., *Fashion-ology. An Introduction to Fashion Studies* [Oxford and New York: Berg, 2005].

Miller, D., *Material Culture and Mass Consumption* [Oxford and New York: Basil Blackwell, 1987].

Mort, F., *Cultures of Consumption: Masculinities and social space in late twentieth-century Britain* [London: Routledge, 1996].

Rodic, Y., *Facehunter* [London: Thames & Hudson, 2010].

Schroeder, J. E., *Visual Consumption* [London: Routledge, 2002].

Sontag, S., *On Photography* [New York: Noon Day, 1977].

Warde, A., 'Dimensions of a social theory of taste', in A. Warde [ed.], *Journal of Cultural Economy 1(3)* [London: Routledge, 2008].

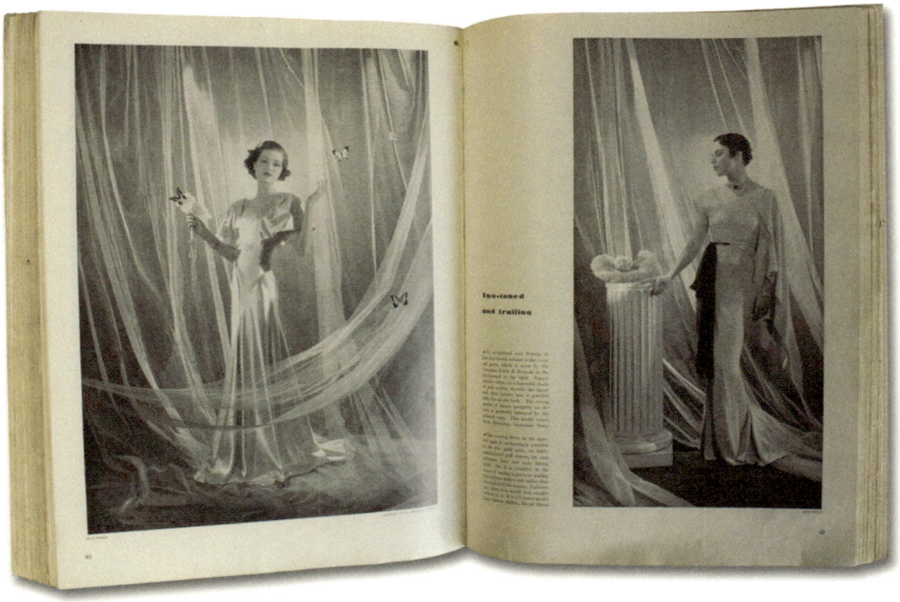

Fig.1:
'Two-Toned and Trailing', *Vogue* UK,
16 May 1934.
Photographs: Cecil Beaton

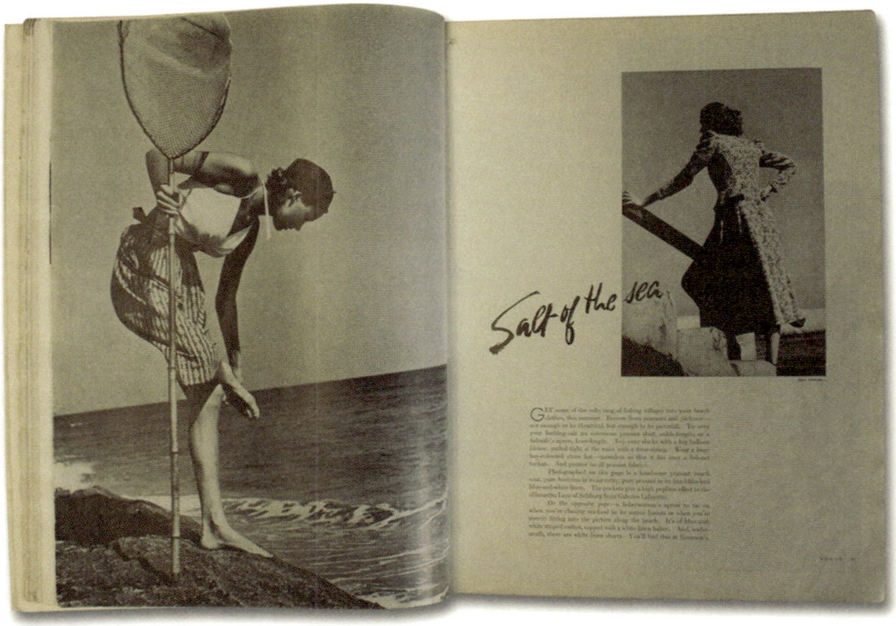

Fig.2:
'Salt of the Sea', *Vogue* UK,
21 July 1937.
Photographs: Toni Frissell

Playing for the Camera
Huizinga's 'Homo Ludens', technology, and the playful body in fashion photography

EUGÉNIE SHINKLE

I'm leafing through a stack of photographs – they look like pictures of children at play. Clad in tights, flowered frocks, or brightly coloured jumpers, they leap and sprint across the frame, kick their legs and wave their arms. Their faces are mostly obscured by clothes or flying hair, and their slender bodies are a blur of motion. In fact, these aren't children – they are the Supreme model agency's hottest girls of the season, and the images are part of Paul Rowland's Fall/Winter 2007 show package.[1] As well as promoting models, the show package also defines an agency's image. What makes this particular show package so interesting is the way it prioritises affect over visual information: identifying the young women is not the point of these photographs. Instead, they work to define an edgy, playful image for the Supreme model agency – and they accomplish this not by means of signification as such, but by embodying a *feeling*.

These three terms – playing, signifying and feeling – are key ones in the following paper, which comprises a number of linked objectives. Its principal aim is to investigate the historical appearance of the playful body in fashion photography, and to suggest ways in which it might be theorised. It examines the difference between the representation of play – the operation of play or playfulness as a signifier – and play as a mode of affective engagement. This distinction is set in the context of early twentieth-century North America and Western Europe. The period between the two world wars was marked by the emergence of a newly mobile, playful body in fashion photography, and also by a growing awareness, within fields such as art, cultural theory and science, of the penetration of the body by technology. In what follows, the notion of play is used as a way of thinking through the modern, fashionable body as a *technologised* body – a body that is explicitly open to engagement with reproductive technologies, such as the camera, and addressed by a growing mass media – and of the fashion image as a cultural actor that is complexly bound up with the embodied agency of both the fashion model and the viewer.

The relatively short history of fashion photography was marked early on by a significant change in the representation of the fashionable body.

Around 1930, the explicitly posed body in fashion photography – a static body arranged as a sort of living sculpture – began to give way to images of a more mobile, active ideal of femininity. Around the same time, Dutch historian Johan Huizinga published *Homo Ludens* [1938], a now-classic text which examines play as a cultural form. In his text, Huizinga provides detailed accounts of a number of culturally familiar play-forms, making a case for play as both socially meaningful and independent of practical and political determinations. Huizinga's concept of play will be used to reflect on the appearance of the newly mobile female body in fashion images – an innovation which took place alongside a dramatic increase in the availability of stylish ready-to-wear garments in the form of sportswear. Under Huizinga's argument, as we will see, these early representations of playful bodies do not exemplify 'true' play, but can instead be understood as signifiers of an ostensibly democratic ideal of fashionable femininity – an ideal that was epitomised by mass-produced clothing and by the standardised female body for which it was designed.

Though the latter interpretation is not incorrect *per se*, Huizinga's argument fails to account for the broader context within which such images circulated. Images of the playful body were distributed through – and dependent upon – a rapidly growing mass media, and were addressed, in multiple ways, to a modern subject that was understood as open to colonisation by technology. Playing for the camera – staging ludic acts specifically for circulation in the mass media – thus involved more than the straightforward representation of a new feminine ideal: it was also concerned with the channelling and transmission of *affect*. Both the model and the consumer of fashion images, I will argue, participated in an *affect economy* in which the body's affective capacities operated as sites of capital investment, and where value was produced through the channelling and modulation of affect by technological means.

Affect is often used as a synonym for feeling or emotion. As it is understood in the following essay, however, affect is a cognitive mode operating between biology and the social, and a way of breaching the critical barrier that is often said to exist between the two. Broadly defined, affect and affective response refer to mental and somatic reactions to various stimuli, experienced in consciousness and registered by the body – mobile forces circulating between body and intellect, conscious and unconscious, mind and physiology. Understood as the root of psychic life and the foundation of meaning, affect is characterised in part by its resistance to expression in language, and it is framed here as a dynamic modality by which new sensibilities and thought patterns make their way into representation.[2] Affect provides a way of thinking about images in terms of their *effect* – not just what they signify or communicate in linguistic terms, but what they *do*, the kinds of sensations that they produce in the viewer. Affect is also theorised here not just in terms of the human body and its capabilities, but in terms of the technologies with which it engages. Affect is a bodily resource, but it is also linked to the way that the body incorporates the nonorganic. As a hybrid concept – a way, as Clough writes, of '[inserting] the technical into felt vitality'[3] – affect acknowledges the complex ways in which the technologically enabled body participates in the creation of meaning.

The concept of the affect economy – and the turn to affect as an analytical trope in critical theory – is typically associated with late capitalism, and with political, economic, and cultural transformations taking place in the decade or so bracketing the turn of the millennium. In what follows, I turn to contemporary figurations of the affect economy in order to understand the historical appearance of the playful body in fashion photography. In so doing, I suggest that the affect economy is not exclusively a recent phenomenon: it can be identified in nascent form in the early decades of the twentieth century. The figure of the technologically colonised body was an important one for artists and writers in the years between the two world wars, and the playful body, as I argue, is an instantiation of this body. Fashion photography of the 1930s and later was concerned not simply with the construction of the model's body as a signifier, but with the transmission of affect – a transaction which involved both the model and the consumer of images.[4] The fashion photography of the 1930s can be understood, in other words, as marking the beginning of a general shift away from images that were designed to be read, and towards images that were also intended to be *felt*.

Although Huizinga's text provides a productive point of departure for the notion of the playful body as a technologically enabled, affective body, these ideas are not articulated openly in *Homo Ludens*. In fact, Huizinga was deeply suspicious of technology and insisted on the autonomy of true play – its independence from ordinary life, from mass reproduction and its technologies. Play, however, is always bound up with other cultural contexts, and technology is key among them. Huizinga failed to recognise the complex and varied interface with technology that characterises play in the context of modernity: more than just a signifier of femininity, the playful body in fashion photography is an index of shifting patterns of engagement between the body, technology and the social.

However, in thinking about the playful body in terms of the circulation of affect, other less clearly articulated aspects of Huizinga's thought emerge as significant. Though it is not developed in any detail in *Homo Ludens*, Huizinga's notion of *lower-order play* is an attempt to account for those forms of play that are not bound by rules. Understood as the simple expression of vitality, lower-order play embodies the essential qualities of pure playfulness and fun – qualities which, according to Huizinga, are not easily captured in language or rational thought. In acknowledging the importance of these less rational, more corporeal dimensions of play, Huizinga assumes [but does not articulate as such] the human subject as an embodied, affective agent. His text thus invites us to think of the playful body in terms of the transmission and circulation of affect, and to extend his argument to the diverse figurations of the technologised body.

Huizinga's *Homo Ludens* and the nature of play

Johan Huizinga's 1938 *Homo Ludens* has enjoyed something of a renaissance in the field of digital game theory of late, but it is less well studied in other fields. Huizinga's text is an idiosyncratic one, noteworthy not just for what it says, but for what it doesn't say. Play, Huizinga writes, is a vital feature of human life and civilisation – a collective, culture-creating enterprise that goes beyond the narrowly psychological or physiological. Although it serves no specific biological or moral function, no practical or rational purpose, play is socially meaningful and important to the formation of a shared culture: it is a creative phenomenon, generating new cultural forms that are retained in memory and passed on in the form of tradition. Play is invested with rhythm and harmony as well as uncertainty and risk, and could thus be said to serve an aesthetic function, although it does not, strictly speaking, belong to the category of the aesthetic. To play is to adopt a singular outlook on life: play 'adorns life, amplifies it and is to that extent a necessity both for the individual – as a life function – and for society by reason of the meaning it contains, its significance, its expressive value, its spiritual and social associations, in short, as a culture function'.[5] Though Huizinga is careful to distinguish play forms from aesthetic forms, his insistence on the cultural autonomy of play is aligned, in many ways, with Modernist claims for the autonomy of art. In order to act as a culture-creating force, Huizinga argues, the 'play-element must be pure. … It must not be false seeming, a masking of political purposes behind the illusion of genuine play-forms.'[6] Forced play is, for Huizinga, a contradiction in terms: play is strictly voluntary, it is a form of freedom, an activity with its own aims and disposition, outside of ordinary life.

Huizinga's study distinguishes between 'higher-order' play, which is marked out by specific rules and conditions, and the less organised, more spontaneous play of children and animals. Higher-order play typically consists of activities such as contests, performances, rituals and masquerades. It also incorporates the plastic arts – which include two-dimensional forms of representation like painting and photography – though by Huizinga's own admission, these fit less easily into the category of play. Bound to matter, and to the limitations of form inherent in matter, Huizinga claims that works of plastic art are unable to embody or express the forms of higher-order play. As I will show, however, they can and do incorporate the affective charge of lower-order play.

In Huizinga's view, the play-element in culture began to decline in the eighteenth century. This was due, he held, to the increasing systematisation of ludic forms such as competitive sports, but also, significantly, to the advancement of technology. Huizinga was particularly apprehensive of modern techniques of reproduction, and of the popularisation of art via reproductive technologies such as photography. Released by technology from the domain of the connoisseur [and the cultural autonomy that this implied] and into the 'broad mass of the simply educated',[7] the creative impulse that typifies play is distorted by the desire for novelty, the influence of advertising, and the modern taste for sensation. As a consequence, Huizinga argues, modern art – and, by implication, modern image culture more generally – is stripped of any genuine play-element.

Dress, technology and media: Aspects of the playful body

The technical difficulty and expense involved in reproducing photographs in print meant that fashion photographs did not feature regularly in magazines until the 1920s. Since the early days of photography, however, fashionable attire had played a prominent role in photographic portraiture, and the legacy of the formal studio pose persists in early fashion photographs.[8] Work by photographers such as Baron Adolf de Meyer featured softly focused images of models posing gracefully in sets strewn with blossoms, poised and tranquil as pieces of classical sculpture. Though photographic styles changed rapidly in the first decades of the twentieth century, with the pictorialist aesthetic of de Meyer and his contemporaries giving way to sleek, Modernist-inspired images, the women featured in the fashion press continued, for the most part, to exemplify a dignified stillness. The so-called '*mannequins du monde*' featured in these early images were not professional models [who were still regarded as somewhat *déclassé*], but society women or stage and screen stars. These early models tended to adopt classical attitudes – leaping, gesturing or appearing overly animated were not in keeping with the dignity of their situation. Edward Steichen's iconic 1927 image of socialite Marion Morehouse in a Pacquin gown shows a young woman posing confidently, her elegantly elongated neck and gracefully curved body emulating the graphic lines of fashion illustrations. Morehouse's classically inspired pose embodied a streamlined, modern ideal of femininity. Later in the 1930s, George Hoyningen-Huene's 'architectonic'[9] images incorporated models within rigorously controlled compositions: 'their personality was never revealed – gesture, composition and lighting were attuned to the ideal.'[10] As a young model in the 1930s, Lisa Fonssagrives used arrested dance movements – 'still-dancing', as she termed it – in front of the camera, and studied portraits in the Louvre to learn 'how to sit, hold her hands, and smile'.[11] Fashion images of this period are marked by a palpable tension between the real and the ideal, between the living body and its representation.

The introduction of mass-produced ready-to-wear in the 1930s and 1940s took place alongside a change in photographic representations of the fashionable body. Although basic ready-to-wear garments had been available in Europe and America from the mid-nineteenth century, the years following the First World War saw a dramatic rise in the manufacture of fashionable ready-to-wear clothing on both sides of the Atlantic.[12] This rise was predicated on improvements in mass manufacturing and also, importantly, upon new fabric technologies that enabled manufacturers to reduce costs while improving properties like strength, drape, handle, laundering and wearability.[13] The sportswear lines conceived in the 1930s and 1940s by American designers such as Claire McCardell and Mildred Orrick 'crystallized ideas of modern ready-to-wear, which was designed to be streamlined and flexible to move with the body'.[14] Although Parisian couturiers like Chanel and Patou had created *sportif* fashions for society women from the first two decades of the twentieth century, as Arnold notes, it was American designers who firmly established sportswear as an affordable fashion choice, defined by its functionality as well as its chic image.

The growing popularity of American ready-to-wear also brought with it a newly dynamic, high-spirited feminine ideal. Movement and gesture – learned, in part, from the movies – became 'a necessary attribute of both femininity and fashionability'.[15] The fluid movement and athleticism of popular and avant-garde dancers like Ginger Rogers, Josephine Baker and Isadora Duncan also helped to change perceptions of the feminine body, and a vital, animated attitude came to be seen as an essential element of modern feminine identity. Women's magazines featured fitness and exercise regimes alongside fashion spreads, encouraging readers to emulate the toned, athletic figure that went along with this newly light-hearted and playful bearing.

Developing the playful image: Munkacsi and the 'fresh air school' of photography

In fashion photography, the studied poses of earlier decades gave way to a different kind of image. Emerging in the 1930s, the 'fresh air school' of American fashion photography gave the model permission to 'live and breathe and move'.[16] Hungarian photojournalist Martin Munkacsi is often credited with the invention of open-air fashion photography. Carmel Snow, then fashion editor of *Harper's Bazaar*, recollected Munkacsi's history-making shoot with model Lucile Brokaw in 1933:

It seemed that what Munkacsi wanted was for the model to run toward him. Such a pose had never been attempted before for fashion [even sailing features were posed in a studio on a fake boat] but Lucile was certainly game and so was I. The resulting picture of a typical American girl in action with her cape billowing behind her, made photographic history. … Munkacsi's was the first action photograph made for fashion …[17]

The spontaneity embodied in Munkacsi's photographs captured the playful, high-spirited demeanour of the new feminine ideal, and his 'snapshot' style was a radical departure from the contrived nature of studio photography. Whether or not Munkacsi's work represented a true first[18] it was highly influential and widely emulated. Toni Frissell's action snapshot images began to appear in *Vogue* around the same time, while Louise Dahl-Wolfe's outdoor shots of the 1930s and 1940s captured a similarly relaxed, independent attitude. In Europe, Jean Moral's images of laughing models walking through the streets of Paris shared the ebullience, if not the physical *élan*, of their American counterparts. Munkacsi's style was an inspiration to later photographers such as Herman Landshoff and Richard Avedon; the animated, playful image of femininity popularised by Munkacsi has since gone on to become a staple of fashion photography.

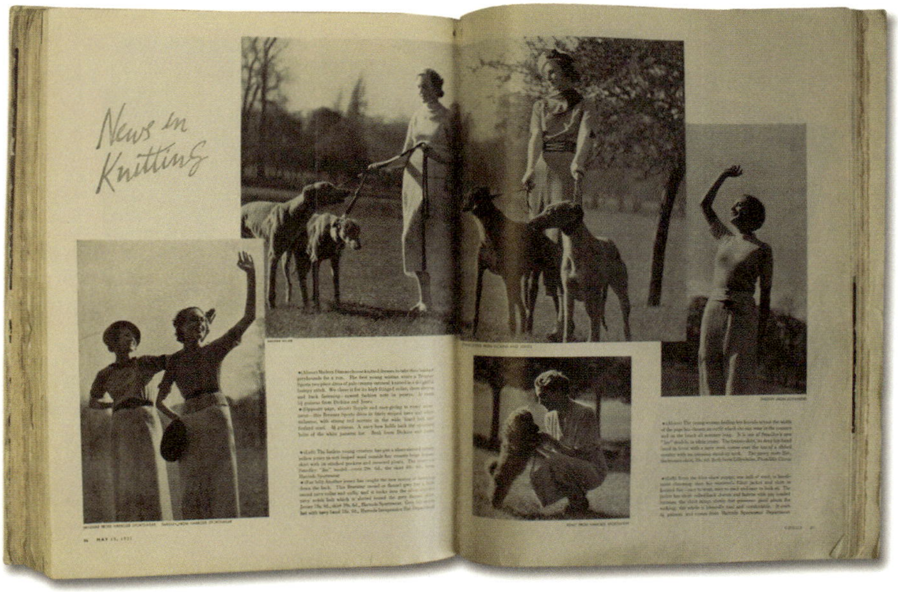

Fig.3: 'News in Knitting', *Vogue* UK, 15 May 1935. *Photographs: George Miles*

Huizinga's gloomy predictions regarding the disappearance of the play-element from modern culture seem out of place here. As well as a form of ludic activity in its most basic sense, we might think of playing for the camera as a form of dance – a performance and display of graceful, choreographed movement, described by Huizinga as 'the purest and most perfect form of play that exists'.[19] For the reader, the playful body signalled a new-found independence: a release from restrictive ideals of feminine comportment, and an embrace of the physical and sartorial freedom promised by new fashion choices. As a signifier, it could be read as an emblem of freedom, of modernity, and of individuality.

In the context of the fashion image, however, play is bound up with commercial interests: as such it is neither spontaneous nor voluntary. And although the playful body heralded a release from earlier attitudes and ideals, it also provided a new means of normalising the fashionable self. As the playful body became synonymous with a chic image, 'women were increasingly schooled by fashion magazines to train their bodies through dance and exercise to produce the fashionable line, and to measure themselves against role models from dance, sport and cinema'.[20] The 'real' settings that were used in fashion photographs of this era encouraged readers to emulate the look and movement of the model in their daily lives, and to bring their own bodies and lifestyles into line with popular images of beauty and vitality. Under Huizinga's argument, what is represented in photographs such as these is not play at all, but simply a veneer – a sign produced on the surface of the body. Marshalled in the service of a normalising feminine ideal, play acts 'to cover up … social or political design'.[21] Rather than engaging in real ludic activity, the model simply *signifies* playfulness. Fashion photography, for its part, encourages readers to adopt a uniformly playful attitude: to perform superficial work on the body's surface, to embody a regulatory ideal disguised as play.

The playful body: Freedom or control?

What, then, to make of the playful body in fashion photography? Is it an emblem of freedom or an agent of control? Huizinga's theory of play suggests a limited and rather cynical appraisal of the significance of the playful body – nor does it help to explain its enduring impact on notions of femininity and fashionability. Part of the problem lies with Huizinga's reluctance to view modern reproduction technology in terms of anything other than its potential to mobilise the most destructive elements in mass culture. For Huizinga, technology was responsible not just for the drawing-down of art, but for the dissemination of the most sinister forms of pseudo-play: phenomena which adopted the appearance of play forms, but which had more ominous social and political motives.[22] Contemporary culture, as he perceived it, was pervaded by such forms, and reproduction technologies were the agents of this deception.

For many of Huizinga's contemporaries, however, the integration of technology into all areas of human living was the very essence of modernity. The figure of the cyborg – the human/machine hybrid – was a prevalent one amongst modernist artists, writers and philosophers in the inter-war years. The Italian Futurist movement sought a release from the oppressive grasp of tradition in the 'reconception of the body as a permeable surface that can interface with technology'.[23] In his famous 'Artwork' essay of 1935, Walter Benjamin made a case for the integration of technology with play. Technology, he claimed, originated in play, in experiments and 'endlessly varied test procedures'.[24] Benjamin argued that the ludic qualities inherent in new technological forms such as the camera would enhance the scope for play in other areas of culture: 'What is lost in the withering of semblance and the decay of the aura in works of art', he wrote, 'is matched by a huge gain in the scope for play [*Spiel-Raum*].'[25] In allowing works of art [and images more generally] to be widely disseminated, technology released them from their dependence on cult value and ritual, extending their revolutionary potential. Huizinga's reluctance to admit the significance of technology contrasts starkly with the opinions of many of his contemporaries, who saw in technology a new way of knowing the world, and who celebrated, in various ways, the correspondence of the body, technology and play.

Clearly, there is more at stake in the appearance of the playful body than the simple signification of a new feminine ideal. The playful body was an index of a more profound transformation in the relationship between the subjects of fashion photography – both the models who posed for the images, and the readers who consumed them – and the technologies of mass representation within which these subjects were incorporated. In order to understand what was at stake in early representations of the playful body – the way such images function and the economy in which they circulate – we need to step forward and examine the work done by the fashion model in the present day.

Playing for the camera: The affect economy and the work of modelling

Contemporary fashion images circulate in an economy that has gone beyond the simple production and exchange of goods. Both the fashion model and the consumer of fashion images participate in the linked spheres of capitalism and what has been termed the *affect economy*. For Patricia Clough, the affect economy extends the project of Foucault's control society, in which the lives of individual subjects are controlled via the circulation of state-sanctioned societal and institutional norms. The affect economy supplements these forms of control with the 'never-ending modulation of moods, capacities, affects, and potentialities … the investment in and regulation of a market-driven circulation of affect and attention'.[26] Here, control is achieved by channelling affect – the transmission and modulation of individual bodily capacities and feelings. In an affect economy, Clough writes, 'value is sought in the expansion or contraction of affective capacity'.[27] Modelling is only one of a spectrum of techniques – typically situated within the spheres of labour, social life and entertainment – in which the body's affective capacities become sites of capital investment.

Workers in an affect economy produce value by modulating and transmitting affect. The term 'aesthetic labour' is often used as a way of describing this kind of work practice. As it is commonly used in the service industries and the corporate world, the term describes the way that employees' physical dispositions and bodily attributes are mobilised for commercial purposes. Joanne Entwistle and Elizabeth Wissinger[28] extend and develop existing definitions of aesthetic labour in their study of the modelling industry, where, as they argue, such labour goes far beyond the superficial signification of ideas or meanings.

Professional fashion modelling involves a complex and subtle play on the model's own personal identity. In order to produce images that will sell, models need to adapt themselves to constantly changing aesthetic trends, and to a multitude of possible images. The model's body is continuously maintained and transformed – through diet, exercise and, sometimes, surgery – in order to increase his or her marketability. Though most [but not all] models must conform to certain physical norms, success is not necessarily dependent on being attractive or beautiful in a conventional sense, but on having a certain, often indefinable, 'look'.

Modelling involves the impalpable, but vital, ability to make an impact, rather than simply communicating a particular message, fuelling a particular desire, or embodying a specific ideal. As well as changing the way her/his body looks, the successful model must also be able to project personality or attitude for the camera. This requirement confounds easy distinctions between the lived body and the body as image. With the possible exception of the supermodel – for whom their perceived 'real' personality is an essential part of their marketability[29] – maintaining a separation between professional and personal selves is by no means straightforward. Rather, it requires the complex management of a body that is simultaneously lived and objectified: the aesthetic labour carried out by the model involves 'seeing the body as *both* externalised object to be worked on *by* the self, as well as an integral aspect *of* the self'.[30] Modelling is an enduring form of work that continues even when the model is not in front of the camera.

The affect economy is dependent upon technology, and the work of the model also comprises a keen awareness of the technological context within which images circulate. In producing content for imaging technologies such as photography, television and the internet, models are required to be open to interaction with and investment by these technologies, capable of entering into 'dynamic interactions' with them, and of participating in the production of value in the form of images and affective flows. Models work to capture and channel attention, 'with the goal of *stimulating and projecting a feeling of vitality or aliveness*'[31] [italics added]. Amplifying and modulating the flow of affect, the fashion model acts as a node, 'embodying an image or stimulating an energy not immediately assimilable to consciousness'.[32] Playing for the camera, then, involves much more than striking a pose. The model's entire embodied self is implicated in the affective economy, interacting with 'technologies that calibrate bodily energies or capacities and feed them into economically productive flows'.[33] The consumer of fashion images, as we will see, must be similarly sophisticated in her interaction with, and openness to, technology. The fashion image [indeed, all media images] is much more than a passive representation – it is a cultural actor that needs to be understood not simply in terms of what it signifies, but of what it *does*, and what its audience does with it.

Concluding thoughts: Huizinga, lower-order play, and the transmission of affect

Framing the work of the model in terms of the embodiment and expression of vitality suggests that we re-examine Huizinga's account of lower-order play. His identification of particular play-forms as lying outside of cultural determination is particularly significant for the present argument. Conceived by Huizinga as an elemental, irreducible form of ludic activity, lower-order play is a primordial expression of vitality that is not exclusive to humans. Lower-order play is the simple expression of an animated body – an inarticulate [but nonetheless meaningful] process of affective discharge. Comprising no set rules or features, lower-order play is an expression of 'pure playfulness'[34] or fun – a category which 'resists all analysis and all logical interpretation'.[35] The essence of play, Huizinga wrote, cannot be reduced to any other mental category, it cannot be summed up rationally, nor can it be easily articulated in language: 'Since the reality of play extends beyond the sphere of human life it cannot have its foundations in any rational nexus ... language possesses no general concept to express it.'[36] Culturally shaped, but based in the precultural circulation and expression of vitality, Huizinga's concept of lower-order play acknowledges the importance of feeling in the formation of meaning, and as such, it has much in common with contemporary definitions of affect. And it is in precisely this sense – as an entity that is continuously shaped and reshaped by the reflexive relation between culture and the precultural – that the playful body is bound up with changing ideas of fashionable femininity.

The dissemination of the new playful feminine ideal was thoroughly dependent upon reproduction technologies such as photography and film. Early fashion photographs can thus be seen to belong to a category of images that Lev Manovich[37] has termed 'image instruments' – images that cannot be thought or experienced apart from the technological context in which they are produced and in which they circulate. Like later media forms, such as the computer, these early image instruments functioned as much more than simple texts. Mark B. N. Hansen[38] argues that such media forms foreground the multisensory character of human perception and invite the embodied user to participate in the production of meaning. Hansen suggests that visual technologies, such as the camera and the computer, extend the body's capacity for 'enframing' images – perceptually completing images by incorporating the subject's own corporeality and sensory memories into their meaning. This completion or performance of an image is a creative act or *poesis*.[39] There is affective work to be done not just in producing such images, in other words, but also in consuming them.

The playful body in fashion photography emerged alongside the increasing standardisation of fashionable dress, and indeed of the body itself – a body that was increasingly under pressure to submit to the pressure of popular ideals of femininity. Images of the playful body offered the viewer the chance to act as a creative agent – to experience the body not simply as a sign, but as an affective instrument, and to experience the image not simply as a representation, but as a mode of feeling. The playful body – trim, toned and energetic – promoted by the fashion press in the 1930s was homogeneous only to the eye. Beneath the surface, however, it expressed a different kind of feminine ideal: one that wasn't fixed in/as an image, but that was embodied as an active, affective agent.

The realist fashion photography of the 1930s, and the playful body that emblematised it, signal much more than a superficial change in ideas of fashionability or photographic aesthetics. It coincides with a profound shift in the nature of fashion photography, and of printed media more broadly – one in which reproduction technologies not only act to represent and construct subject identities, but also focus on the production and channelling of affect. It also marks a point in the history of fashion media where the fashionable body – both that of the model, and that of the consumer of fashion images – comes to be understood as a technologically mediated, affective body. Most popular culture, writes Henry Jenkins, is 'shaped by a logic of emotional intensification. It is less interested in making us think than it is in making us feel. Yet that distinction is too simple: popular culture, at its best, makes us think by making us feel.'[40] Huizinga's text – both what it says, and what it suggests – makes it possible to grasp the playful body in fashion photography in terms of the reflexive relationship between thinking and feeling: between what the model plays for the camera, and the way that the image comes to life, the way that it acquires resonance, cultural vitality and cultural persistence.

ENDNOTES

1 A show package is a form of promotional material sent around by model agencies to designers, casting directors and stylists, with a view to securing bookings for highly coveted places in the season's runway shows. It contains 'show cards' with images and statistics of girls represented by the agency.

2 See I. Armstrong, *The Radical Aesthetic* [Oxford and Massachusetts: Blackwell, 2002]; B. Massumi, *Parables for the Virtual: Movement, Affect, Sensation* [Durham and London: Duke University Press, 2002]; M. B. N. Hansen, *Bodies in Code: Interfaces with Digital Media* [Cambridge and London: Routledge, 2006]; and M. B. N. Hansen, *New Philosophy for New Media* [Cambridge and London: Routledge, 2004].

3 P. T. Clough, 'Introduction' in P. T. Clough [ed.], *The Affective Turn: Theorizing the Social* [Durham and London: Duke University Press, 2007], pp. 1–33, p. 2.

4 Though not discussed in the present work, the fashion photographer, as well as other members of the creative team, is also part of the affective dynamic that characterises the production of fashion images.

5 J. Huizinga, *Homo Ludens: A Study of the Play-Element in Culture* [Oxford: Routledge, 2002], p. 9.

6 *Ibid.*, p. 211.

7 *Ibid.*, p. 202.

8 See W. Ewing, 'Perfect surface', *Aperture*, 122 [1991], pp. 6–19.

9 N. Hall-Duncan, *The History of Fashion Photography* [New York: Alpine Book Company, 1979], p. 58.

10 H. Quick, *Catwalking: A History of the Fashion Model* [London: Hamlyn, 1997], p. 54.

11 M. Gross, *Model: The Ugly Business of Beautiful Women* [New York: Warner Books, 1996], p. 47.

12 This rise was due in large part to improved channels of communication, advances in technology, and a rise in the purchasing power of the middle classes. See A. De La Haye, 'The dissemination of design from haute couture to fashionable ready-to-wear during the 1920s', *Textile History*, 24:1 [1993], pp. 39–48; and P. Scranton, 'The transition from custom to ready-to-wear clothing in Philadelphia, 1890–1930', *Textile History*, 25:2 [1994], pp. 243–73.

13 See A. Farren and A. Hutchison, 'Cyborgs, new technology, and the body: the changing nature of garments', *Fashion Theory*, 8:4 [2004], pp. 461–75.

14 R. Arnold, 'Movement and modernity: New York sportswear, dance, and exercise in the 1930s and 1940s', *Fashion Theory*, 12:3 [2008], pp. 341–58, p. 341.

15 *Ibid.*, p. 346.

16 Quick, *Catwalking*, p. 60.

17 S. Morgan, 'America: creating the impromptu attitude', *Aperture*, 128 [1992], [special issue on Martin Munkacsi], pp. 46–61, p. 47.

18 Toni Frissell claims to have independently conceived a snapshot style around the same time, based around her own sporty lifestyle. See Hall-Duncan, *The History of Fashion Photography*, p. 77.

19 Huizinga, *Homo Ludens*, p. 164.

20 Arnold, 'Movement and modernity', p. 343.

21 Huizinga, *Homo Ludens*, p. 205.

22 'Modern social life is being dominated to an ever-increasing extent by a

quality that has something in common with play and yields the illusion of a strongly developed play-factor. This quality I have ventured to call by the name of Puerilism, as being the most appropriate appellation for that blend of adolescence and barbarity which has been rampant all over the world for the last two or three decades.' Huizinga, *Homo Ludens*, p. 205. Here, and elsewhere, Huizinga refers implicitly to the spread of fascism in Europe.

23 S. D. Hashimoto, 'Technology, corporeal permeability, ideology', *Communication Theory*, 15:1 [2005], pp. 10–22, p. 16.

24 W. Benjamin, 'The work of art in the age of its technological reproducibility', in H. Eiland and M. W. Jennings [eds.], *Walter Benjamin: Selected Writings Vol. 3: 1935–38* [Cambridge, Massachusetts and London: Harvard University Press, 2002], p. 107.

25 *Ibid.*, p. 127.

26 Clough, 'Introduction', p. 19.

27 *Ibid.*, p. 25.

28 See J. Entwistle and E. Wissinger, 'Keeping up appearances: aesthetic labour in the fashion modelling industries of London and New York', *Sociological Review*, 54:4 [2006], pp. 773–93.

29 R. Vogel, 'Strike a pose', *Vogue (UK)*, 172:9, no. 2498 [2006], p. 174.

30 Entwistle and Wissinger, 'Keeping up appearances', p. 785.

31 E. Wissinger, 'Always on display: affective production in the modelling industry', in Clough [ed.], *The Affective Turn*, pp. 231–60, p. 235.

32 *Ibid.*, p. 243.

33 *Ibid.*, p. 232.

34 The higher forms of play, Huizinga writes, 'are generally much easier to describe than the more primitive play of infants and young animals, because they are more distinct and articulate in form and their features more various and conspicuous, whereas in interpreting primitive play we immediately come up against that irreducible quality of pure playfulness which is not, in our opinion, amenable to further analysis'. Huizinga, *Homo Ludens*, p. 7.

35 *Ibid.*, p. 3.

36 *Ibid.*

37 See L. Manovich, *The Language of New Media* [Cambridge, Massachusetts and London: MIT Press, 2001].

38 See M. B. N. Hansen, *New Philosophy for New Media.*

39 The term *poesis* is used here in its Platonic sense, as a powerful form of creativity and an appeal to the sensual.

40 H. Jenkins, *The Wow Climax: Tracing the Emotional Impact of Popular Culture* [New York and London: New York University Press, 2007], p. 3.

BIBLIOGRAPHY

Arnold, R., 'Movement and modernity: New York sportswear, dance, and exercise in the 1930s and 1940s', *Fashion Theory*, 12:3 [2008].

Benjamin, W., 'The work of art in the age of its technological reproducibility', in H. Eiland and M. W. Jennings [eds.], *Walter Benjamin: Selected Writings Vol. 3: 1935–38* [Cambridge, Massachusetts and London: Harvard University Press, 2002].

Clough, P. T., 'Introduction' in P. T. Clough [ed.], *The Affective Turn. Theorizing the Social* [Durham and London: Duke University Press, 2007].

De La Haye, A., 'The dissemination of design from haute couture to fashionable ready-to-wear during the 1920s', *Textile History*, 24:1 [1993].

Entwistle, J. and E. Wissinger, 'Keeping up appearances: aesthetic labour in the fashion modelling industries of London and New York', *Sociological Review*, 54:4 [2006].

Ewing, W., 'Perfect surface', *Aperture*, 122 [1991].

Farren, A. and A. Hutchison, 'Cyborgs, new technology, and the body: the changing nature of garments', *Fashion Theory*, 8:4 [2004].

Gross, M., *Model: The Ugly Business of Beautiful Women* [New York: Warner Books, 1996].

Hall-Duncan, N., *The History of Fashion Photograph* [New York: Alpine Book Company, 1979].

Hansen, M. B. N., *New Philosophy for New Media* [Cambridge and London: Routledge, 2004].

Hashimoto, S. D., 'Technology, corporeal permeability, ideology', *Communication Theory*, 15:1 [2005].

Huizinga, J., *Homo Ludens: A Study of the Play-Element in Culture* [Oxford: Routledge, 2002].

Jenkins, H., *The Wow Climax: Tracing the Emotional Impact of Popular Culture* [New York and London: New York University Press, 2007].

Manovich, L., *The Language of New Media* [Cambridge, Massachusetts and London: MIT Press, 2001].

Morgan, S., 'America: creating the impromptu attitude', *Aperture*, 128 [1992], [special issue on Martin Munkacsi].

Scranton, P., 'The transition from custom to ready-to-wear clothing in Philadelphia, 1890–1930', *Textile History*, 25:2 [1994].

Quick, H., *Catwalking: A History of the Fashion Model* [London: Hamlyn, 1997].

Vogel, R., 'Strike a pose', *Vogue (UK)*, 172:9, no. 2498 [2006].

Wissinger, E., 'Always on display: affective production in the modelling industry', in Clough [ed.], *The Affective Turn*.

Surpassing the Reified Film Star

A poetic-linguistic glimpse of indescribable life

INGEBORG THAANUM CARLSEN

Introduction

The Danish poet Christel Wiinblad has published a collection of poetry mainly about icons of modern culture: Mick Jagger, Pete Doherty, Marilyn Monroe, Leonard Cohen. Closely linked to visual media are Audrey Hepburn and Marilyn Monroe, whose starring in the films *Breakfast at Tiffany's* [1961] and *Some Like It Hot* [1959] are the background, or object, of the two poems that will be analysed in this paper. Hepburn and Monroe are described as they each manifest themselves in a certain scene in each movie.

In the case of Hepburn, the poem slows down the pace of the film to be able to peel back every detail of the actress in a single scene, possibly in order to find life in the waifish star. And in the case of Monroe, the poem jumps from the overwhelmingly beautiful smile of the actress in the chosen scene to encompass the entire, unnerving story of the actress's life with pills and alcohol. The tempo of the poems is thus on one side slow, on the other side fast, but both can be captured through the theory of the *ekphrasis* genre.

Traditionally seen as a mimetic genre, the linguistic, rhetorical and post-modern theoretical developments of the twentieth century have not diminished the interest of poets for ekphrasis. Indeed, the aspiration of language and its inherent temporality towards the immediate sensibility and the spatiality of the visual arts has expanded the scope of the ekphrastic genre into what the literary theoretician Murray Krieger has formulated as an ekphrastic principle: 'those other manifestations of the spatial impulse within poem-making that seek to fulfill the original ekphrastic impulse in the history of the verbal arts in the West.'[1]

The case of Wiinblad is explored with the use of a range of classical rhetorical figures in order to comprehend the incomprehensible in the reified film stars.

The workings of ekphrasis

The literary response to images unfolds in time due to the fact that language as medium is temporal. Furthermore this response participates in a conversation that traverses eras. A poet is bound by the literary tradition and by the literary canon, a web or weave which abides by its own rules and expands around the poet. Two of Wiinblad's poems form dialogues with famous films and the stars of the films. These poems are analysed in the frame of literary close-reading, especially theories looking at interartial relations.

The poet lives and writes in a web of influences that includes cinema, music, theatre, painting, sculpture, photography, as well as literature. Poets and other artists have at all times made use of techniques and material from other cultural areas than their own. The avant-garde of the early twentieth century and the post modernists of the late twentieth century employ techniques such as assemblage, installation, and mixing of genres and material from the everyday world to unfold their broad inspiration and tell the story of a new way of looking at the world.

The theory behind the following analysis is that of ekphrasis. The ekphrasis genre is, briefly, a verbal and temporal representation [or: re-presentation] of a visual and spatial representation. Another definition of ekphrasis could be that formulated by Murray Krieger: 'a literary genre, or at least a topos, that attempts to imitate in words an object of the plastic arts'.[2] In order to fit more properly to modernist and post-modernist poetry, and integrate knowledge from post-structuralist theoretical developments, this definition by Krieger is further extended into 'the ekphrastic principle' so as to encompass 'those other manifestations of the spatial impulse within poem-making that seek to fulfill the original ekphrastic impulse in the history of the verbal arts in the West ...'[3] Although the genre or the concept of ekphrasis dates back to Antiquity, modern understanding of the genre and of the ekphrastic principle is what lies at the heart of this analysis.

The etymology of the word is 'the detailed and lively description in words of a place or another visual thing'.[4] An early understanding of literary ekphrasis thus saw liveliness [*enargeia*] as a demand upon language: Poetry should strive for a naturalness, liveliness and immediacy similar to that of the visual arts. In this demand lies a philosophy of the visual arts being closer to nature and providing direct access for the viewer to the world [or the truth or 'reality'].[5] In his extensive work on the relation between visual art and poetry, *The Sister Arts*, Jean Hagstrum offers a great deal of attention to the paragone between the two arts, which especially took place in the Renaissance and can be understood as the fight between poetry on one side and painting [and maybe sculpture] on the other to be the more natural and immediate art, the one art that makes it possible for a viewer/reader/listener to have an experience of direct contact with an object.[6] The close relation/competition of poetry and painting/sculpture is taken a step further when Lessing, in 1766, defines specific areas of interest for the two arts. According to Lessing they don't need to compete. Each medium has its limits and possibilities that govern what can be told and shown through its works.[7] No matter which author or theory is mentioned here, there are a great many volumes of research around them; nuances and discussions flow. The aim of this brief summary of the history of the theory of ekphrasis is to introduce a more post-structuralist way of using ekphrasis. And as this paper is not about the genre or a presentation of the genre in full, these nuances and discussions will be left to others. Modern theoretical works on ekphrasis show great interest in the linguistic medium and the developments in linguistic theory through the twentieth century. From the theory of the sign dating to Ferdinand de Saussure over the pragmatic theory of, for instance, John R. Searle,[8] to post structuralism,[9] language has been at the centre of studies of human interaction. As ekphrasis is a linguistic medium trying to adopt visual qualities, the theories of language will of course have an influence on poetry. Consequently, a further introduction to Annette Fryd's theory of the iconoclastic, linguistic surpassing of the visual will be fundamental to this discussion.

A highly illustrative example of how ekphrasis works is demonstrated in Danish poet Henrik Nordbrandt's 'Kina betragtet gennem græsk regnvejr i Café Turque' ['China viewed through Greek rain at the Café Turque']. Here Nordbrandt uses the image of an almost emptied coffee cup being filled by rain in an outdoor café, thereby gradually exposing a Chinese image at the bottom as the dissolving coffee turns translucent – all described in the poem. The first and the second stanzas tell: 'the drizzle / falls in my coffee / till it turns cold / and runs over / till it runs over / and turns clear / so that the image at the bottom / appears. // the image of a man / with a long beard / in China, in front of a Chinese pavilion / in rain, torrential rain / that is hardened / in streaks / across the windblown façade / and across the man's face.'[10] Linguistically the poem uses the rhetorical figure of the *chiasmus* to stop time as well as prepositions such as 'in front of', 'over', 'across' and 'beneath' to create a feeling of space. And there is a close description of the scene not only at the bottom of the cup, but also of the café and the street. It creates a picture with words. Furthermore if the lines of the poem are centralised [i.e. aligned along a central axis] on the page, the shape of a pagoda reveals itself. In different ways the Danish poet makes use of stylistic features that belong to the world of ekphrasis, or at any rate the ekphrastic principle.[11]

The Danish poet Christel Wiinblad [b. 1980] published her first collection of poetry in 2008. It is called *49 forelskelser. Portrætdigte* [*49 Loves. Poems of Portraiture*].[12] Most of the poems are named after and describe well-known cultural personalities. When reading the poems one has to imagine the persons described, since only two photos occur in the book, one of the poet herself taken by the Danish photographer Thomas A. and one showing a youthful portrait of the English rock star Pete Doherty by an unknown photographer. Nevertheless, many of the persons lending their names to titles of Wiinblad's poems are easy to imagine in an iconic role in a specific movie or posing in a certain way on the performance stage or in a movie still. Readers of the poems would in all likelihood be able to see in their mind's eye image-like objects of the visual phenomena described in the poem.

Wiinblad's collection includes poems called 'Audrey Hepburn' and 'Marilyn Monroe'. These have subtitles that tell the reader exactly where to find the described images, which are frames from the famous films. In *Breakfast at Tiffany's*,[13] Hepburn [as Holly Golightly] leaves a cab and stands by the window at the famous jeweller's. Monroe [as Sugar] is caught more or less undressed as she is taken aback when one of her new, rather masculine, colleagues, played by the female-impersonating Jack Lemmon, calls her name through the sleeper in *Some Like It Hot*.[14]

Both actresses are post-war media icons. This makes the poems directly accessible to most readers. It is interesting to see that Wiinblad describes features of Monroe similarly to those chosen by another Nordic poet, Tua Forsström.[15] Hair, semi-nudity and bodily ruin are at the core of the description.[16] A depiction based on the portrait of an unknown person would create another kind of poetic experience. The poem would usually be more sympathetic and would hold the reader's attention by the universal existential content rather than recognition of a singular icon that touches a familiar chord in the viewer or reader.

Wiinblad's poems deal with being and identity in an image-satiated culture, and how a contemporary literary aesthetics take place in a world of images.

These two poems are central to this discussion as they are the only ones that point at specific gestures, or in this case to specific pictures that the poems deal with. Among Wiinblad's other poems are, for instance, poems about the general impression of some rock musician on stage. In the case of Hepburn and Monroe, the poem points out that particular scene, and almost frame, where it finds its star. The theory of ekphrasis chosen is that about the iconoclastic way of writing and reading an ekphrasis. It is relevant because of the theme of the poems. When the poet chooses film icons as subject-matter of her poems it is interesting to see how a play of iconicity and iconoclasm takes place. As part of that play the specific linguistic and rhetorical devices will be closely examined since they form the tool of the iconoclasm.

Iconoclasm and surpassing of the figurative

In 1999 the Danish researcher Annette Fryd published *Ekfraser. Gunnar Ekelöfs billedbeskrivende digte* [*Ekphrases. The image-describing poems by Gunnar Ekelöf*].[17] Fryd contributes an analysis and a theory of how language in the work of one poet [Swedish Gunnar Ekelöf] acts as an iconoclastic tool. On the one hand it aims at stripping an image of its figurative elements to uncover an unutterable place or message, while on the other, it is seen how language, as material with its graphic and auditive aspects, has an ability to achieve some characteristics normally ascribed to the visual arts, as, for instance, immediate sensibility. These features of language are all present at the same time [in Ekelöf at least] as the iconoclastic stripping, and hence result in the production of not an image, but another sensible thing or art object.

Fryd's theory is about poems operating on the background of Byzantine icons, a motif-genre with specific contents and special rules, one important element of which is the description or presentation of the invisible – the sacred. Another important element of the Byzantine icon is the status of time. According to Ekelöf, time, and especially the figurative elements that all together tell a story, is characterised by simultaneous succession, which means that different parts of the story [from different times in history] are juxtaposed. The icon is not static. Since the visual arts and language are fundamentally different in what their specific mediums can present, the question of how to present the invisible is present in a transformed way when the poet explores ekphrastic areas. How is it possible to represent something from another order? Can poetic language surpass the visual and the figurative in order to present or describe the unutterable, the invisible, the indescribable, the unrepresentable – that which can be perceived, but not described?

The dream of surpassing materiality is confronted with linguistic materiality – as mentioned: the graphic and auditive features of language. These features are at the same time the stuff that makes the poem get closer to an original understanding of ekphrasis: the mimetic aim of language. Whereas the poem does not paint a picture, the auditive and graphic aspects can stop the temporality of language, or at least make some pauses in the flow of time.

Analysis

Prior to analysis, English translations of the two poems cited are followed by a short introduction to the movies that have been described in Wiinblad's poems.

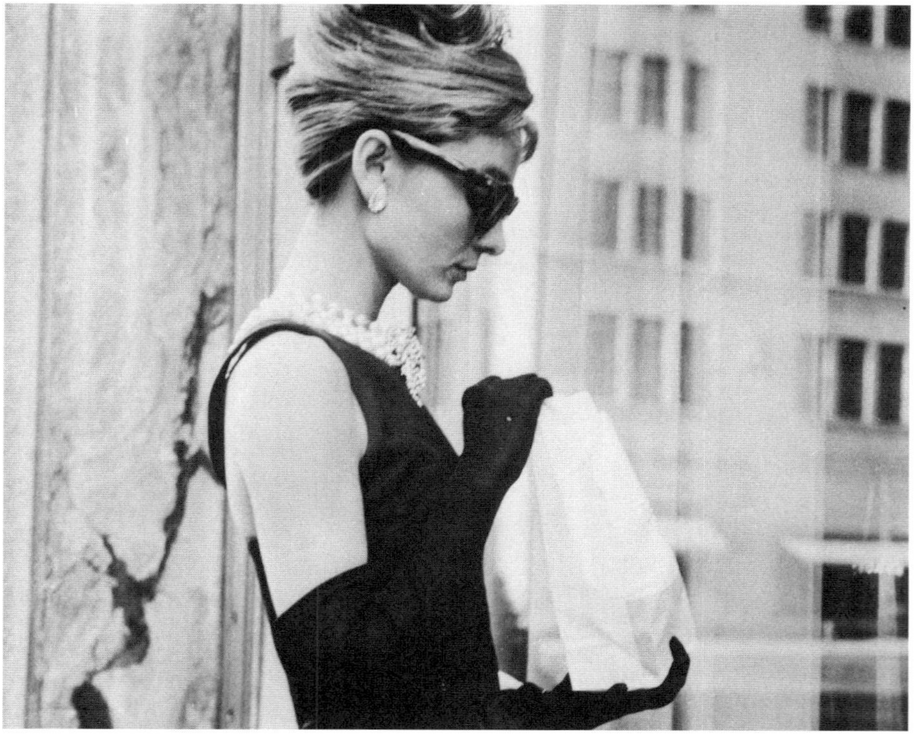

Fig.1: Side view of Audrey Hepburn on location on Fifth Avenue during shooting of *Breakfast at Tiffany's.* [Photo courtesy of All Over Press]

Audrey Hepburn
2[18] [as seen through Holly Golightly in *Breakfast at Tiffany's*]

gracefully, silently and more delightful
than pigeons landing
        she steps
out of the cab
and sips the morning coffee with milk
as melancholic and spoiled she
struts over to the windows
        and their big chaste dreamsale

and look, her hand shakes
just a bit as of fear
but really because of the sugar from the croissant
as the body is no longer
        used to consuming food

and carefully and meticulously
as would she measure
        her future bridal couch
she places her just a bit too large
and perfectly wonderful feet on the ground

and here and now in the morning light
her delicate bony shoulders are uncovered
since she starves herself
        so as to seem really
as superhuman, fragile and slender
as a lonely
        and all too mature child[19]

In *Breakfast at Tiffany's* Audrey Hepburn plays the high-class prostitute Holly Golightly, who dreams of a better life – the American dream. The film is based on the 1958 novella by Truman Capote which tells the story of the rootless, party-going Holly from the countryside who falls in love with a not-so-bestselling writer, Paul.[20] She nevertheless insists on her life among rich, though unserious, men. Finally she accepts her love of Paul.

The film differs from the short story, where she leaves the United States as the result of a romantic liaison. Furthermore, the atmospheres in the film and in the short story are different. Wiinblad's poem catches Audrey Hepburn in the well-known morning scene in front of the windows at the famous jeweller Tiffany and Co's, from which the film has taken its name. She is wearing an elegant evening gown. Around her neck she carries five rows of large pearls that stretch from her shoulders down along her back. Her dark hair is taken up and she wears sunglasses. She bites into a croissant, or some other kind of bread, and in her other hand she carries a to-go coffee. In the described morning scene, which is also the beginning of the film, Hepburn is at no instance seen directly from the front. She leaves the taxi and moves with her back to the audience away from the camera. The next cut shows Hepburn, still from her back, but also from below, when she looks up towards the front of the shop. The next cut shows Hepburn walking in small, stiff steps towards the closest window, but now the perspective is normal. The small steps are due to a very narrow, long dress. The camera catches Hepburn from the right, and we see how she bites the bread. The panning camera makes us see Hepburn's mirror image. After that the camera is behind the shop window looking out, and this single take is the only segment in this sequence where we see her face, but it is seen through the glass – and of course the camera – and Hepburn of course still wears her sunglasses. Hepburn continues down the road, still with her back to the camera and the viewer.

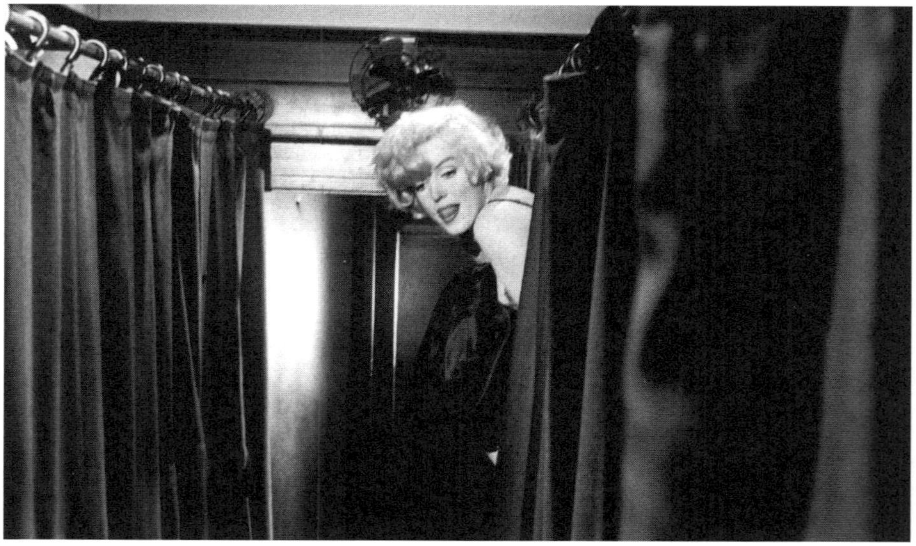

Fig.2:
Marilyn Monroe on location looks out from her berth in the sleeper during shooting of *Some Like It Hot*.
[Photo courtesy of All Over Press]

Marilyn Monroe
1[21] [as she as Sugar pulls her dress over her head in the sleeper in *Some Like It Hot*]

her smile [22]
is like light
on the verge of *most fiercely bright* –
        so white
that it fairly shrieks
of *unbearable* and *perfect*
        and would be more
than tiresome
in the long run

had it not
been for the darkness
        and the blackness
that lurk and grow
slimy and weighty
like bones and trash
that even now
        stink foully of *rotten*

and had it not
been for her frailty,
for the booze
the obesity
and the pills
        her beauty would
have been too awful

too overwhelming
and unmanageable
like too much
spirit without body
        like a butterfly
        without pins.[23]

Sugar, played by Marilyn Monroe, sings in an all-girl band, which needs a couple of musicians before a tour. Joe [played by Tony Curtis] and Jerry [played by Jack Lemmon] are unemployed musicians. They dress up as women and get the jobs. Already on the platform looking for the right carriage of the train that will take the band on tour, Sugar's new colleagues are fascinated by her very special power of attraction. Later, while she undresses in her sleeper on the first evening, Jerry calls 'Good night' to Sugar. She responds politely and surprised by putting her head out in the passage. Her pale skin, her blonde, short hair style – like marshmallow, her voluptuous curves and her almost transparent slip oppose her eyes' innocence.

Through the layers of an icon

Wiinblad moves through several layers to see and describe Hepburn and Monroe. The first layer in each poem is the subtitle. These are: '2 [as seen through Holly Golightly in *Breakfast at Tiffany's*]' and '1 [as she as Sugar undresses in the sleeper in *Some Like It Hot*]'. To look at and understand the actresses Hepburn and Monroe requires a distance. The poet's voyeurism is worked through via the language and the text. The fulfilment based on distance and observation or looking is passionately lived in the poems. Other layers are the roles [Holly and Sugar], the films, interpretations of the films, history.

By stripping Hepburn and Monroe of their beauty and elegance and replacing it with clumsiness on the part of Hepburn and decay on the part of Monroe, Wiinblad gets through some of the layers that the poetic voice has placed between the reader and the objects of description. The idea of the layers that the poem has to work its way through is connected with the ekphrastic genre and with the theme of the poems, i.e. post-World War II media icons. The first stanza of 'Audrey Hepburn' is an example: 'gracefully, silently and more delightful / than pigeons landing / she steps / out of the cab / and sips the morning coffee with milk / as melancholic and spoiled she / struts over to the windows'. Graceful steps are supplanted with strutting as, later in the poem, her feet are 'just a bit too large / and perfectly wonderful ...' The first stanza of 'Marilyn Monroe' describes a smile that is so beautiful that it will make you go crazy if it is not balanced. Luckily it is. The second stanza goes: 'had it not / been for the darkness / and the blackness / that lurk and grow / slimy and weighty / like bones and trash / that even now / stink foully of *rotten*'.

One possible interpretation of such descriptions is that we are confronted with women who are complex characters. Another way of looking at it is the ekphrastic gaze. Following Fryd's theory, Wiinblad's poems strip bare the chosen frames of the movie to find what lies beneath the beauty, the elegance, the stories: in short, the iconicity of the two women. The ekphrastic gaze is linked to a voyeuristic attitude as it depends upon a distance and upon observation and looking. At the heart of the ekphrasis there is a distance and a fulfilment: the poet longs to be able to do what an artist of the visual arts can do. As long as the poet is confined within language the visual impulse cannot be fulfilled, at least not in a simple way. The objects of the poems, Audrey Hepburn and Marilyn Monroe, are media icons of the flourishing era after World War II. As such we all seem to know them. Their biographies are common knowledge as are their productions. To reach beyond the iconicity, the thing-ness, although the whole story is there in a single moment, requires a poetic encounter, a poetic technique and ekphrastic longing.

As already noted, Wiinblad's two poems are concerned with two particular sequences of films. The poems refer to these sequences both by mentioning them directly in the subtitles of the poems and by describing the actions of the two actresses. The resultant slowing down of the pace, made possible by the close and elaborate descriptions of Hepburn in particular, changes the moving picture into static photographs, more or less corresponding to individual frames in a film. The poetic speaker of Wiinblad's poems thus provides herself with an opportunity to dwell on the pictures. The film is a visual representation characterised by temporality. Moreover the star system of Hollywood [that was still extant and had an influence on the spectator when *Some Like It Hot* and *Breakfast at Tiffany's* were shot] made great efforts to stage the lives of actors to correspond with the majority of their roles.[24] The idea of this correspondence makes the spectator feel that he or she knows the actors and actresses as private persons.

Audrey Hepburn – the perfect threshold

Besides telling us who Hepburn is behind Holly Golightly – elegant and clumsy, starves herself, child and mature at the same time, dreams of the traditional marriage – the poem tells a story of its own struggle to become a poem – its own genesis. One central, rhetorical figure is accumulations. The poem piles up adjectives and adverbs in the first and the fourth stanzas in the descriptions of Hepburn as if to imitate the coincidental contents of a snapshot. At the same time the poem uses the four stanzas in a taut, classical way by building up to a climax. The first, the second and the third stanzas use verbs in the active. The person described is the acting force of the scene: 'she steps / out of the cab', 'struts over to the windows', 'she places her just a bit too large / and perfectly wonderful feet on the ground'. Then in the fourth stanza 'her delicate bony shoulders are uncovered', that is, without her own consciously purposive action.

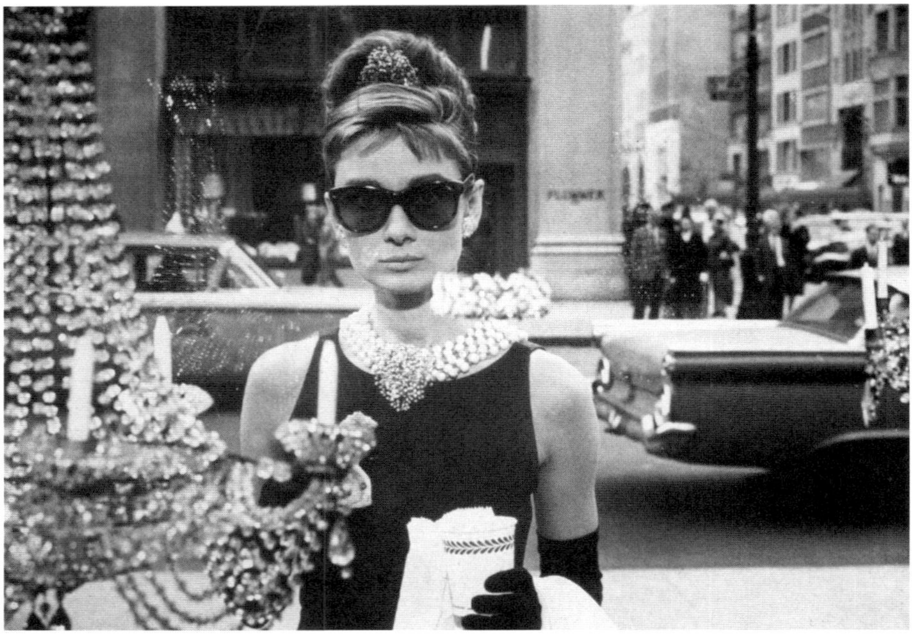

Fig.3: Audrey Hepburn as Holly Golightly seen from within Tiffany's in *Breakfast at Tiffany's.* [Photo courtesy of All Over Press]

The following sentence in the active does not describe an element of the movie, but rather an underlying story about the actress. As a contradiction of the accumulations and their sense of chance, the poem's classical structure suggests a linear story or plot. The experiment with the accidental could be the poem's attempt to get a glance of Hepburn's life. Through the ekphrastic gaze 'she' is caught in her dream and in her starvation and in a pose where something that she cannot have an influence on uncovers her. An uncovering is also an act of making something naked, which furthermore associates transparency. The poem does not have any direct descriptions of colours, but in the first stanza there is a move towards a colour: 'the morning coffee with milk'. Depending on the amount of milk the contents of the cup will be some nuance of brown or beige, which can be interpreted as the colour of skin. The nakedness and the thereby alluded transparency is either the poetic speaker's device to establish a poem or it is the goal towards which the poem reaches. Seen from another perspective, the reification is not the work of the poet. It is rather inherent in the iconicity, part of which is Audrey Hepburn's problem with food dating back to her starvation during World War II: 'the body is no longer / used to consuming food'. This last sentence of the second stanza could be read as the indication of a body that is no longer human. The poem talks about 'the body', not 'her body', as if the object in question is not a person, but a thing. Starvation and the media industry have turned her into a thing, an object. So when something uncovers Hepburn in the fourth stanza, it follows from the already manifested 'thingness' of the actress. And the actress's action[s] in the first three stanzas, that seem so stiff, are actions that are part of the thing rather than a human being's deliberate movements. Creating the snapshot feeling in the description of a frame from a film is the poet's way of getting at the indescribable. What happens when, for instance, the poet uses accumulations is the creation of the snapshot feeling, i.e. the feeling or experience that this photo, or this poem, has a more random genesis. We feel that it has not been staged or planned. The photographer, or the poet, took the photo, snapped the poem, and got a bit closer to the invisible life of the star.

Marilyn Monroe – unfathomable beauty pinned in a pile of waste

The poem *Marilyn Monroe* begins and ends in metaphorical modes. Monroe's beauty is so overwhelming that it needs translation. It also has to be balanced by the decay that the poem accumulates in the second and third stanzas. The first metaphorical device is actually a *comparatio* [the comparatio makes a comparison of a thing with another thing that is familiar and that holds some similarity and logical connection to it]. Monroe's smile is compared with light: 'her smile / is like light / on the verge of most fiercely bright – / so white / that it fairly shrieks'. The third verse seems to be a defining of the light. A closer inspection of the rest of the stanza teaches that more interpretations are available: 'of unbearable and perfect / and would be more / than tiresome / in the long run'. 'Like light' could be read as an interpolation or it can be the direct term of comparison to 'smile'. According to the syntactical indeterminacy either the smile, the light, both coupled, or the comparatio in itself is just on the verge of something else, maybe on the verge of life behind thing. Wiinblad marks some of the words in italics: most fiercely bright, unbearable and perfect. It is usually seen as an objectionable practice in poetry to use [too many] adjectives. Though Wiinblad does use adjectives, she marks these in italics and thereby tells us that she knows that she breaks away from proper poetry. The marking could be understood as reading instructions. The adjectives suggest very broad categories. Readers know what a perfect smile and a perfect beauty are. Wiinblad's use of the word suggests a total universe to the reader's mind, a definite image of a woman. The same could be said of 'most fiercely bright' and 'unbearable'.

Fig.4:
Marilyn Monroe on location in her berth in the sleeper during shooting of *Some Like It Hot*.
[Photo courtesy of All Over Press]

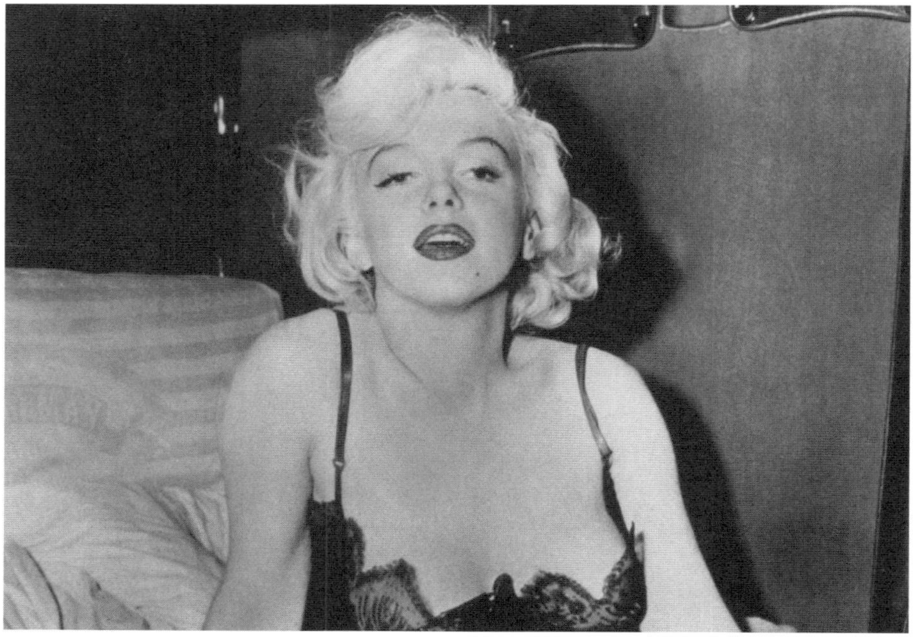

At the end of the poem a new metaphor is available: 'and had it not / been for ... / her beauty would / have been awful // too overwhelming / and unmanageable / like too much / spirit without body / like a butterfly / without pins.' It is only through the link with 'awful' that Monroe's beauty can be seen as compared to a butterfly without pins. The direct comparison is between awful and too much spirit without body and a butterfly without pins. We nevertheless see Monroe as this butterfly. Both the subordinating construction of the second stanza and the more accumulative reeling off of the third stanza are ways to imitate the snapshot. Although the sentence of the second stanza is not as much a catalogue as the list of the third stanza the effect is the same. A lot of descriptive adjectives and adverbs are accumulated without any proper system – like in a snapshot. The feeling is imitated, i.e. the idea of the non-composed and random is illustrated through language. Perhaps again in this poem the accumulations are the poem's way towards the indescribable.

One verse of the poem goes beyond, or rather ahead of, the situation described. In the second stanza it says: 'like bones and trash / that even now / stink foully of rotten'. What is meant by 'now'? Is it the now of the writer or the reader? Is it the now of a more generalised posterity? Or is it a now that comes after the moment of the film but before the decay? The present tense of these verses clashes against the ending of the poem where the pluperfect operates, but maybe it does so in a subjunctive manner. The dominating tense of the poem is the present. The different uses of different past tenses hold a more subjunctive style so as to make a form of comparison with the goal of explaining Monroe's beauty.

Monroe is too beautiful and her beauty too awful to be observed directly. Her enigmatic qualities make her attractive and at the same time make her slip away from description and observation. She is as complex as Hepburn, but she is more indeterminate and less accessible. The difficulties describing her result in a rhetorical show comprising metaphorical devices, accumulations and hyperboles.

All too tangible? Conclusion

By applying the theory of the ekphrasis, especially the iconoclastic-inspired version, to two contemporary Danish poems we have seen that a contemporary poet can find use in an ancient, yet still developing genre and the themes of that genre, viz. time and space, life and lifeless, to make her way into the poetic tradition.

When Wiinblad relates to a materially concrete and specific culture, namely that of the rock music and the cinema of the twentieth century, she finds this attractive, but also in some respects all too tangible. Whether the stars are seen on stage or on film the observer-poet is confronted with something real: voices, their sweating, their movement, in a word their materiality. It is cast right against Wiinblad's eyes and body. And although the film stars may be dead, we speak of them in a manner as if they were still alive. We see a photo of Marilyn Monroe and say: 'This is Marilyn Monroe', not: 'This was Marilyn Monroe' or 'This is a photo of Marilyn Monroe'. The present tense of the verb and the omission of the word *photo* or *picture* indicate how we experience life in the lifeless. The dead persons of a photo or a film are to us very much alive, when we stand before the photo or watch the film. The effect is attraction to the human character of the stars, a love and fascination often dependent on distance since it is impossible for [for instance] Wiinblad to meet those persons as individuals, who, after all, died long before she was born [or because a living rock star of today will likely as not be living his life in complete isolation from ordinary fans, including a Danish poet]. The attraction to the images combines with knowledge of their actual lives, both moving and repulsive, to form a complex love. Born in 1980, Wiinblad grew up surrounded by this culture. To some extent it determines who she is and what and how she writes.

Wiinblad's exploration of her designated love of all those stars of popular culture as well as serious literary culture follows a classic ekphrastic technique. In the poem about Audrey Hepburn the already lifeless, film icon-thing comes to a further stop, when time and life are stopped, both in the way the poetic speaker makes the film stop, or at least slows down the pace, to make it possible to make a close inspection of a few frames, and in the way the linguistic tools at hand catch Hepburn in her threshold role of not entirely being an innocent child while as yet not having become a mature woman. This is where the poem likes to see and love Hepburn: without the life that will change the poetic encounter. And Wiinblad is attracted to Monroe's sublime beauty, which she compares to a delicate butterfly, but above all to the dead butterfly that has had the pins removed. It is no longer dressed up in its pins – her assumed smile – it [that is: she] has been broken down to the medicine, the booze and the waste that Monroe is made of and ends in. The comparisons and accumulations are ways to get a glimpse of the real Monroe, while Monroe the icon frees herself of her body and escapes where no words can touch her.

The power of the accumulations used in Wiinblad's poems lies in their creating a feeling in the reader that opposes the staging of the films and of the life of the film stars. It seems to be accidental, that 'frailty', 'booze', 'obesity' and 'pills' pile up beneath each other in the Monroe poem. Such an accumulation suggest an accidental style, which could be a rhetorical way of stripping the image of staging in order to get closer to the life of the icons that is invisible as long as they are things in the minds of the films.[25]

ENDNOTES

1 M. Krieger, *Ekphrasis. The Illusion of the Natural Sign* [Baltimore and London: The Johns Hopkins University Press, 1992], p. 9.

2 *Ibid.*, p. 6.

3 *Ibid.*, p. 9.

4 A. Fryd, *Ekfraser. Gunnar Ekelöfs billedbeskrivende digte* [Copenhagen: Museum Tusculanums Forlag, Københavns Universitet, 1999], p. 47; Krieger, *Ekphrasis. The Illusion of the Natural Sign*, p. 7.

5 Fryd, *Ekfraser. Gunnar Ekelöfs billedbeskrivende digte.*

6 J. Hagstrum, *The Sister Arts* [Chicago: The University of Chicago Press, 1958], pp. 66–90.

7 G. E. Lessing, *Laokoon: oder über die Grenzen der Malerei und Poesie* [München: Carl Hanser Verlag, 1974], pp. 102–3.

8 J. R. Searle, *Expression and Meaning: Studies in the Theory of Speech Acts* [Cambridge: Cambridge University Press, 1981].

9 J. Derrida, *Of Grammatology* [Baltimore: Johns Hopkins University Press, 1997].

10 H. Nordbrandt, *Syvsoverne* [Copenhagen: Gyldendal, 1969], p. 11.

11 *Ibid.*, pp. 11–12.

12 C. Wiinblad, *49 forelskelser. Portrætdigte* [Århus: Athene, 2008].

13 *Breakfast at Tiffany's*, DVD recording, Paramount Pictures, 2001 [1961].

14 *Some Like It Hot*, DVD recording: Special edition, S. F. Film & Video, 2002 [1959].

15 T. Forsström, *Fiskenes himmel* [Århus: Husets Forlag, 1995], p. 41.

16 It is not known as to whether Wiinblad has read Forsström.

17 Fryd, *Ekfraser. Gunnar Ekelöfs billedbeskrivende digte.*

18 The number indicates that this is the second of two poems about Audrey Hepburn.

19 Wiinblad, *49 forelskelser. Portrætdigte*, p. 11.

20 T. Capote, *A Capote Reader* [London: Penguin Books, 1987], pp. 228–81.

21 The number indicates that this is the first of two poems about Marilyn Monroe.

22 'her smile' is the grammatically correct translation of 'smilet på hende', but it lacks one important possibility of interpretation. The Danish sentence could be understood as 'her smile', but also as 'the smile on her', possibly meaning an artificial smile that Monroe puts on habitually or professionally. The second proposition seems possible when considering what Adam Victor writes about Monroe's smile: 'Marilyn's trademark quivering smile was the product of Emmeline Snively's comment that Norma Jeane did not have "enough upper lip between the end of your nose and your mouth". The head of the Blue Book Modelling Agency suggested that she "try smiling with your upper lip drawn down", advice Marilyn put to good use for the rest of her life.'

23 Wiinblad, *49 forelskelser. Portrætdigte*, pp. 30–1.

24 R. deCordova, 'The emergence of the star system in America', in C. Gledhill [ed.], *Stardom. Industry of Desire* [London and New York: Routledge, 1991], pp. 17–29; T. Harris, 'The building of popular images: Grace Kelly and Marilyn Monroe', in Gledhill [ed.], *Stardom. Industry of Desire*, pp. 40–4.

25 Fryd, *Ekfraser. Gunnar Ekelöfs billedbeskrivende digte*, p. 14, pp. 32–9; A. D. Miller, 'Apostrophes to Light. The Ekphrasis of Photography from the nineteenth century to the Present' [unpublished PHD dissertation, Det Humanistiske Fakultet, Københavns Universitet, Copenhagen, 2010], pp. 256–8.

BIBLIOGRAPHY

Benjamin, W., 'A short history of photography', in A. Trachtenberg [ed.], *Classic Essays on Photography* [New Haven, Connecticut: Leete's Islands Books, 1980].

Breakfast at Tiffany's, DVD recording, Paramount Pictures, a Jurow-Shepherd Production, directed by Blake Edwards, screenplay by George Axelrod, based on the novel by Truman Capote, 1961 [2001].

Capote, T., *A Capote Reader* [London: Penguin Books, 1987].

Castle, A. [ed.], *Billy Wilder's Some Like It Hot. The funniest film ever made: the complete book* [Köln: Taschen, 2001].

deCordova, R., 'The emergence of the star system in America', in C. Gledhill [ed.], *Stardom. Industry of Desire* [London and New York: Routledge, 1991].

Derrida, J., *Of Grammatology* [Baltimore: The Johns Hopkins University Press, 1997].

Edwards, S., *Photography. A Very Short Introduction* [Oxford: Oxford University Press, 2006].

Forsström, T., *Fiskenes Himmel* [Århus: Husets Forlag, 1995].

Fryd, A., *Ekfraser. Gunnar Ekelöfs billedbeskrivende digte* [Copenhagen: Museum Tusculanums Forlag, Københavns Universitet, 1999].

Hagstrum, J. H., *The Sister Arts* [Chicago: The University of Chicago Press, 1958].

Harris, T., 'The building of popular images: Grace Kelly and Marilyn Monroe', in C. Gledhill [ed.], *Stardom. Industry of Desire* [London and New York: Routledge, 1991].

Heffernan, J. A. W., *Museum of Words – The Poetics of Ekphrasis from Homer to Ashbery* [Chicago: University of Chicago Press, 1993].

Krieger, M., *Ekphrasis. The Illusion of the Natural Sign* [Baltimore and London: The Johns Hopkins University Press, 1992].

Lessing, G. E., *Kunsttheoretische und Kunsthistorische Schriften* [München: Carl Hanser Verlag, 1974].

Miller, A. D., 'Apostrophes to Light. The Ekphrasis of Photography from the nineteenth century to the Present to the Present' [unpublished PHD dissertation, Det Humanistiske Fakultet, Københavns Universitet, Copenhagen, 2010].

Nordbrandt, H., *Syvsoverne* [Copenhagen: Gyldendal, 1969].

Sandbye, M., *Kedelige billeder* [Copenhagen: Rævens Sorte Bibliotek, 2007].

Sandbye, M. and E. Steffensen, *Sex, løgn og fotografi. Essays om kunst, fotografi, snapshots og virkelighed* [Copenhagen: Rævens Sorte Bibliotek, 1995].

Searle, J. R., *Expression and Meaning: Studies in the Theory of Speech Acts* [Cambridge: Cambridge University Press, 1981].

Some Like It Hot, DVD recording: Special edition, S. F. Film & Video, 2002 [1959]. Screenplay by Billy Wilder and I. A. L. Diamond, suggested by a story by

R. Thoeren and M. Logan, director of photography Charles Lang Jr., produced and directed by Billy Wilder. Original movie: USA: Metro-Goldwyn-Mayer: Ashton Productions; S. I.: Mirisch Company, 1959.

Spoto, D., *Enchantment. The Life of Audrey Hepburn* [London: Arrow Books, 2006].

Victor, A., *The Complete Marilyn Monroe* [London: Thames & Hudson, 1999].

Wiinblad, C., *49 forelskelser. Portrætdigte* [Århus: Athene, 2008].

Wilder, B. and I. A. L. Diamond, *Some Like It Hot. A Screenplay* [New York: The New American Library of World Literature Inc., 1959].

Afterword

DR JO TURNEY

This book has developed from a much wider discourse surrounding the interaction between people and their clothing, both in terms of production [manufacture, customising, styling] and consumption [buying, wearing, not-wearing], entitled 'Wardrobe'. A wardrobe is a thing, but it is also an idea, an expression of identity and ideology as well as a sign of behaviour, expression of social norms and expectations that go beyond fashion and its systems. We all wear clothes, and in a post-modern, post-structuralist world, we are increasingly aware of the immediacy of their potential for communication. Clothing creates meaning, and never before has the expression 'clothes make the man' been more pertinent. From this basic premise, the significance of clothing has extended beyond mere body covering to the projection of the self and one's position within a wider world. This has led to the over-consumption of clothing [we have more clothes than we could ever wear] and we, in the Western world, waste or throw away vast amounts on an annual basis. So, clothing is both significant in terms of its symbolic potential, but is equally problematic. Wardrobe asks 'why?' and poses this question within an inter-disciplinary and international framework.

This early Wardrobe study has facilitated an investigation into different ways of approaching clothing through its wearing, both in the contemporary world and over time as recorded through photography. *Images in Time* provided a forum for the discussion of representations of clothing as worn, addressing the iconography and iconology of the photograph and the clothed subject within. Like clothing, the photograph is both ordinary and special. It is a familiar aspect of our material culture and as such is a thing that is infinitely accessible. Used by both the professional and the amateur, the photograph circulates images and messages to be read and viewed by those unable to witness the event. The photograph documents events, people and places, capturing moments that otherwise would remain unrecorded. It is a medium of the everyday, and, as with the clothing we wear, provides narratives of seemingly everyday experiences, norms, technologies, trends and styles that demonstrate a historicity.

Of course the phrase 'the camera never lies' is much like 'clothing demonstrates personal identity' and is highly contentious; photographs are staged and the clothing one wears when captured *on camera* can be considered as costumes supporting a performance. The photograph is not evidence, but is a representation of how clothing was worn, for what occasion and as a means of addressing specific agendas. With closer analysis, as this investigation has acknowledged, the camera tells many and varied stories to an equally disparate audience. By addressing and uncovering these stories held within the Wardrobe, the ordinary can really become extraordinary, and theory given practical application.

The Wardrobe network is a Scandinavian endeavour, and is a leading force in the development of this discipline. Drawing together scholars from a variety of disciplines and from all of the Nordic nations, the network aims to provide a forum for the discussion of people and their clothes that extends beyond fashion studies and design histories.

One might pose the question 'why Scandinavia?', and as a non-Scandinavian perhaps I am best placed to address this. Scandinavia has a rich history of colonising the world; indeed, as an English person I am often reminded by Scandinavian colleagues that there is probably a Viking in my family tree…Yet it is this mentality that has fuelled an explosion in design and clothing practices as well as scholarly activity that has taken the fashion world and associated industries by storm. It is not without evidence that Iceland claims to be 'the coolest place on earth', nor that Copenhagen is the 'Paris of the North'. Distinctive national styles are in evidence wherever you go in Scandinavia, and these are not restricted to trendy boutiques or local designer-name brands, although these are abundant, but extend to everyone who wears clothes. And, as it is very cold, that really is everyone [sauna excepted].

Clothing is big business. In Scandinavia there is no bad weather, merely bad clothing, an epithet the British could learn from, but one which is taken very seriously. Drawn from a heritage of fitness for purpose, local myth and legend, and a quest for a distinctive national identity, clothing in these parts creates a trajectory by which business merges with the consumer and vice versa. From this holistic position, the relationship between production and consumption are entwined, facilitating a discourse of object relations with shared concerns. Likewise, the intervention of the State in the long establishment of design, technology and consumer science groups and bodies, which involve both producers and consumers, creates an arena for mutual respect and product development.

The significance of the State is unquestionable; political acknowledgement that design and product development is central to the health and wealth of the nation has created funded investigation into what national design is, should be, and how it is to be promoted. This approach to design, and clothing in particular, has raised questions about how clothing is consumed, one of the key themes of discussion for the Wardrobe network.

This is not, though, an exercise in navel gazing; although rooted in Scandinavia and Scandinavian thinking, the concerns of the network are far reaching and operate on a global scale. Built on foundations of co-operation and collaboration, the network addresses themes that affect everyone, in particular over-consumption, environmental and ethical concerns, as well as the recording of oral testimony and the display of everyday dress.

The Wardrobe network offers participants workshops, conferences and discussion groups, one of which [*Images in Time*] forms the basis of what I hope to be the first of many Wardrobe studies. The papers in this volume represent a small selection of the papers presented at the *Images in Time* conference, Reykjavik, 2009. Contributors to and participants within this project are offered our thanks for widening the discourse surrounding both photography and people and their things. This is not the end, just a pause for breath.

June 2011

EDITORS

Æsa Sigurjónsdóttir

Æsa Sigurjónsdóttir works as assistant professor at the Faculty of Icelandic and Comparative Cultural Studies, University of Iceland. Recent publications include contributions to *Berg Encyclopaedia of World Dress and Fashion* [2010], *Icelandic Art Today* [2009], and her book *Fashion and Identity in Dress and Photography: Iceland 1860–1960* [National Museum Iceland, 2008].

Michael A. Langkjær

Michael A. Langkjær has a PhD in history and is a lecturer at the Saxo Institute, History Section, University of Copenhagen. His field of research since 2006 is fashion and costume history, focusing on 'rock military style' in Anglo-American popular culture. Recent publications include '"Then how can you explain Sgt Pompous and the Fancy Pants Club Band?" Utilization of military uniforms and other paraphernalia by pop groups and the youth counterculture in the 1960s and subsequent periods', *Textile History*, 41:1 [2010], Supplement: *Textile History and the Military*, pp. 182–213., and 'Not Entirely Subversive: Rock Military Style from Hendrix to Destiny's Child', in J.L. Foltyn [ed.], *Fashions: Exploring Fashion through Culture* [Probing the Boundaries at the Interface Series, Oxford, The Inter-Disciplinary Press, 2011], pp. 201–236. He is Reviews Editor of *Catwalk: The Journal of Fashion, Beauty and Style.*

Jo Turney

Jo Turney is the course leader for MA Investigating Fashion Design at Bath Spa University. She is the co-author with Rosemary Harden of *Floral Frocks* [Antique Collector's Club, 2007] and the sole author of *The Culture of Knitting* [Berg, 2009]. She is currently the contributing editor of *Fashion and Crime* [I. B. Tauris, 2012]. She is particularly interested in everyday practices and the ways in which the ordinary becomes extraordinary. She is currently investigating the relationship between dress and deviant behaviour, as well as trans/national clothing practices and identities.

CONTRIBUTING AUTHORS

Charlotte Bik Bandlien

Charlotte Bik Bandlien is an anthropologist recently returned to the academic sphere after several years in visual communication. She currently works as a researcher at the National Institute for Consumer Research in Norway with projects related to new tendencies and new theoretical approaches to material culture. She is contributing editor to the fashion journal *Personae* [www.personae.no].

Henning Bender

Henning Bender has an MA in history from the University of Copenhagen [1970]. He worked at the National Archives and at the University [economic history] from 1970–1974. From 1974–2009 he was director of the City Archives of Aalborg and the Danish Emigration Archives. He has written books and articles on the history of emigration, industry and photography. He is retired [2009] and lives on the island of Bornholm.

Ingeborg Thaanum Carlsen

Ingeborg Thaanum Carlsen, MA in literature and linguistics from the University of Copenhagen, is a Head of Section at the Ministry of Employment in Denmark. Her MA thesis was about the ekphrasis genre in the work of Danish poet Henrik Nordbrandt. She is presently working on themes of the snapshot aesthetics in art photography and fashion photography.

Anna Dahlgren

Anna Dahlgren, PhD in art history, currently holds a postdoctoral fellowship at Institutet för folklivsforskning, Nordiska Museet funded by Stiftelsen Riksbankens Jubileumsfond and the Royal Swedish Academy of Letters, History and Antiquities. She writes and teaches on different aspects of photography, among them fashion photography, and is currently working on a book that investigates the photo album as a medium in a cultural historical perspective.

CONTRIBUTING AUTHORS

Lidia Marte
Lidia Marte is a critical ethnographer with research interests in the anthropology of representation, critical cultural studies, and food-place-memory, particularly as it pertains to African-diasporas in the Americas. Marte has an MFA in Photography and Media Studies, completed her PhD in cultural anthropology at the University of Texas in Austin in 2008, and is currently an adjunct instructor of Cultural Foundations at St Edwards University, in Austin, Texas.

Per Nielsen
Per Nielsen is an assistant lecturer, Department of History, University of Copenhagen, a research fellow, National Museum, Copenhagen, and author of articles about the history of the Danish colonies.

Tone Rasch
Tone Rasch is a curator and leader for the photo archive at the Norwegian Museum of Science, Technology and Medicine in Oslo. She has published articles about textile and clothing production in the nineteenth-century, the production and consumption of plastic rainwear in the 1950s and 1960s, and fashion and textile design in the same period. She has also contributed to the *Berg Encyclopedia of World Dress and Fashion, Volume 8* about home production and Norwegian dress. She is now co-operating with the Polish photo archive Fundacja Archeologia Fotografii on a web presentation that includes the Sohlberg Foto studio's fashion photography.

Stephanie Sadre-Orafai
Stephanie Sadre-Orafai is Assistant Professor of Anthropology at the University of Cincinnati. Her research focuses on transformations in contemporary US racial thinking and visual culture through the lens of expert visions within and beyond the fashion industry. She has published essays on casting, model development and fashion reality television and is beginning work on a comparative project on image and knowledge production practices in fashion and criminal justice.

CONTRIBUTING AUTHORS

Merja Salo

Merja Salo is professor of Photography and Visual Communication at Aalto University School of Art and Design in Helsinki. She is responsible for the doctoral studies of photography and teaches history and theory of photography as well as photojournalism. She has published *A History of Finnish Fashion Photography* [Muodin ikuistajat, Taideteollinen korkeakoulu, 2005]. She is also a practising photographer and has recently published a photo book called *Automaisemia – Carscapes* [Edition Patrick Frey and Musta Taide, 2011].

Eugénie Shinkle

Eugénie Shinkle is Senior Lecturer in the Department of Photography and Film at the University of Westminster. Originally trained as a civil engineer, she went on to study photography, art history, and critical theory, obtaining her PHD from the Slade School of Fine Art in 2003. Her research interests include fashion photography, landscape photography, and digital games, with a special focus on the haptic and embodied dimensions of image perception. She has published and lectured widely in the field of digital game studies and photography, and is the editor of *Fashion as Photograph: Viewing and Re-Viewing Images of Fashion* [I. B. Tauris, 2008] and *Emerging Landscapes: Between Production and Representation* [Ashgate, 2012]. She has been exhibiting her photographic work internationally since 1993.

ACKNOWLEDGEMENTS

The editors and authors of this book would like to offer their heartfelt thanks to the following people in the completion and production of this book: Lise Skov, the Nordic Wardrobe network and Nordforsk without whom the book would not have been conceptualised nor the contributors brought together. Likewise we would also like to thank the University of Iceland and the National Museum of Iceland for their support and hospitality, and Bath School of Art and Design for its commitment to the project.

We would also like to acknowledge the dedication and expertise of everyone at Wunderkammer, in particular Dr Graham McLaren, Anna McLaren, Viv Kenchington and Jo King, and offer our deepest thanks to Paul Minott for the beautiful book design.

The editors Æsa Sigurjónsdóttir and Michael A. Langkjær wish to thank Cherine Munkholt, editor at the Danish National Research Foundation's Centre for Textile Research for proof-reading the draft version of our introduction to the present volume.

Ingeborg Thaanum Carlsen would like to acknowledge the generous support of the Danish Research Foundation's Centre for Textile Research in connection with the purchase of usage permits for the illustrations in her contribution.

Without the assistance of these people and institutions this project would not have come to fruition. Thank you all.

Index